Privilege at Play

Recent Titles in

Global and Comparative Ethnography
Edited by Javier Auyero

Violence at the Urban Margins
Edited by Javier Auyero, Philippe Bourgois, and Nancy Scheper-Hughes

Concrete Jungles
By Rivke Jaffe

Soybeans and Power
By Pablo Lapegna

Occupying Schools, Occupying Land
By Rebecca Tarlau

Privilege at Play

Class, Race, Gender, and Golf in Mexico

HUGO CERÓN-ANAYA

OXFORD
UNIVERSITY PRESS

OXFORD
UNIVERSITY PRESS

Oxford University Press is a department of the University of Oxford. It furthers
the University's objective of excellence in research, scholarship, and education
by publishing worldwide. Oxford is a registered trade mark of Oxford University
Press in the UK and certain other countries.

Published in the United States of America by Oxford University Press
198 Madison Avenue, New York, NY 10016, United States of America.

Library of Congress Cataloging-in-Publication Data
Names: Cerón-Anaya, Hugo, 1975– author.
Title: Privilege at Play : class, race, gender, and golf in Mexico /
Hugo Cerón-Anaya.
Description: New York, NY : Oxford University Press, [2019] |
Includes bibliographic references.
Identifiers: LCCN 2018049119 (print) | LCCN 2019013339 (ebook) |
ISBN 9780190931629 (Universal PDF) | ISBN 9780190931636 (Electronic Publication) |
ISBN 9780190931605 (hardback : alk. paper) | ISBN 9780190931612 (pbk. : alk. paper)
Subjects: LCSH: Golf—Social aspects—Mexico. | Golf—Mexico—History. |
Athletic clubs—Social aspects—Mexico. | Discrimination in sports—Mexico—History. |
Social classes—Mexico—History. | Mexico—Social conditions.
Classification: LCC GV985.M4 (ebook) | LCC GV985.M4 C47 2019 (print) |
DDC 796.3520972—dc23
LC record available at https://lccn.loc.gov/2018049119

9 8 7 6 5 4 3 2 1

Paperback printed by Webcom, Inc., Canada
Hardback printed by Bridgeport National Bindery, Inc., United States of America

For Teo, Isa, and Sandra in no particular order—thank you for all your support and love.

Contents

Acknowledgments

NO INTELLECTUAL PROJECT is an individual project, and therefore I developed this book with the help of a large number of generous people. Some of them directly intervened in the project, reading early or later drafts of the book. Others kindly shared with me their time, hearing details of different pieces of the book, offering incisive comments about my arguments and evidence. Some people, after hearing about my research, shared with me valuable scholarly references that I had not yet discovered. Others regularly sent me news and popular articles recently published addressing the relationship between golf and multiple forms of privilege. Lastly, some people constantly encouraged me to keep researching and writing, reminding me about the value of my work. The daily struggles to put my ideas on paper sometimes made me forget the relevance of the topic, but the encouragement I received from colleagues and friends refreshed my memory, motivating me to keep working. I am greatly indebted to all the generous people who made me feel less isolated during the time it took me to develop this book—thank you. The order of appearance of names in the following paragraphs does not reflect any hierarchical order.

I would like to offer my gratitude to the Consejo Nacional de Ciencia y Tecnología (CONACyT), Mexico, for the doctoral scholarship and the economic support to conduct part of the fieldwork. Without this funding, I could not have completed my doctoral degree and carried out this research. This project started long ago while I was studying at the University of Essex. There I shared with John Scott a comment about a brief article I found describing how the Mexican government punished the most important regional economic elite by conducting a tax audit in a golf club. At that moment, I thought of the information as an amusing anecdote. However, John immediately suggested that I think about the topic from a sociological perspective. I would not know at the time that the article would eventually evolve into my doctoral dissertation and later on into a book—thanks, John, for your support and help, first during my master's degree and later through my PhD. I would also like to extend my gratitude to Colin Samson, who became a strong supporter of my work during my time at Essex and afterward. I would also like to extend a warm thank you to my peers Carlos Gigoux, Megan Ward, and Rie Suzuki, who always made my life at Colchester cheerful.

I spent a considerable amount of time as a visiting doctoral scholar at the University of Manchester, where Mike Savage and Karel Williams kindly welcomed me at the Centre for Research on Socio-Cultural Change, a site that hosted an exciting, vibrant, and truly global intellectual community. At Manchester, I would also like to thank my peers Ebru Soytemel, Tara Martin Lopez, and Isabelle Darmon for your help and friendship. Moving to the United States right at the time of one of the worst economic recessions was a daunting experience. I would like to thank Orin Starn for his generous support and advice during this time. My gratitude during those moments also extends to Erica Nastasi, Judith Lasker, and Nicola Tannenbaum, who directly and indirectly supported my work. They heard some of the earliest oral descriptions of this book through the voice of my students, who, I learned many months later, informally and enthusiastically talked with other professors at Lehigh University about a class that discussed the relation among capitalism, racialization, masculinity, and everyday social relations. The words of these students and the receptive ears of Erica, Judith, and Nikki meant a lot to me. Special thanks to my students in multiple classes, who, after being warned that my courses do not provide answers but offer a multitude of unresolved questions, have decided to stay, extensively read, and help me think aloud about some of the topics developed in this book.

I am particularly indebted to my colleague Bruce Whitehouse, who kindly read the final draft of this book, offering sharp comments and pointing out intellectual pitfalls. Your comments helped me developed a stronger book and reinforced a thought I have long suspected: disciplinary borders are sometimes a matter of futile disputes. I would also like to extend my gratitude to Megan Sheehan, who generously looked at early drafts and, despite her busy schedule, always had time to sit down and talk about my ideas and arguments. Barbara Zepeda Cortés read a draft of the epilogue—thank you very much for your help and constant encouragement. I would like to extend my gratitude to the members of the Department of Sociology and Anthropology and the Latin American and Latino Studies program at Lehigh University, particularly to Yuping

Zhang, David Small, John Gatewood, Ziad Munson, Sarah Stanlick, Matt Bush, and Mariana De Maio. I deeply value your words of encouragement and support.

I would also like to offer a thank you note to Carlos Vargas-Ramos, who invited me to join the "Whiteness in the Americas" writing group at Hunter College. When I joined the community, the academic knowledge displayed and sharp criticism offered on each other's work did not surprise me; after all, these are common characteristics among most scholars. However, what greatly surprised me was the degree of collegiality, humility, and generosity that all members of the group demonstrated. People carefully read one another's work, providing detailed analysis, sharp criticism, and well-informed comments, yet always in a considerate manner. Using a metaphor from the world of sports, people in this group play rough but never in bad faith. Therefore, I would like to personally thank Ana Ramos-Zayas, Ulla Berg, Zaire Dinzey-Flores, Hal Barton, Stan Thangaraj, Katy Lopez, Juan Usera, Suzanne Oboler, Tshombe Miles, Hilda Lloréns, and Airin Martinez. Their comments and criticisms, and above all their company, significantly contributed to the development of this book—thank you.

I am also much indebted to Xavier Auyero for believing in this project and for offering great advice on how to make my work available for students and scholars in Latin America. I would also like to thank James Cook, acquisition editor at Oxford University Press, for his advice and support in shaping the book. My gratitude extends to the anonymous reviewers who offered great comments to improve the arguments of the book as well as the editorial and marketing teams at OUP, Suganya Elango, Christina Nisha Paul, Emily Mackenzie, and Seth Cotterman, thank you for all the work you put behind this book. I would also like to offer a thank you note to Kate Bullard, Research Program Development Officer at Lehigh University, who invited me to participate in multiple writing retreats and encouraged me to apply for a Faculty Research Grant. This fund offered me the economic support to work with Jennifer Eggerling-Boeck, whose sociological imagination and fantastic editorial skills dressed up the prose of this book. Jennifer always found ways to express my exact thoughts in more beautiful words—thank you. My gratitude also extends to Sarah White, who read a final version of the manuscript—I greatly appreciate your comments and, above all, deeply respect your desire to work for a more just world.

Some of the theoretical arguments presented in the book started as conversations in the virtual reading group on Bourdieu that I organized with a group of junior scholars scattered around different time zones on two continents. Richenda Herzig, Jean Boucher, and Viviane Riegel—thank you very much for your enthusiasm and engagement reading together Bourdieu's work. I would also like to thank Salvador Vidal-Ortiz and Sara Crawley for their generosity, encouragement, and advice. Your support has meant a lot to me—thank you. My gratitude also extends to the *Journal of Contemporary Ethnography* and *Ethnography*, where earlier versions of Chapter 2 and Chapter 6 were respectively published. I also would like to thank Aracely Monroy Pérez at the Archivo Histórico y Museo de Minería A.C., who efficiently helped me to identify three of the images reproduced in the first chapter of the book. Donna Gayer did a fantastic job recreating an old promotional map of a golf club, and Carrie Baldwin-SoRelle helped me track down the copyright of one of the pictures included in the book—thank you for your help.

I would also like to say thank you to my parents, Angélica Anaya Reyes and Serafín Cerón Santillan, for your love and strong support during all my life. I did not realize how challenging, frustrating, and rewarding parenting is until life turned me into a father. Thank you for supporting me. My deep gratitude extends also to my witty and supporting partner Sandra, who, despite her own academic work, participated in this project since the beginning. Thank you for your love, encouragement, and support, particularly in those gloomy days in which the project seemed stuck. Sandra, beyond our relationship, I admire your work. My gratitude extends to my children, Isa and Teo, who asked me every third day or so if I had finished the book because they wanted to play with me. Despite my constant disappearance on weekends to work on this book, Teo and Isa always offered me their unrestricted love and support—this book is for you.

Finally, I would like to thank the golfers and workers who kindly offered their time to talk with me, sometimes for hours, about the world of golf in Mexico. Without you, this work would not be possible. Particularly, I would like to offer this book to those journalists and caddies who, after hearing more about my research project, encouraged me to write a critical analysis about the sport. One of them openly told me, "someone needs to write a more critical history of golf, most of the books already published tell the same [uncritical] stories." I hope that you find another perspective on the royal and ancient game of golf in these pages.

Privilege at Play

Introduction

GOLF

There is a funny TV ad about a [brand of expensive cars], which compares buying one of these cars with the cost of playing golf. The ad goes like this: There is a guy looking at one of these cars and someone next to him invites him to play golf. The guy looking at the car starts mentally adding up the cost of playing golf—the cart, green fee, caddy, food, drinking, betting—and then a voice-over says the monthly payment of the car, suggesting that it is cheaper to buy an expensive car than to play golf. This is correct; golf in Mexico is [an] expensive [sport].

—HORACIO, *an upper-middle-class golf player in his late forties*

Introduction

The Mexican state experienced its worst economic crisis in modern times in 1982, when the international price of oil—its most important commodity—collapsed, leaving the government in bankruptcy, unable to repay its debtors. Almost immediately, massive amounts of national and international capital began to flow out of the country, threatening to further depress the already grim position of the regime. Amid the economic panic unleashed by the crisis, the Mexican government announced the immediate nationalization of the banking system, which, at the time, was owned exclusively by affluent Mexicans. This decision further exacerbated the chaotic situation. Ignoring the government's instructions, bank clients packed the local branches of their financial institutions in an attempt (in almost all cases unsuccessful) to recover their savings. The decision also shocked and enraged powerful financial and business groups. The economic elite in the northern state of Nuevo León—a particularly tight group whose members possessed some of the largest fortunes in Mexico and had long perceived themselves as the economic engine of the country (Saragoza 1988)—was furious.

This affluent group felt betrayed and humiliated by the government's decision and immediately initiated an unprecedented rebellion by funding and organizing a national strike, a move that had only been attempted by trade unions and leftist political parties in previous historical moments and which had always resulted in harsh repression and dead bodies on the workers' side. The Mexican government rapidly retaliated by sending customs agents and tax auditors to the region's most prominent golf club, one of the most prestigious and exclusive clubs in the country. The agents seized 120 golf carts that were privately owned by members and had been imported illegally. In the following days, after the government extended the tax audits to directly target several members of the club, the elite dropped their plans for the strike (Maza 1984).

I became aware of this episode as I was conducting preliminary research on economic elites in late twentieth-century Mexico. After reading this story I wondered why the Mexican government, in the midst of the worst economic and political crisis in modern times and a seemingly rebellion of the upper class, chose to attack one of the most powerful regional elites via a golf club. Was the government trying to intimidate and humiliate these wealthy individuals? Why do so at a golf club? More generally, I began to wonder why golf is popularly associated with wealth. Why is this sport played by affluent people in Mexico? What makes this game different from other sporting practices? Has golf always been associated with upper-class communities, or was this a recent development? Thus, my initial interest in economic elites, privilege, and class inequalities led me to a research project on golf.

In search of answers to these questions, I discovered that despite golf's strong connection with the expansion of capitalism (Cerón-Anaya 2010; Cock 2008), its link with multiple forms of imperialism (Cole 2002; Stoddart 1999), and its strong affiliation with elites all over the world (An and Sage 1992; Cerón-Anaya 2017; Gerth 2011; Hirst 2001; Inglis 2019; Kendall 2008; Pow 2017; Salverda and Hay 2014; Sherwood 2012), golf is one of the most underresearched athletic games in the sports literature.[1] Further, I learned that while golf has a relatively small global audience compared to soccer, basketball, or boxing, it offers some of the highest economic rewards among all professional sports according to the *Forbes*

---

1. Throughout the rest of the book I use the terms games, athletic games, physical games, and sports as synonyms. For a discussion of the historical differences between games and sports, see Guttmann (1994).

"World's Highest-Paid Athletes" ranking (Badenhausen 2012, 2013, 2014, 2017; *Forbes* 2015, 2016). I also found that golf is a truly global game, a title reserved for only a handful of sports that are played in all corners of the world (baseball and football, for example, are not global sports; see Kelly 2007; Maguire 1991). However, unlike any other global game, golf requires the transformation of large tracts of land and has spread a type of upper-class lifestyle rooted in an Anglo-American aesthetic across the world (Klein 1999).

In a recent interview, U.S. President Donald Trump expressed some of the ideas that have been long associated with golf. When asked if golf is an elitist sport, he responded, "It may be elitist, and perhaps that's what golf needs. Let golf be elitist" (Roberts 2015). He then elaborated on what he viewed as the positive side of elitism, understanding the concept as a type of aspirational goal that makes people work harder to achieve a "better status" in life. He said, "Let people work hard and aspire to someday be able to play golf. To afford to play it." In line with his frequent racialized rhetoric and a long history of racialization of the sport (Mitchelson and Lazaro 2004, Demas 2017), the U.S. president then drew a boundary between those who could "naturally" play golf and those who, no matter how hard they worked, would never been able to do so, noting, "They're trying to teach golf to people who will never be able to really play it. They're trying too hard. Because of the expense of playing, and the land needed, golf is never going to be basketball" (notably, the sport of basketball is strongly associated with African American athletes). Although these comments may seem unreasonable and President Trump is known for making extreme and often untrue statements, his words echo a set of racialized and class-based tropes that have long been connected with golf (Collinson and Hoskin 1994; Demas 2017).

The exclusivity associated with golf makes it a strategic site to analyze the confluence of upper-class interests, racialized narratives, and unequal gender dynamics in a myriad of geographical and historical contexts (An and Sage 1992; Cave 2008; Cerón-Anaya 2010; Cock 2008; Crosset 1995; Gerth 2011; Inglis 2019; Le 2010; Lowerson 1994, 1995; Pow 2017; Sherwood 2012; Starn 2012; McGinnis, McQuillan, and Chapple 2005). Before continuing with the introduction, however, I want to clarify that this book should not be regarded as an accusation against golf and golfers but rather as an illustration of how structures of privilege become embedded in the most banal and mundane practices, hiding their true nature behind masks of intelligence, hard work, good choices, discipline, and meritocracy. Some of the arguments wealthy golfers expressed about poorer people are likely also presented, in almost identical ways, in other spaces of privilege such as elite universities, top corporate circles, or among high-ranking bureaucrats. While I am not arguing that all other spaces function in the very same way, I am asserting that there is a considerable degree of overlapping between these sites. Therefore, this is neither a book about golf nor an anti-golf treatise but rather a critical exploration of how dynamics of domination and subordination are simultaneously openly articulated and obscured in the context of a privileged space, such as golf, in Mexico. Following Collins's argument (2015), the present book uses golf as a case study to examine the multiple layers that constitute power relations and articulate social inequalities.

Studying Up

As a sociologist, I have long been curious about the relationship between social inequalities, marginalization, and poverty. These topics are particularly relevant in countries marred by extreme class differences, and Mexico is just such a nation (Castillo Negrete 2017, Esquivel 2015c). Mexico City is home to extreme wealth: it has the honor of being the city with the second largest number of private helicopters per capita in the world, after Sao Paulo, Brazil (Quesada 2016). Further, in 2016, 15 Mexicans were billionaires and one was on the *Forbes* list of the top 10 wealthiest individuals in the world. At the same time, the salaries of Mexican workers are the lowest of all members of the Organisation for Economic Co-operation and Development (OECD 2017), and almost half of the population lives in poverty (CONEVAL 2014). In popular discussion, these extreme disparities are commonly interpreted in terms of differences in intelligence, hard work, good choices, and discipline within a system of meritocracy, based on the assumption that the poor lack all these qualities and habits.

While scholars of Mexico have examined these social disparities extensively from the perspective of the excluded (Adler-Lomnitz 2014; Arzate Salgado 2005; Boltvinik and Mann 2016; Diaz-Cayeros, Estévez, and Magaloni 2016; Eckstein 1977; Lewis 1961; Mahar 2011; Middlebrook and Zepeda 2003; Reygadas and Gootenberg 2010; Székely 2005; Teruel and Reyes 2017), they have rarely explored social inequality from the point of view of the privileged (Alder Lomnitz and Pérez Lizaur 1987; Camp 2002; Iturriaga Acevedo 2016; Nutini 2008). This criticism also applies to research on most other countries (Cattani 2009; Donaldson 2003; Hay and Beaverstock 2016; Khan 2012; Savage and Williams 2008; Twine and Gardener 2013). Social scientists have overlooked the fact that wealth and poverty are interrelated, not isolated, processes. The production of one necessarily requires the creation of the other, in both a concrete way (i.e., workers must produce objects for consumers) and a symbolic way (i.e., no one is poor until confronted with someone wealthier). In other words, without the existence of wealth, poverty is not a condition of exclusion but a way of living (Dinzey-Flores 2017). Poverty, therefore, is not a self-contained condition but rather the manifestation of a set of relations between poor and rich people (Bourdieu and Wacquant 1992; Elias 1991; Emirbayer 1997; Marx 1993 [1858]).

Despite the interrelated nature of poverty and wealth, social scientists have a relatively nuanced understanding of the tastes, pastimes, consumption practices, socialization patterns, educational aspirations, perceptions of gender, notions of violence, and racial ideas of the lower classes but a very shallow understanding of the corresponding attitudes, beliefs, and behaviors among dominant groups. It is possible that the vast knowledge generated about the poor has unwittingly facilitated the development of more effective mechanisms of social control and subjugation (Foucault 1995), while the restricted insight into the upper strata has allowed these groups to increase their power and influence under neoliberal capitalism. This argument becomes more convincing in light of recent studies of wealth concentration at the top of the class hierarchy in a myriad of global contexts (Donaldson and Poynting 2013; Friedman and Laurison 2019; Gaztambide-Fernández 2009; Gerth 2011; Hay and Beaverstock 2016; Hay and Muller 2012; Piketty 2014; Pow 2017; Ratcliff 2019; Reeves 2017; Rivera Lauren 2015; Sherman 2017). The limited understanding scholars and policymakers have about these groups might have inadvertently let them benefit greatly under the current capitalist system.

Since the 1970s, the study of business organizations has produced a solid body of "study up" literature on Mexico. Although this work is certainly important, it is limited: almost all of these studies have explored institutional settings (Anzaldua and Maxfield 1987; Arriola 1991; Babb 2002; Basañez 1990; Camp 2002; Centeno 1994; Garrido 1994; Luna 1992; Minushkin 2002; Puga 1994; Schneider 2002; Tirado 1998), and most researchers have focused on formal political interactions. In other words, these studies shed light on the organizational activities of local economic elites, specifically the ways that think tanks, business associations, and company boards produce class inequality. Further, most of this literature has privileged the analysis of interactions between economic elites and the nation-state, such as the connection between private organizations and the state and the influence economic elites have on policymaking. Thus, while this literature is undoubtedly valuable, it is incomplete. Researchers have rarely focused on informal and personal interactions (Camp 1982), even though, historically, Mexico is a country in which policies, procedures, and institutional dynamics have been organized in personal, unsystematic, and unregulated ways (Smith 1979). Given Mexico's historical patterns, it is necessary to complement institutional and macro-scale research with qualitative data that reveal concrete forms of exclusion, specific mechanisms of inclusion, and distinct power dynamics involved in the constitution of privilege in this nation. (I expand on the complexities this task entails in the Appendix.)

Scholars must balance studies of institutional dynamics with analyses of informal relations in order to explore the "back stage," to use Goffman's famous term (1959). The back stage is the area in which people unwind and express their true feelings and ideas, and most of what occurs there is not concealed because it is not meant to be public. This area is where a golfer might reveal, off the record, that clubs do not support caddies in their attempts to become professional players "because [despite their outstanding skills] caddies remind golfers of their maids and chauffeurs," where a journalist can rave about caddies' lack of taste and the need to discipline them, and where golfers revel in the exclusivity of their sport. The back stage is also the site where caddies complain about golfers' lack of honor, where women explain their marginal status in terms of blatant sexism on the part of their male colleagues, and where members of golf clubs openly complain about other members' lack of "class." Using qualitative data, this book thoroughly explores the back stage, offering an analysis of the organization of a leisure space for the upper-middle and upper classes in Mexico City.

In response to the longstanding appeal to shift the focus of scholarly analysis from the poor to the wealthy—from the classical texts of Mills (1956), Domhoff (1967), and Nader (1972) to the more contemporary entreaties of Savage and Williams (2008), Cattani (2009), Gaztambide-Fernández (2009), Khan (2010), Ostrander (2010), and Sherwood (2012)—the current book contributes to a wider understanding of society by "studying up." This book illuminates the lives and social dynamics of the powerful rather than focusing exclusively on the lives of the marginalized, although the experiences of the latter are also examined. The book studies affluent people's notions of honor, language, competition, humor, fashion, athleticism, etiquette, and morality to examine how class, racial, and gender dynamics inform social hierarchies in contemporary Mexico City.

Privilege at Play reveals how wealth and status become natural conditions for some individuals, allowing them to believe that poverty is exclusively the result of personal actions and attributes rather than structural conditions. Based on ethnographic research conducted in exclusive golf clubs as well as in-depth interviews with club members and lower-status employees, the book analyzes inequality from an often-overlooked perspective by focusing on the privileged rather than the underprivileged. This viewpoint permits to demonstrate the multilayered condition of power, showing how the golf course is a site shaped by class as much as gender dynamics. For example, the organization of space and the distribution of playing times inside clubs, and even the word "golfer," are elements based on masculine standards. Most players are aware of this reality. Unsurprisingly, a male golfers once told me that, "in golf, everything is designed for men" and a female player humorously remarked that golf stands for "Gentlemen Only Ladies Forbidden," statements that capture the gender dynamics that typify this sport (for a broader discussion about sports and masculinity see Messner 1988, 1992 and Messner and Sabo 1990).

Privilege however is not only based on class and gender elements. Following a small but growing literature, this book claims that racial perceptions influence the distribution of resources, opportunities, and status in Mexico (Moreno and Saldívar 2016; Nutini 1997; Navarrete 2016; Serna 1996; Sue 2013; Villarreal 2010; López Beltran 2017; Mora 2017). Notwithstanding, this does not mean that a strict color line exists in this country. Instead, I assert that racial dynamics always operate in conjunction with class relations. *Privilege at Play*, hence, is a study of wealth, racial hierarchies, and gender inequalities in today's Mexico City. Drawing on historical data, the book also shows that privilege must be studied in terms of historical relations of power, highlighting the ways these interactions shape today's society. It is worth restating that this study is not an indictment of any individual nor a sport; instead, it demonstrates that social privilege and exclusion are processes that are both structurally organized and individually expressed.

A Segment of the Elite

According to the Mexican Golf Federation (FMG), there are 27,631 golfers in the entire country (IGF 2017). Most of these players live in one of Mexico's three largest urban centers: Guadalajara, Monterrey, and Mexico City. Including its surrounding metropolitan area, Mexico City has a population of around 20 million inhabitants and contains the largest concentration of golf players and clubs. However, even if all the golfers in Mexico were in the capital city, they would make up only 0.00013 percent of the city's population. What's more, in this megalopolis there are no public courses—the sport is exclusively played at private clubs (see Chapter 2). The price of membership varies significantly at the 13 private golf clubs in the city and its metropolitan area, with two clubs having one-time membership fees greater than $100,000 and the less expensive club charging around $7,000 (Rodriguez 2014; Saliba 2003). According to participants, however, the cost of membership in most clubs ranges from $16,000 to $35,000.

The upscale condition of the sport becomes even more evident when the cost of joining a club is compared with the economic reality of the average population in this country. As indicated before, nearly half of the population lives below the poverty line (CONEVAL 2014), and workers, on average, earn the lowest salaries of any other member state of the OECD (OECD 2017). The average annual income (after taxes) is only $15,314 (OECD 2017). A regular family, therefore, would have to save their entire income for five months to pay for a membership in the least expensive club. Moreover, the membership fee does not include other expenses related to the sport such as annual club maintenance fees, personal equipment, golf lessons, food, drinks, and caddy service; additionally, some clubs have minimum monthly food expenses. It comes at no surprise that the few references to this sport in the academic literature point out that golf in Mexico is not a middle-class game but a pastime almost exclusively played by the upper-middle and upper classes (Nutini 2008:125), a situation that is replicated in most parts of the world (An and Sage 1992; Cock 2008; Gerth 2011; Gewertz and Errington 1999; Inglis 2019; Salverda and Hay 2014).

In the Mexican case, limited research on dominant groups makes it hard to determine with precision the percentage of the population that belongs to the upper-middle and upper classes. Estimates of the combined proportion of these two groups range from slightly more than 10 (Gilbert 2007) to 6 (AMAI 2018) percent of the total population. The considerable variation in the price of a membership in the 13 clubs existing in the city inevitably generates the question: Are all golfers part of the elite in Mexico? While members of the two clubs charging more than $100,000 for membership belong to the local elite, it seems unclear whether members of the least expensive club could also be part of the same group. In purely economic terms, it is possible to separate golf clubs into two different categories: upper and upper-middle class clubs, with the former, but not the latter, being part of the elite. Notwithstanding, this division does not reflect the close relations members of these two class groups described during the interviews. After all, people in highly affluent clubs put me in contact with their friends in less affluent ones and vice versa.

The small number of studies on dominant groups suggests a high degree of overlap between the upper-middle and upper classes (Alder Lomnitz and Pérez Lizaur 1987; Iturriaga Acevedo 2016). In his study of the Mexican noble class, for instance, Hugo Nutini (2008) argued that the aristocracy—defined as individuals who could trace back their lineage to members of the nobility in the colonial area (1521–1821)—have enough social distinction to interact on equal terms with members of the upper class. Financially, however, aristocrats are located at the same level as the upper-middle class. The latter has accumulated enough wealth and status to detach from the middle class, getting closer to the upper class.[2] In spite of the differences in wealth and status, the aristocratic, upper-middle, and upper classes share common spaces and possess multiple similarities to the extent that it is possible to treat them as a form of superordinate social class, Nutini maintained. The work of Larissa Alder Lomnitz and Marisol Pérez Lizaur (1987), on a Mexican aristocratic family, and the study of Eugenia Iturriaga Acevedo (2016), on the dominant classes in the southern Mexican state of Yucatán, offer more evidence about the affinities the upper-middle and upper classes share.

Borrowing the Bourdieu-inspired definition of an elite that Khan (2012) proposes, which also coincides with the above arguments, an elite is a group that possesses a "disproportionate control over or access to resources" that are accumulable, transferable, and, more importantly, that can be exchanged for other highly valuable assets. These characteristics provide members of the elite with great advantages in relation to most other individuals in society (Khan 2012:362). Under this definition, the

---

2. The middle class is wealthier than the lower classes, yet it is still characterized by a high degree of economic vulnerability (see Atkinson and Brandolini 2014; Esquivel 2015a, 2015b; Morales Oyarvide 2016; Teruel and Reyes 2017).

sheer majority of clubs—including those where the ethnographic work was conducted—belong to individuals who have access to and control over resources that are out of reach for about 90 percent of the Mexican population. This does not mean, however, that all golf players perceive each other as equals. As the book demonstrates, these highly affluent clubs are sites where different understandings of privilege symbolically compete with each other. The outcomes of these symbolic competitions are not trivial, they have very real and material consequences.

It is noteworthy that golf does not represent the only sport that attracts highly affluent individuals and that not all members of the Mexican elite play it. Golf clubs are one of multiple sites and activities where the upper-middle and upper classes articulate their interests and reproduce a sense of social uniqueness. There are other privileged spaces, such as upscale schools and charitable foundations, where members of the elite articulate other arguments to explain the composition of dominant classes and their own position on them (Alder Lomnitz and Pérez Lizaur 1987; Nutini 2008). Therefore, the group analyzed in this book is just one segment of the elite. One more caveat is necessary. Most of the participants interviewed for this project were older club members, people in their fifties and sixties. The fact that I openly asked participants to put me in contact with higher-ranked corporate executives and business people who were also golf players strongly influenced the age group of the sample. The comments and explanations I collected from these participants, therefore, were inevitably shaped by the perspective older upper-middle and upper class people have of society.

Thinking about Space

When I started the current research, I knew that a golf club existed in the area of Mexico City where I had lived for more than 20 years. Yet I had never seen it, nor did I know anyone who had seen it. I was perplexed by my inability to translate my knowledge of the area into the practical ability of identifying the exact location of this club. Although I knew a course was situated somewhere in this part of the city, I had no idea how to find it. I eventually used aerial maps of the city that I found on the Internet to determine the exact location of the club. The maps revealed that there were actually two courses in the area; I later learned that one of these clubs was one of the oldest and most prestigious golf clubs in Mexico. The difficulty I had pinpointing two large tracts of land in a familiar area of the city prompted me to think about the role of space and spatial dynamics in the reproduction of privilege. These early thoughts remained unexplored for a long time but resurfaced when I began the fieldwork.

My interactions with golfers and caddies inside golf clubs inspired me to further consider the importance of space to relations of power. On one occasion, for example, a golfer invited me to conduct our interview at the snack bar at his prestigious and long-established golf club. The snack bar was a pleasant area. Its minimalist architecture, including its panoramic glass walls, allowed for a superb view of the mature course from any of the about 10 tables located in the place. The scenery—neatly spaced old trees, verdant green turf, and the hilly contours of the course spreading out in front of the bar—momentarily transported me to Britain (where I had attended graduate school), which was a particularly odd sensation given that I was halfway across the globe, in the middle of Mexico City. Later, as part of my fieldwork, I visited newer clubs. These sites did not have the same effect but rather gave me the sensation of being in a generic Anglo-American space. In these cases, the hypermodern aesthetic of a club house, a spacious golf course, and the pervasive presence of immaculate green turf (similar to the grass found in any upper-middle or upper class suburban development in the United States) generated a very different spatial feeling than I had experienced in almost any other public space in Mexico City.

These incidents repeatedly brought several questions to mind: Why does the spatial arrangement of golf clubs communicate a specifically Anglo-American aesthetic? Do aesthetic principles influence the organization of social hierarchies? Does colonialism shape the lush vegetation that characterizes these elegant golf clubs? During the fieldwork period, I began to have more and more questions about the role of space in the reproduction of privilege and the underprivileged. For example, my early inability to identify the precise location of a golf club in the area where I had spent my entire childhood came back to me during an interview with a caddy who described arriving late the first time he visited the club (for a job interview) because none of the workers or passersby in the area could tell him how to get to the club (I elaborate on this story in Chapter 1). I found it remarkable that in a city characterized by a lack of large public areas and green parks, golf clubs could remain invisible to the average city dweller.

My fieldwork experiences made me realize that the organization of space communicates more much than aesthetic elements. Spatial arrangements facilitate the organization of social hierarchies and, hence, the reproduction of privilege. The separation of caddies and golfers, for example, was commonly interpreted as the product of unavoidable class-based differences. The spatial arrangements inside clubs contribute to cement these ideas, as the caddies' house—the space reserved for caddies—was always visually hidden from club members. The invisibility of the caddies' waiting area allowed players to reproduce derogatory narratives that attribute lack of work ethic, immoral behaviors, and limited intelligence to these workers. Yet, in a more profound way, club members' frequent articulation of arguments that assigned these workers a "natural" otherness suggested that the exclusion was based on a combination of class and racialized connotations.[3] The racialization of workers was an intriguing theme, considering that Mexicans espouse a strong belief that race (as a concept) and racism (as its manifestation) do not exist in their country. Despite the supposed absence of a racial order, the organization of space constantly conveyed racialized dynamics. The connection between class and racial ideas slowly became clear as I began to pay more attention to how space was used to justify the inherent inferiority of lower-class workers. At this point, a visible pattern of racialization of lower-class people, including the spaces they occupied, became intelligible.

Class and racialized dynamics are not the only forces that shape these privileged spaces. The fieldwork also revealed how a gender hierarchy impacts spatial dynamics inside golf clubs. At most clubs, for example, women were banned from the bar, which commonly functioned as a site for male golfers to socialize. The exclusion of women from this site prevented male players from learning about the outstanding golf abilities, witty conversation, endurance, and charming personalities of women golfers. The bar, however, was not the only place that "gently" pushed women aside. The customary distribution of playing time, which turned most clubs into masculine sites during the early mornings (prime playing time), was another spatial dynamic based on gender. This temporal separation, which male golfers portrayed as being based on "biological" differences between women and men, was an expression of the hegemonic masculinity that informs the organization of space and time inside clubs.

The current argument about space does not suggest that there is a mastermind purposefully determining the organization of space or that

---

3. The term racialization does not claim that race exists as a scientific reality. Instead, it captures how people use a wide range of ideas, perceptions, and arguments to attribute alleged inherent differences to human groups. Racialized statements recur to a myriad of phenotypical or biological markers to validate social distinctions, implicitly or explicitly reproducing the unscientific idea of race. For an extended analysis of the term see Barot and Bird (2001), Saldívar (2014), Murji and Solomos (2005), Omi and Winant (2014), Goldberg (2002).

people follow spatial arrangements in a robotic fashion without any sense of agency. Instead, throughout the book, I show how everyday interactions and perceptions are unwittingly informed by the arrangement of space. Because of its presumed triviality, space can build social differences into everyday interactions, subtlety transforming historical relations of power into apparently normal and natural characteristics of social life. To paraphrase Thomas Gieryn (2000), space is not simply a background but rather another component of the game, a force with a detectable effect on social life. Throughout the book, I constantly think about space.

Thematic Organization

The book is structured in the following manner: Chapter 1 considers the ways that historical dynamics have profoundly marked today's relations of privilege, offering an analysis of the development of golf in Mexico throughout the twentieth century. This section pays particular attention to the connection between golf and modernity. Exploring this relationship allows us to examine two interrelated processes: the expansion of capitalism and the introduction of Anglo-American racialized ideas to Mexico. These elements are fundamental to understanding some contemporary trends. The second part of the chapter describes the mid-twentieth-century transformation of Mexican golf clubs from Anglo-American enclaves to communities of upper-middle- and upper-class local people. Paradoxically, this transformation preserved some of the class-based and racialized dynamics established by wealthy Anglo-American immigrants during the early twentieth century.

Chapter 1 ends by chronicling golf's rapid expansion by the end of twentieth- century and beginning of twenty-first-century Mexico—when more golf courses were built in a span of about 20 years than in the previous 90 years. This development is associated with the neoliberal shift this country experienced during the 1990s. Despite the increase in golf infrastructure, however, the sport retained many of its exclusionary practices. The historical explanation clarifies why golf is commonly considered a game of the middle class in the United States but in current-day Mexico is played exclusively in private clubs that cater to those in the higher rungs of the class hierarchy. The analysis of the relationship between golf and modernity, and the racialized dynamics that emerged from this connection, helps one understand the tremendous symbolic power golf possesses in Mexico today.

Chapter 2 analyzes the class composition of golf clubs, demonstrating that class dynamics cannot be reduced to economic relations. The first part of the chapter shows how players commonly framed the broader golf community in terms of similarities, illustrating how these clubs offered a common ground for members of the upper-middle and upper classes to come together in a space that noticeably excluded the middle and working classes. This does not mean, however, that all golfers and golf clubs were regarded as equal. The section elaborates on the tensions and antagonism that existed between players situated at the extreme ends of the internal socioeconomic hierarchy, i.e., between golfers belonging to the least expensive and most exclusive clubs.

The second part of the chapter analyzes how clubs erected firm social boundaries with the outside world, creating spaces that are invisible to the larger city but hypervisible to the internal group. For example, despite their massive proportions, golf clubs are often imperceptible to the average city dweller. In contrast, the spatial arrangements inside clubs are organized in a way that generate a sense of openness and communal visibility. The chapter ends by illustrating that class is not the only principle that shapes this privileged sites. Gender dynamics also informed privilege. Female club members, for example, faced many restrictions that effectively reduced their visibility inside the clubs. This process fosters a narrative that perceived women as inherently weaker and incompetent players.

Chapter 3 provides an analysis of the everyday dynamics that reproduce privilege inside golf clubs, starting with the way ordinary speech is used to reinforce class hierarchies between players and workers. For example, while club members only used first names when introducing, referring to, and addressing other golfers, workers were expected to use multiple forms of linguistic subordination when interacting with golfers. These everyday verbal exchanges solidified the substantial class differences existing inside the community. The chapter also shows that club members widely believed that golf is a sport linked to honor, honesty, intelligence, and civility, a narrative that reflects golfers' perception of themselves. This account allows players to claim a form of athletic exceptionalism for golf, justifying exclusionary practices based on arguments that transcended wealth.

The second part of the chapter explores the internal class tensions created by the rapid expansion of golf in recent years. The growth of the sport has attracted newly rich golfers as well as global corporations, both of whom are interested in using the game to bolster their image. Long-time golfers viewed some of these changes in negative terms because they believed that economic assets had displaced other forms of capital that had traditionally defined the sport, such as social and cultural goods. These changes have not resulted in a more welcoming and open pastime. Instead, they reflect the way in which neoliberal capitalism has forced out traditional social markers in favor of financial assets in contemporary Mexico.

Chapter 4 presents the thesis of the racialization of class, which maintains that racial understandings are deeply intertwined with class principles in Mexico. The analysis starts by showing how despite the assumption that mestizaje eradicated all racial ideas, people still employ a wide range of racialized notions in everyday interactions. Second, it demonstrates how the class system profoundly influences these racial ideas. These arguments, however, do not assert that the wealthier a person is, the whiter they are perceived to be. Instead, the chapter discusses why racial notions change from more fluid cultural assumptions at the bottom and middle part of the class hierarchy to more rigid biological views at the top of the socioeconomic order. The transformation is linked to both the changing nature of capital and the average phenotypical composition of the upper classes. The chapter ends by using a series of concrete ethnographic examples to illustrate how the argument of the racialization of class operates in everyday life.

Chapter 4 contributes to a growing literature aiming to re-examine traditional understandings of race in Mexico (and Latin America). In this country, some scholars have argued against the use of the term race in favor of the term ethnicity, based on the assumption that whereas race implies a fixed biological understanding, strongly rooted in racist views, ethnicity is a malleable concept focused on cultural differences, which, at least theoretically, are more flexible. This academic debate has centered on the significance and precisions of the term race. Chapter 4, however, aims to shift the focus of the dispute from the *meaning* and *accuracy* of the term to its *effects* on everyday life, by examining the racialization of ordinary relations and the influence of the class system on this process.

Chapter 5 uses caddies to examine the racialization of class argument, also showing how spatial dynamics played a fundamental role in expressing racialized perceptions. The chapter starts by demonstrating how the low status of caddies inside golf clubs is connected to the working-class origins of these workers. Notwithstanding, club members commonly explained the

impoverished condition of caddies via a set of seemingly inherent characteristics, such as immoral attitudes and lack of ambition. In the same vein, despite caddies' deep knowledge of the sport—and outstanding skills in some
cases—none of the golfers I spoke with said, or even implied, that caddies
could be considered golfers. On the contrary, most players maintained that
caddies were innately unable to understand the sport based on their *otherness* concerning club members. These widespread narratives illustrate how
the outsider condition of caddies was based on both their lower-class origins
and a process of racialization that naturalized their exclusion.

The second part of the chapter expands on the analysis of space and
spatial relations by examining driving ranges (inexpensive sites where
golf players can practice hitting the ball) and the caddies' house (the
area where caddies wait to be called to the course to work). This section
describes how club members commonly belittled these sites, assigning
them a set of negative class and racialized characteristics. The spatial analysis shows how in a society where racial categories are not always openly
acknowledged, people frequently resorted to class and spatial allegories to
articulate concealed racialized arguments.

Chapter 6 uses the concept of hegemonic masculinity to explain the
subordinated position female players experienced in these clubs, despite
having affluent backgrounds similar to their male peers. The chapter
first describes how women golfers occupied a higher-class position and
white(r) racial identity than most lower-class women and men, elements
that grant them a dominant position in society. Despite their advantaged
role, however, the class-based hegemonic masculinity prevailing in golf
clubs produces a multitude of mechanisms that keep women in a marginal role. The gender distribution of playing time and the exclusion of
women from the bar are two examples used to illustrate how hegemonic
masculinity articulates a multitude of practices that emphasize women's
"inadequacy" and "deficiency." These elements reinforce a narrative that
portrayed women as incompetent athletes by nature.

The chapter expands the discussion of space by elaborating on its
relationship with time, showing how hegemonic masculinity strongly
influences the organization of time and space inside golf clubs. Despite
these structural conditions, however, some women successfully challenged the practices that sought to control them. Ironically, women's
ability to generate more equal gender relations was limited by the same
privilege that benefited them in the broader society. In other words, if female golfers were to disrupt the set of relationships that placed them in a

subordinate position within the world of golf, they could potentially also transform the class and racial hierarchies that allowed them to occupy a very comfortable place in Mexican society at large.

The Epilogue demonstrates that the interwoven relation between class, race, gender, and privilege greatly interests ordinary people. Using the 2018 presidential election in Mexico, the Epilogue shows how the broader issues analyzed in this book played a central role in the public debates during the political campaigns. This section represents a renewed "call to arms" for social scientists interested in studying privilege. We cannot fully understand impoverished groups without examining the other face of the same coin, the privileged.

This book includes a methodological Appendix that explains how I gained access to golfers and golf clubs in Mexico. Of particular importance, the Appendix elaborates on several instances in which I only partially disclosed the motives of the research, such as when I presented my project as an analysis of the relationship between business and golf, when I answered the inevitable question of whether I was a golfer affirmatively, and when I informed caddies that the research focused on the recent history of the sport. While these instances might seem to suggest that I deliberately deceived participants throughout the fieldwork (an unethical practice), I use the Appendix to offer a more nuanced understanding of my choices, situating the research in the broader context of the "studying up" literature and joining the appeal for a shift away from traditional understandings of the ethical/unethical discussion.

It is worth noting that the names of all participants are pseudonyms and multiple details have been modified to keep the privacy of informants. The goal of this book is not to expose people but to make the affluent world of golf in Mexico visible to outsiders. I sought to gather information about privileged Mexicans and present it in a way that helps those outside of this group understand this privileged space. Yet, as Elijah Anderson argued (2011:xvi), "No ethnographer presents exact truths, all accounts of social experience are rendering." Thus, this book is unavoidably my own interpretation of the exclusive universe of golf in contemporary Mexico City.

Finally, I would like to clarify that the picture included in the cover of the book is not from Mexico City, but Sao Paulo in Brazil. During my fieldwork, I witnessed multiple scenarios in the clubs I visited that reminded me so much the paradoxical relationship between wealth and poverty captured in this image. Hence, this picture truly reflects the way privilege and underprivileged inevitably constitute each other.

1

The History of Golf in Mexico

As much as the modern [Western] state has been about increasing bureaucratization and rationalization, about increasingly sophisticated forms of democratization and social control, about the rule of law and the control of capital, it has [also] been about increasingly sophisticated forms and techniques of racial formation.

—THEO GOLDBERG (2002:49)

Introduction

I grew up on the northern side of Mexico City in a neighborhood that included working-class, lower middle-class, and middle-class families. Since my teenage years, I somehow knew that there was a golf course in the general vicinity. Only when I began reading about the history of golf in Mexico did I learn there were, in fact, two golf courses nearby, one of which was one of the oldest and more prestigious clubs in the country. Even though the clubs covered large swaths of land, I found myself unable to pinpoint exactly where these two courses were located or determine how to reach them. While I considered myself a *pata de perro* (literally, a dog's leg), which in the local slang means someone who is very familiar with the surrounding neighborhoods because they are constantly wandering around the area, my inability to locate these two golf courses made me doubt about my knowledge of the city. In the end, I had to search the Internet for aerial maps of the city to find these two large pieces of land that were seemingly invisible, even to a prior resident of the area.

I started by perusing a wide-angle aerial map of the city. All tracts of land appeared as indistinguishable green areas—public parks, ecological preserves, state-owned land, and golf clubs were all just large green spots on the screen, and I was unable to distinguish between public and private land. I then zoomed in to the point at which the names of streets, buildings, and parks as well as other details popped onto the screen. At this scale, the physical map became a social geography, revealing power dynamics through the public–private ownership of the land, a distinction between accessible to all versus accessible to few. Using the map, I was finally able to identify the exact locations of these two golf clubs within my childhood stomping grounds. I realized that these private clubs were considerably larger than most of the public parks in the area.

More importantly, when I zoomed in further, all the way to a pedestrian's view of the city, the golf courses disappeared from the screen, leaving few traces of their existence for anyone walking by to notice. For one club, when I shifted to a pedestrian's view, the neat and modern landscape, including a lake, trees, bushes, and lush vegetation that evoked a rural British scene, was replaced by a tall wall covered with graffiti and poor-quality murals promoting politicians and political parties (which are commonly painted without the consent of the owner). When I zoomed in near the second club, the periphery of the club was delimited by a large stone wall that was covered with graffiti in some sections. As in the other case, the wall completely blocked people's view of the manicured landscape on the other side of the barrier, reinforcing social distance.

The pedestrian views of the aerial map highlighted a surprising aspect of one of these clubs, just how obscured its entrance gate was, given that its members were extremely distinguished and the club's fees were extremely expensive. In the other club, a private guardhouse blocked the flow of cars and people into both the residential area adjacent to the course and the entrance to the club itself. For those allowed to proceed beyond the guardhouse (where regular urban dwellers did not normally go), an inner chain-link fence allowed for a clear view of the course. Thus, this modern green oasis was only visible to people who could justify their presence (i.e., workers) or demonstrate their belonging (i.e., club members or home owners) to the private guards. These two golf clubs remained almost invisible to the constant flow of pedestrians walking around their perimeters, the workers traveling across the city on public buses, and *patas de perro* who wandered around the city with no intention other than exploring their surroundings.

Surveying the neighborhood via the aerial maps made me realize that I had walked past these clubs countless times without ever realizing they were right next to me. The ability to see these sites from the air while they remain invisible to pedestrians shows that golf clubs have adapted to the city's transformations by maintaining an isolated condition via obstructions that block outsiders from viewing the course. These architectural barriers, in the form of tall walls, thick bushes, obscured entrances, and guardhouses, effectively make large pieces of land invisible to the average city dweller. Most of the people who walk, run, cycle, drive, or ride a bus alongside the perimeters of these courses are unable to recognize them as golf clubs—they could just as easily be a playground at a school, a park, a recreational area at a church, a preserve, a row of backyards, or the grounds of a local business. The mature trees that elicit a tranquil landscape inside the course are simply generic treetops when viewed from outside.

After exploring these maps, I was unsure how to describe the clubs' "seen" (to a small number of members) versus "unseen" (to a large number of passersby) qualities. I wondered whether the aerial maps captured the social experiences of those living near the clubs. Was the dramatic gap between an aerial view and a pedestrian view simply the result of a technological misrepresentation of social life? Did my need to use Internet maps merely reflect my poor understanding of the urban geography? These questions about space and golf remained buried in my field notes until I interviewed Tom, a caddy in his mid-twenties who had been working at a high-end golf club for five years. When I asked him what his friends and family members thought of his job as a caddy, his answer highlighted the unseen nature of the clubs and reminded me of my experience with the aerial maps. First he explained,

> [People] ask me, "What do you do for a living?" So, I answer, "I am a caddy in a golf club." So, people ask again, "What's that?" So, I need to explain to them, "Have you ever seen on TV sports news, when they talk about golf? There are dudes who carry the bags, I am one of them, yeah . . . the lackey." So, I am the servant, [laughs] we all [caddies] are servants.

Tom's statement emphasized the large class distinctions existing between caddies and golfers; he then continued by referencing the unseen nature of the courses, noting that the club where he works, despite its centrality and massive proportions, is unknown by workers in the vicinity. He recounted,

> The first time I came here for the job interview, I arrived late, because people around here [using public transportation] don't know about the club. So, I arrived at the nearby metro station [and asked],

"Hey, where is the golf club?" Nobody could tell me where it was. [People asked me] "Is there a golf club here?" And I said—"Yeah, there is one" [People responded]—"No, I don't know anything about it."

Tom had reached the nearby subway station without any problem, but once there he found that the people in the area, street vendors, waiters in the local eateries, and taxi drivers, could not tell him how to reach the club, which was located only one mile (a mere 15-minute walk) from the subway station. Ordinary people's lack of awareness of the existence of a large piece of property adjacent to the spaces of their everyday lives brought to mind my own experience dealing with the (in)visibility of golf clubs. Out of curiosity, I decided to stop at the metro station Tom mentioned on three different occasions to see whether anyone there could give me directions to the golf club.

The street vendors who erected their stalls outside the station each day knew nothing about the club. When I asked people working at three different inexpensive eateries near the entrance to the station, two waiters and a waitress all were unable to offer me directions, claiming that they were new to the area or the job. Paradoxically, an extensive piece of property less than a mile from their job site was not visible to them. One suggested asking the taxi drivers parked outside the station, conferring upon them a degree of expertise on the matter. I asked nine taxi drivers the same question, and only one could offer specific directions. He directed me to a private guardhouse less than half a mile away and told me I would be able to reach the door to the club through that street. Notably, he said "the door" and not "the worker's door." The main door to the club was approximately one-quarter mile farther down the street, over an artery carrying high-speed traffic. None of the other eight taxi drivers could offer me exact directions to the club, and one even answered, "I don't know of any golf club around here."

The inability of ordinary people, including my own experience, to recognize a large tract of centrally located land helped me grapple with the central puzzle of my project: How does privilege materialize during everyday interactions? The more I advanced in the ethnographic fieldwork and conducted interviews, the more it became clear that this inquiry needed to be accompanied by other questions in order to capture the intersectional dimensions of privilege. My work, therefore, also addresses the following questions: To what extent and in what ways are upscale social spaces, like golf clubs, exclusively organized by class? Despite the widely believed notion that race (as a concept) does not exist in Mexico, do racial perceptions inform social arrangements inside upscale sites? How does gender influence the distribution of social dynamics in exclusive social clubs? And how does spatial interactions inform relations of privilege? The current chapter, however, seeks to offer a long-term perspective to these questions.

The chapter analyzes the history of golf in Mexico, showing a long-term pattern of class and racialized dynamics associated to the sport. The first part describes how wealthy Anglo-American immigrants brought golf to late nineteenth-century Mexico. This section explains how the early development of golf was connected to the spread of modernity, capitalism, and Anglo-American racialized ideas.[1] The second part chronicles the transformation that golf experienced after the 1940s when a growing number of affluent Mexicans joined this sport. The chapter ends by showing how the neoliberal policies introduced by the late 1980s significantly expanded the number of golf clubs existing in the country. Despite the considerable expansion, however, golf is still the preserve of the upper-middle and upper classes in today's Mexico.

The History of Golf

Golf arrived in Mexico in the 1890s with the establishment of the Tampico Country Club and the Pachuca Country Club (Wray 2002). These two clubs were funded by wealthy U.S. and British immigrants working for the Anglo-American conglomerates that controlled local extracting industries (i.e., mining and oil). In 1900, the San Pedro Golf Club was the first club to open in the vicinity of the capital city (Wright 1938). San Pedro was located in Tacubaya, one of the most exclusive suburban towns on the outskirts of Mexico City, which was advertised as the "Monte Carlo of Mexico" (Massey-Gilbert 1901:69). The memberships of these clubs were composed exclusively of affluent businessmen, political figures, and other prominent members of the Anglo-American community; among them,

---

1. Modernity refers to the historical process that replaced agrarian societies, organized under non-democratic systems, and built on traditional norms with capitalist economies, based on democracy, and arranged around class dynamics. Multiple scholars have questioned the assumed positive character of modernity (see Foucault 1995; Goldberg 2002; Harvey 2003; Robinson 2005).

for example, were D. P. Bennett, director of the Mexican National Railway; J. J. Moylan, director of the Mexican Lumber Company; and Powell Clayton Jr., son of the U.S. Ambassador to Mexico. According to the 1901 Massey-Gilbert Blue Book (a city directory), no Mexicans were members of the San Pedro Golf Club.

In 1901, a second club, the Mixcoac Golf Club, was established in Mexico City. Like San Pedro, the club was in the vicinity of the "Monte Carlo of Mexico," and its members were also affluent businessmen from the Anglo-American community. Prominent members of the Mixcoac Golf Club included Paul Hudson and A. J. Hunter, directors of the *Mexican Herald* and the International Bank, respectively. Unsurprisingly, the 1901 Massey-Gilbert Blue Book shows that San Pedro and Mixcoac were composed of U.S. and British immigrants working for rail companies, real estate corporations, trading firms, retail business, and financial enterprises. The strong connection between golf and capitalism should not be a surprise. By the late nineteenth century, at a time when sports were exported from Britain to new locations, golf was a game already identified with actions and themes such as fighting against nature, taking risks, strategic thought, calculation, being resilient in the face of misfortune, individualism, ethics, responsibility, and trust. All these tropes strongly resembled the daily activities, situations, paradoxes, and dilemmas faced by modern businessmen (Cerón-Anaya 2010; Moss 2001).

In 1905, San Pedro, Mixcoac, and the nearby Cricket Club merged to form the Mexico City Country Club (commonly called "the Country Club"). The new club relocated to the village of Churubusco, which was about a 20-minute trip from the city center by a recently installed electric tram. Grove Johnson, a fellow at the Royal Institute of British Architects (Wright 1938), designed a lavish clubhouse. The club was officially inaugurated by Mexican President Porfirio Díaz during a glamorous party in 1907. At the time, a U.S. traveler described the Mexico City Country Club as follows:

The grounds are admirably laid out and the extensive golf-links in the rear of the building add to their attractiveness. The artificial lake is fed by artesian water. The entrance hall terminates in a grand dance-hall. The cantina is decorated in Old Flemish. There is a commodious gymnasium with baths. The building is the finest of its class in the Republic. (Terry 1911:407)

Later that year, the club hosted a reception for Elihu Root, the first U.S. secretary of state to visit Mexico (Morales and Caballero 1908). The club's selection as a site to welcome such an important guest indicates the great status the Country Club enjoyed among wealthy Anglo-American immigrants. It is worth noting that this club broke with the traditional patterns of settlements among local elites in Mexico City, since the Country Club was far away from where the local elites lived. During the late nineteenth century, many members of the local aristocracy and the upper class moved their residences from the colonial center of Mexico City to the southeastern periphery (Nutini 2008). In contrast, the Country Club's new location, Churubusco, was south of Mexico City and was not even considered a suburb at the time.

The Anglo-American capitalists who established the club decided to move it far from the homes of local Mexican elites. This decision resembles the colonial patterns of residential segregation that emerged in multiple locations across the world at the time, including Dakar, Cairo, Johannesburg, Leopoldville, and Algiers (Goldberg 2002; Said 2006). In each of these cases, white colonial settlers created their own modern spaces for living and entertainment far from the local elites, allowing only a few locals to join them—for example, by restricting residential areas only to members, who needed to be U.S. or British citizens. Later in the chapter, I further explore the way in which the boundary between the modern golf club and the non-modern surrounding areas was linked to the racialization of people and space.

In 1910, the Mexican Revolution disrupted the pleasant world of golf in Mexico. The civil war was connected to, among other things, the structural economic inequalities that allowed the massive concentration of wealth that had produced golf clubs. In 1914, the Zapatista Army, one of the most progressive factions in the conflict, besieged Mexico City and occupied the Country Club. The *American Golfer* described the presence of the Zapatistas at the club with great horror:

All rules and regulations consistent with country club formalities were pitched into the discard. Coarse, vulgar, perspiring soldiers, wearing hobnails and spitting tobacco at long range with unerring accuracy, pranced into the grand salon, there to toss their kits upon the inlaid floors and halt for as many nights as they could hold the Club against pursuing invaders. (Davis 1935:31)

When William Mitchell and Eugene Bailey, president and vice-president of the club, visited the site with the goal of persuading the revolutionary army to leave their property, "both gentlemen, unharmed, but denuded of their clothing returned to Mexico City in barrels. Neither of them could be induced to revisit the club until the out of town membership petered out in 1915" (Davis 1935:62). Notably, the image of the vulgar, sweaty, violent, and tobacco-spitting Zapatista soldiers portrayed in the magazine seems to evoke exactly the opposite characteristics of the seemingly refined, clean, mannered, and self-regulated golf player. The former represented the antithesis of modernity, whereas the latter epitomized the embodiment of modernity, including a set of racialized assumptions; I will return to the point later.

By the 1910s, golf had become the preferred pastime of modern capitalists in Britain and the United States (Cerón-Anaya 2010; Lowerson 1994, 1995; Napton and Laingen 2008;Vamplew 2012), to the extent that this sport was also used as a way to *educate* people about capitalism. For instance, David R. Forgan, the president of National City Bank and one of the key speakers at the 1910 annual convention of the New York Bankers' Association, used golf to illustrate risks in the banking industry. Forgan began his speech about the banking field with the following comparison: "Besides having bunkers, bankers, like golfers, are in danger of water hazards and bad lies" (*United States Investor* 1910:46). In the same year (1910), at the annual convention of the Pennsylvania Banker's Association, D. S. Kloss, the secretary of the organization and one of the main speakers at the meeting, suggested that attendees should use golf to develop "closer personal relations among neighboring bankers" (*United States Investor* 1910:16). Hence, it is not surprising that the *American Golfer* viewed with such disdain the presence of *coarse, vulgar, perspiring*, and quasi-socialist Zapatista soldiers at the Country Club in Mexico City.[2]

The Mexican Revolution disturbed the development of modernity, capitalism, and golf throughout the entire country. Some clubs were abandoned while others were temporarily occupied (Wright 1938). Yet by the end of the armed conflict in 1921, Mexican society had returned to its "normal" order. An article published in the November 1921 issue of *Golf Illustrated* declared, "Those who think of Mexico as a country of

---

2. Land reform was the main objective of the Zapatist movement, but, unlike other factions during the arm conflict, the Zapatistas wanted to promote collective forms of land ownership (see Womack 2011).

revolutions, which so many are prone to do nowadays, would scarcely expect to find a distinctly modern idea exemplified so finely as it is in the Mexico City Country Club" (14). The article included pictures of Mexican President Álvaro Obregón paradoxically celebrating the centennial anniversary of Mexico's independence at the Country Club, an organization that accepted locals not as equal subjects but almost solely as subordinated workers. The images showed important local political figures and international diplomats mingling at a magnificent and well-attended party.

In 1926, the Mexico Golf Association (MGA) was formed and put under the authority of the United States Golf Association (an arrangement that continues today). The group comprised seven clubs: Mexico City Country Club, Chapultepec Heights Country Club, Guadalajara Country Club, Pachuca Country Club, Tampico Country Club, Monterrey Country Club, and Oro Golf Club (Wright 1938). Following a common fashion at the time, these clubs were exclusively connected to the local culture via their names, as they were exclusively composed by wealthy Anglo-American immigrants (pattern that followed a colonial practice). The lack of locals among the membership in these clubs might be the reason why the organization was called "Mexico" Golf Association rather than "Mexican," as few members of the association were in fact Mexicans. For example, Anglo-American executives working for the local subsidiary of the United States Smelting, Refining & Mining Company controlled the Monterrey Country Club, and the Oro Golf Club was home to executives of the London-based El Oro Mining and Railway Company. No specific company controlled the clubs in the two main cities in the country, Guadalajara and Mexico City. The strategic locations of these metropolitan areas attracted a wide variety of prominent Anglo-American businessmen, accepting also a small number of Mexicans from the local economic and political elites (Huerta Nava 2005; Wright 1938). The spirit of capitalism was of course linked to these golf clubs via the activities of almost all of their members.

The steering committee of the MGA was composed entirely of members of the Anglo-American immigrant community. The main force behind the creation of the group was Harry Wright, a Virginian who was also closely involved in the creation of the American Chambers of Commerce (Rodriguez Diaz 1975). Harold Campbell, another member of the MGA steering committee, was later president of the American Chambers of Commerce on two different occasions (Rodriguez Diaz 1975). Nelson Rhoades was a third key figure involved in the MGA. In addition to being a golf enthusiast, Rhoades was a partner in the law firm James R. Garfield and Nelson Rhoades of Cleveland. Due to the social connections of Rhoades's associate James R. Garfield (son of U.S. President James Abram Garfield), the firm had close ties with members of the U.S. government, Standard Oil, and important financial circles in New York (Hart 2002).

By the late 1930s, the MGA had grown from 7 to 16 clubs (Wright 1938). Like the original clubs, all the new clubs were created and controlled by wealthy Anglo-American immigrants working for extractive, real estate, or financial firms. For example, the Cananea Golf Club, situated in the northwestern state of Sinaloa, was linked to the mining conglomerate of William Rockefeller. The Alondra Golf Club in the southeastern state of Veracruz was connected first to the British-owned Aguila Oil Company and later to the Anglo-Dutch oil company Shell. The Tlahualilo Golf Club (situated next to the largest cotton production complex in the world) was tied to the New York–based Tlahualilo Company. And the Torreon Country Club in the northern state of Coahuila was associated with the Baruch Brothers Investment Bank of New York (Hart 2002). Once again, this scenario illustrates how golf became the quintessential game promoting the modern spirit of capitalism.

Racial Modernity

In the early twentieth century, the aesthetic of the golf course was reminiscent of aristocratic British taste, and thus the golf course seemed not to be an obvious manifestation of the spirit of modernity. However, the course itself was palpable evidence of the wondrous possibilities of modernity. Although the aesthetic of the golf course concealed its modern nature behind a paradoxical reverence of pristine nature, a golf course in Mexico was material proof of the power of modernity to recast any landscape to fit human desires. Modernity made the existence of a lake, a small forest, and green lush hills possible even in the middle of a strikingly different terrain, showing that nature could be dominated and controlled at will. In the world of golf, the modernist trope that urged "man" to conquer nature was not just a metaphor but a material reality expressed in every contour of the course. Hitting a light rubber ball with an aluminum club on a grassy tract of land that resembled the British landscape rather than the local terrain (and which by extension represented capitalism) was an experience that only a modern rational mindset could create. Yet modernity and reason were not the only elements that defined this space.

Modernity and the Process of Racialization

The connection between modernity and golf was a central aspect of the sport. However, as David Harvey argues,

> One of the myths of modernity is that it constitutes a radical break with the past. The break is supposedly of such an order as to make it possible to see the world as a tabula rasa, upon which the new can be inscribed without reference to the past—or, if the past gets in the way, through its obliteration. (2003:1)

Modernity did not represent a radical break with the past; rather, it came preloaded with a whole range of notions included racial perceptions (Appelbaum, Macpherson, and Rosemblatt 2003; Wade 1995). As Weinstein (2015) explained, the scientific racism of the nineteenth and early twentieth centuries,[3] which was produced primarily in northern Europe and the United States, articulated a set of notions that linked northern Europe and North America with a set of positive ideas about progress, reason, and modernity. This narrative subtly connected modernity, rationalization, the landscape, and race in an almost *natural* way. In other words, the narrative assumed that the connection between North American and European territories, the birth of modernity, and the racial identity of the people living in these areas was not a mere coincidence, rather the economic progress of these regions resulted from an interdependence. Considering the scientific racism at the time, Native and African Americans were excluded from any positive assumption about geography and modernity.

This process of racialization, which posited strong links between progress, geography, and whiteness (as well as between stagnation, geography, and non-whiteness) was not a modern invention. These ideas were first intertwined during the configuration of the colonial world and, therefore, preceded and influenced the development of modernity (Gall 2004; Go 2016; Goldberg 2002; Omi and Winant 2014; Robinson 2005). The modern process of racialization connected a whole range of positive characteristics to Western European and North American nations—excluding

---

3. Scientific racism is the belief that accurate scientific evidence exists to support the division of people in different racial groups and that these groups naturally differ from each other regarding behaviors, ethics, morals, and intelligence, among other traits. Modern science has proved the inaccuracy of these ideas, but some scientists considered them correct in the nineteenth and early twentieth centuries. (For a discussion of the topic in Latin America see López-Durán 2018; Loveman 2014; Stepan 1991.)

Mexico—based primarily on their racial composition (Goldberg 2002). Thus, whiteness and its constellation of beneficial attributes became linked to modern Western European and Anglo-American states and, by extension, to those who could legitimately claim these nationalities based on a particular phenotypical appearance (Ngai 2004; Schrag 2011).

The racialization of the West as predominantly white, and non-Western states as predominately non-white, was deeply connected to the development of the rational spirit of modernity. As Theo Goldberg's quote at the beginning of the chapter suggests, the development of the rational spirit of modernity, expressed in the development of modern nation-states, was also connected to "increasingly sophisticated forms and techniques of racial formation" (2002:49). This process strongly associated modern morals, values, ideas, and material elements with individuals and processes emanating from the West; everyone and everything else was consigned to one of a seemingly endless number of states of unaccomplished modernity (non-modern, pre-modern, primitive, barbarian, savage, traditional, etc.). Modernity was assumed to be an intrinsic characteristic of Western European and Anglo-American individuals and communities, as well as their practices and traditions.

This strong association between modernity, the West, and whiteness permeated the practice of sports. The 1904 Olympic Games in St. Louis, Missouri, for example, included a special set of "contests" called "Anthropological Days" in which Pygmies, whose bodies were the antithesis of the Western body, engaged in athletic competitions that usually devolved into carnivalesque spectacles (Brownell 2008). A newspaper headline at the time—"Barbarians meet Athletic Games"—highlighted the anti-modern racial stereotypes applied to the Pygmy athletes (Eichberg 1990). Sports played a key role in the global spread of racial formation because the deficient performance of non-white individuals in modern athletic competitions was viewed as conclusive evidence of the impossibility of non-white subjects to discipline their bodies through rational physical activities (Brownell 2008; Gems 2006).[4] When Western athletic games began to travel to new global destination during the nineteenth century,

---

4. Nowadays in the United States, non-white bodies are seen as superior athletes, but inferior with regard to intelligence, which is seen as a more important characteristic. In other words, African Americans are stereotyped as athletes (and entertainers) rather than doctors or lawyers. However, in the late nineteenth and early twentieth centuries, non-white bodies were associated with a lack of modern athleticism.

they were accompanied by deep-seated ideas that linked modernity and progress with pre-modern racial perceptions.

Golf, Modernity, and the Process of Racialization

Golf, like any other sport, was a democratic game—winning was based on clear and rational rules rather than any sort of identity. Golf clubs in Mexico did not have signs stating, "Only whites allowed." Yet, in an insidious way, the entire space of golf, both the course itself and its immediate surroundings, reflected Anglo-American racial thinking. Several specific aspects of the club—the landscape, the architecture of the clubhouse, the street names in the nearby development, the club's stationery and promotional materials, and the trophies—highlighted an assumed racial hierarchy with Anglo-Americans at the top and indigenous groups at the bottom. Following Goldberg (2002), the power of race was magnified by the fact that it was so obviously both everywhere and nowhere.

While most sports (e.g., soccer and baseball) embraced generic modern athletic aesthetics such as geometric perimeters of action, a highly visible scoreboard, and uniforms for practitioners, golf embraced a specifically Anglo aesthetic. Golf required foreign landscapes to be obliterated and then reshaped in the image of the British landscape. The course was not only a site molded by the practices of modernity (i.e., technology and the human desire for control) but also a site that aesthetically emulated a British landscape.[5] Course developers' subordination of nature was not simply an attempt to create a *beautiful* landscape for play, but rather an effort to universalize a *particular* aesthetic—the British countryside—which became the universal aesthetic of golf and a symbol for the modern nature of the game. Thus, early golf architects across the globe sought to dominate nature in order to transform sections of Mexico City, Cairo, Johannesburg, Bangalore, Bangkok, Sao Paulo, Buenos Aires, Panama City, and other major cities into replicas of the British landscape (Klein 1999).

At the Mexico City Country Club, golf's Anglo-American racial affiliation was also evinced in the architectural contours of the clubhouse, which evoked the "Spanish-inspired" style of extravagant mansions in California (Wright 1938). The "tiled Belgian-glass roof," "spacious grounds," and "commodious gymnasium with baths" (Terry 1911) offered players and

---

5. In the second half of the twentieth century, architects in the golf world aimed to mimic a more generic Anglo-American landscape (see Klein 1999).

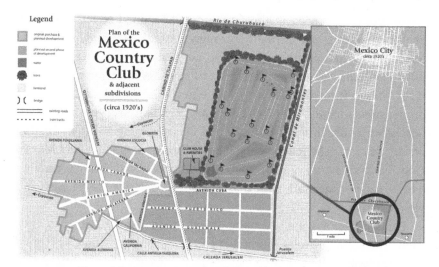

FIGURE 1.1 Plan of the Mexico Country Club and Adjacent Subdivisions, c. 1920's
Source: This is a recreation of an original plan developed by Escude and Potts, Engineers and Contractors, Callejón del Espíritu Santo 9, P.O. Box 331-DF (c. 1920's), included in Krauze, Moreno, and Speckman Guerra (2005:144).

their guests the opportunity to inhabit a site that, aesthetically, was closer to the modern Anglo-American and Western European worlds than to the non-modern Mestizo/Indian context of the local area.

The Anglo-American racial thinking was not only present in the club's architectonic details, it was also reflected in the modern urban development area constructed around the club (Figure 1.1) for the purpose of housing club members, which the rules of the club stated should be at least 75 percent U.S. or British citizens (Wright 1938).[6]

The biggest plots of land, which were laid out near the southern end of the course, were divided by three streets that the developers had named "Cuba," "Puerto Rico," and "Guatemala" (names that might have evoked colonial images among Anglo-American golfers). In front of the main gate at the southwest corner of the club, six streets emerged from a roundabout and continued through a residential area that included slightly smaller plots. The central street was named "America," and the other five were "England," "Ireland," "Scotland," "Canada," and "Germany." Four smaller streets, "Dakota," "Virginia," "California," and "Pennsylvania," crossed the larger streets. By the early twentieth century, each of the

---

6. The remaining 25 percent of members could be any other nationality.

nationalities referenced in the four European-named streets (England, Scotland, Ireland, and Germany) strongly evoked a white identity in the Mexican context, even though this had not always been the case (Schrag 2011). Ironically, the plots on the streets named after the colonized states of Cuba, Puerto Rico, and Guatemala were never developed, while the plots on the streets named after European countries that had sent large numbers of white immigrants to the United States became host to a thriving residential area. The letterhead and promotional materials of the Mexico Golf Association emphasized again the process of racialization through which Anglo-American enthusiast golfers perceived themselves and viewed locals.

Figure 1.2 shows the letterhead of the Mexico Golf Association circa 1926. The scene includes four figures and three objects framed by a majestic landscape with two large mountains in the back (the volcanic mountains of the Popocatepetl and Iztaccihuatl, which surround Mexico City). In the foreground there are two figures and two objects: a tall man in an active position, a smaller (possibly young) man in a passive stance, an agave plant, and a cactus. The passive man, situated next to a donkey, is dressed in traditional indigenous (Native American) attire (a large hat and clothes made of coarse white cloth) and carries a bag of clubs, indicating that he is a caddy, not a golfer. The figure's passive stance metaphorically situates him closer to the donkey (which is in a similarly passive stance) and to the natural objects in the composition (e.g., the cactus and the mountains) than to the active figure.

MEXICO GOLF ASSOCIATION

FIGURE 1.2 Detail of the letterhead produced by MGA, c. 1926

Source: Image found at Fondo Norteamericano, Sección Dirección General, Serie Correspondencia, Sub-serie General, Volumen 54, expediente 120, Archivo Histórico de la Compañía de Minas Real del Monte y Pachuca (AHCMRMyP), archivo a cargo del Archivo Histórico y Museo de Minería, A.C. (AHMM,AC).

In contrast to the caddy, the central figure is dressed in a distinctively modern outfit, holds a club in his hands, and is looking toward the horizon, possibly searching for the ball he just hit. The other two figures are in the background of the scene, between the male golfer and the indigenous caddy. Both are dressed in modern clothing, hold clubs in their hands, and are in active positions, suggesting that they are also playing the game. One is clearly a woman, based on the hat and dress, while the other appears to be a young boy. These three figures suggest a hierarchical social order in which the central male figure takes the lead role and the woman has less status, indeed, almost the same status as the young boy. I will return to the influence of gender in the organization of golf later in the book.

The golfers are all portrayed in active positions, in sheer contrast to the other (submissive) elements in the scene, including the indigenous caddy and the donkey. Although the faces of the four figures are not defined enough to distinguish phenotypic patterns, the clothes and manners indicate a separation between active/passive, energetic/lethargic, and modern/non-modern. The three golfers clearly embody the first set of characteristics, while the caddy embodies the second, almost as if these characteristics were naturally connected to their bodies. This artistic representation of the world of golf in early twentieth-century Mexico perfectly reflects the racial perceptions about Mexico that were broadly accepted in the United States at the time. As Hart (2002:42) noted, "American businessmen and politicians contrasted the 'hard working and independent' virtues of the Anglo–Saxons with the 'laziness and docility' of the Mexicans." The racial hierarchy portrayed in the scene reflects the deep-seated racial ideas that organized the worldviews of affluent Anglo-Americans in Mexico at the time. The stationery depicts in visual form the expectations, assumptions, and stereotypes about who could and could not play golf—in other words, who could and could not become a modern subject. While the aesthetic tastes of the Mexico Golf Association changed in the following decade (the 1930s), the group's racial ideas did not.

The next version of the association's letterhead (Figure 1.3) featured a more modern design, including updated clothing for the golfers. However, the central organizing ideas of the composition remained the same. The fashion and active posture of the male golfer in the foreground evoke notions of agency and purposefulness. While the several figures in the background do not possess identifiable phenotypical features, certain characteristics clearly place them into two distinct groups. Three are

FIGURE 1.3 Detail of the new letterhead produced by MGA, c. 1936

Source: Image found at Fondo Norteamericano, Sección Dirección General, Serie Correspondencia, Sub-serie General, Volumen 54, expediente 120, Archivo Histórico de la Compañía de Minas Real del Monte y Pachuca (AHCMRMyP), archivo a cargo del Archivo Histórico y Museo de Minería, A.C. (AHMM,AC).

wearing large hats and are either serving others or standing idly: the first carries a bag of clubs, the second holds the flag that marks the hole, and the third is sitting on a donkey. The four other figures in the background are wearing knickers (pants cut off at the knee, a style that was strongly associated with golf); three of them are resting their bodies on their clubs as they wait (a momentarily idle position), and one is about to hit the ball. The figures with the big hats are passive characters who are not very different from the other ornamental elements in the composition.

In 1937, when the MGA organized its 12th National Amateur Tournament, the poster promoting the event (Figure 1.4) reflected the modern/non-modern, white/non-white, and culture/nature dichotomies of colonialism (Dirks 2000). In the foreground there is a map of a highway connecting the United States and Mexico as well as two modern cars, suggesting fast travel between San Antonio and Mexico City (possibly also Acapulco, though at the time this city was not yet the tourist destination it would become in the following two decades). The poster portrays two seemingly identical golfers—one in the United States and one in Mexico City—each about to hit a ball. The U.S. golfer is flanked by two men, a black caddy serving the golfer and an amused cowboy looking on, while the golfer in Mexico is accompanied by a boyish caddy dressed in traditional indigenous fashion.

The fast, modern, technological world associated with golf that is pictured in the foreground stands in contrast to the traditional, non-modern, ancient world of Mexico that is represented in the background by images of timeless figures of an ancient nature. These images reference pre-Hispanic (prior to 1519), colonial (between 1521 and 1821), and

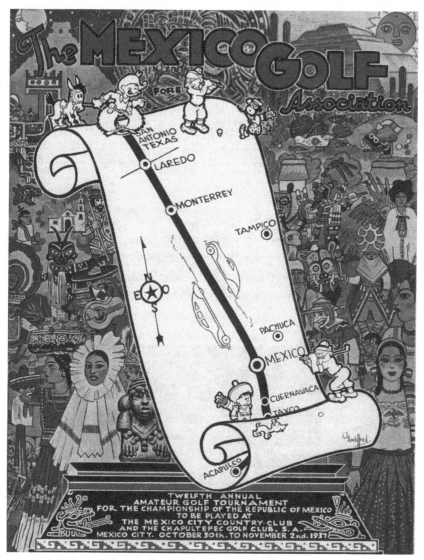

FIGURE 1.4 Promotion material of the 12th National Amateur Tournament, 1937

Source: Image found at Fondo Norteamericano, Sección Dirección General, Serie Correspondencia, Sub-serie General, Volumen 54, expediente 120, Archivo Histórico de la Compañía de Minas Real del Monte y Pachuca (AHCMRMyP), archivo a cargo del Archivo Histórico y Museo de Minería, A.C. (AHMM,AC).

post-colonial historical moments (after 1821)—i.e., across more than five centuries, as well as the entire country—by portraying festive clothes from multiple geographical areas including the south, center, and north of the country. The poster suggests a dichotomy in which the culture of Mexico is ancient and timeless while the culture of Anglo-America is modern and technological, conveying notions of romanticization and infantilization of Mexican society. The image reflects a recurrent trope in Anglo-Americans' perceptions of Mexico: Mexico is ancient and static while Western countries are modern and dynamic.

Another example of the racial character of golf's aesthetics is evidenced by the trophies MGA created in the late 1920s for the winners of the association's annual competitions. Long-time president Harry Wright described the Challenge Cup (Figure 1.5), "one of the most unique of the trophies," in the following way:

> It is nearly three feet high. Its bowl, one foot in diameter, has an elaborate frieze of delicate workmanship representing Tiger and Eagle knights, armed not with their traditional weapons, but with peaceful golf clubs in their carcaxes [bodies]. Macuilxochitl, god of pleasure, who presided over the sporting events of the Aztecs in the

FIGURE 1.5 Challenge Cup, c. 1928
Source: Courtesy of Wright (1938:49).

Valley of Anahuac, is seen handling his mashie [a type of golf club] as he contemplates the crater of Popocatepetl and decides that from (sic) all time he will hold the record for "a hole in one." The entire valley of Mexico is depicted in the background as the Aztec golf course. The old Teocalli [temple] of the ancient city of Tenochtitlan and the famous pyramids of San Juan Teotihuacan are among the interesting details. On each side of the cup are two beautifully wrought handles depicting Quetzalcoatl, the Plumed Serpent god of the Toltecs. A golf ball, mounted on the top of the cup, forms the base for Centeotl, the water goddess, where she stands with an iron club in her hand, symbolic of the hazards she has triumphantly crossed. (Wright 1938:46)

Wright described the cup as the masterpiece of Jacinto Vigueras, a local artist who "has applied himself since childhood to this ancient Aztec craft" (1938:46). Given the reification of victory that the cup represented, the cup and the description above might initially seem like a compliment to the local culture. However, in the context of early twentieth-century affluent Anglo-American golfers in Mexico, this object was linked to the modern/non-modern colonial and racialized dichotomy embraced by the world of golf. The cup is the only pre-Hispanic–themed artistic manifestation I encountered, in either Harry Wright's history of golf in Mexico (1938) or any other early account, that garnered recognition. Descriptions of the aesthetics of the clubhouses or any other space linked to golf always portrayed these spaces in terms of their modern and technological spirit, which was simply a way to refer to its Anglo-American/European aesthetic nature, including the racial ideas evoked by these tropes. Artistic manifestations of indigenous groups, even in their pre-colonial glory, were never included in buildings, the landscape, or any other artistic objects among golfers.

McClintock argued that "the mapping of Progress depends on systematically inventing images of archaic time to identify what is historically new" (cited in Weinstein 2015:34). The Challenge Cup, the stationery of the MGA, and the posters promoting golf events in early twentieth-century Mexico were instances of precisely this practice; these images and objects served to juxtapose the archaic local nature and the new Anglo-American culture. The only roles for indigenous people in the sport were as references to the past or as workers. The Challenge Cup trophy may be the ultimate aesthetic reflection of a racialized order, and the golf ball mounted at the top was a clear representation of the presumed *natural* hierarchy of this world.

The Modern History of Golf

Throughout the course of the ethnographic fieldwork, I constantly found myself being lectured about the foundational myths of golf, among them the idea that golf arrived in Mexico by the mid-twentieth century. The transcribed interviews commonly include a variation of the phrase, "let me explain this, the history of golf in Mexico starts when President Alemán introduced golf to Mexico by the 1950s. . . ." With the exception of six golf players who were very knowledgeable about the history of the sport, most other golfers repeated this widely believed narrative that assigns Mexican President Miguel Alemán the honor of being the importer of golf to this nation. Despite the historical inaccuracy of the statement, the role of this president popularizing golf among the upper-middle and upper classes paradoxically signaled a deep transformation in the organization of this sport and a stunning continuity in the association between golf, modernity, and racialization.

1940s–1970s

The dynamics of golf clubs changed during the mid-twentieth century when many of the groups that had originally introduced the sport to Mexico left the country during World War II, as global industrial and trading activities considerably decreased and more men and women were required to join the war efforts. As members left, clubs began to suffer financially. For example, the Monterrey Country Club, founded by the American Smelting and Refining Company, was defunct by the late 1940s (Wray 2002). The war, however, was not the only factor that influenced the transformation of the sport. In Mexico, as in many other countries in the Global South, there was a growing sentiment of nationalism. Starting in the 1940s, the Mexican state launched multiple initiatives aimed at generating a strong sense of national pride, and sports were part of this plan (Arbena 1991). Rather than promoting native sports—the ball games indigenous groups played in pre-colonial times—the state actively adopted and sought to Mexicanize modern sports first created in Western nations. Thus, ironically, nationalism was enhanced not via "the rejection of European and

North American athletic forms but in trying to perform these [sports] as well as or better than the source nations" (Arbena 1991:362).

The economic problems many golf clubs encountered during the 1940s and the push to excel at Western athletic games coincided with the election of Miguel Alemán (1946–1952), the most right-wing president in Mexico after the Mexican Revolution (1910–1921). Alemán was popularly known as the "Businessman President" because of his pro-capitalism and pro-business positions, which represented a shift from the pro-worker and socialist sympathies of some of his predecessors. This president was an avid golfer who promoted the sport during his time in office. As ex-president, Alemán became the head of the newly created Consejo Nacional de Turismo (National Council for Tourism), a state-funded organization that promoted the creation of tourist destinations. It was through this public organization that Alemán sponsored the creation of a large number of private golf clubs around the country.

Between the 1950s and 1970s, golf became one of the preferred sports of the upper-middle and upper classes in most parts of Mexico (Morales y Favela 1996). The great allure golf possessed among the upper rungs of society was based on three elements. First, golf was still one of the best examples of the modern nature of sports. For example, although modern stadiums for sports, such as soccer, also required the transformation of the landscape into novel sites where fans could enjoy a communal modern experience (Elsey 2011), golf was the only sport that allowed people to have such a modern experience both as a player and in a small group at the same time. Golf hence provided not only a modern and capitalist experience but also a sense of distinction because it was played in an intimate and exclusive setting.

Second, the allegoric connection between golf and capitalism became even more important by the mid-twentieth century. For example, the October 1954 issue of the magazine *Fortune* reminded its readers that "golf is one of the most delightful dodges for multiplying contacts, for ingratiating oneself with clients, and for enhancing one's business prestige" (14). More revealing, on July 13, 1977, the *Wall Street Journal* published an editorial titled "Of Golf, Capitalism, and Socialism," in which Armen Alchian, a distinguished professor of economics at the University of California, Los Angeles, used old arguments to explain why golf was a positive capitalistic enterprise. He asserted, "Golf's ethic, principles, rules, and procedures of play are totally capitalistic. [. . .] Like life, it is often unfair and unjust, with uninsurable risks. More than any other sport, golf exploits the whole capitalist spirit." Hence, golf was still viewed as the quintessential athletic embodiment of the modern spirit of capitalism.

Third, although Anglo-Americans now accounted for a smaller proportion of golfers in Mexico, the sport firmly maintained the early twentieth-century racialized legacy. In lieu of formal rules or overt stipulations excluding players based on skin color elements, the high cost of the game effectively preserved the racialized dynamics of the sport. This preservation was possible because of the paradoxical racial organization of Mexican society. Despite the widespread myth that racial distinctions do not exist in Mexico, "the overwhelming majority of the lower classes are phenotypically Indian, while the great majority of the upper classes are phenotypically European" (Nutini 1997:54). While this particular characterization of racial dynamics in Mexican society refers to late twentieth-century patterns, the pictures in books and magazines describing the world of golf indicate that the portrayal would also accurately illustrate the decades between the 1940s and 1970s (Castellanos 1999; Horta 1989; Krauze, Moreno, and Speckman Guerra 2005; Morales y Favela 1996; Wray 2002). Therefore, building on the legacies of the Anglo-American sportsmen who had introduced the game to Mexico, playing golf became a class as much as a racialized marker in the local context during second half of the twentieth century. (I elaborate on these topics in the following chapters.)

End of the Twentieth Century

The 1982 oil crisis described in the introduction to this book left the Mexican government with little power to negotiate its way out of the economic catastrophe, because oil, its most valuable asset, lost its value. The state hence was one of the first nations to be "drawn into what was going to become a growing column of neoliberal state apparatuses worldwide" (Harvey 2007:29).[7] The ascent of neoliberalism radically transformed both

---

7. Following Harvey (2007), neoliberalism is a political and economic theory that maintains that human well-being is best achieved by liberating entrepreneurial freedoms in a context characterized by free markets, free trade, and strong private property rights. The state needs to limit its role to support and protect these three pillars, even by force if needed. Outside of early intervention creating markets when they do not exist (in regard to, e.g., environmental contamination, education, social services, and healthcare), the state must be kept to a bare minimum.

the Mexican national context and the sport of golf. Specifically, the restructuring of the state in alignment with the neoliberal project led to the radical dismantling of environmental policies, the transformation of communal land into individual property, the sale of the most important state-owned assets, and the arrival of large amounts of foreign investments (Harvey 2007; Weaver et al. 2012). The state, for example, stopped supporting small farmers via agricultural subsidies, which resulted in the displacement of these rural workers by large agro-industrial corporations.

This scenario generated an unprecedented boom in the construction of golf courses, aiming to cater to both Anglo-American tourists as well as locals interested in consuming products and practices linked to the new global era. To illustrate the expansion of the sport, between 1895 and 1980 a total of 87 golf clubs were constructed in Mexico, while between the 1980s and the early 2000s more than 102 courses were added to the national golf infrastructure—i.e., more courses were constructed between the last decades of the twentieth century than in the previous 85 years. In today's Mexico, the old allegoric connection between modernity, capitalism, and golf has been slightly reinterpreted, offering a more inclusionary tone—the new narrative presents contemporary globalization as an era of endless possibilities for everybody (see Thomas Friedman's bestseller *The World Is Flat*). Yet some exclusionary patterns, such as class-based segregation, gender subordination, and the deep-seated racialized dynamics of the sport, persist. During much of the time I spent at golf clubs, I was one of the few dark-skinned individuals who was not cleaning, serving, or maintaining the club; despite their love for the sport, women held a second-class status in the world of golf; and I did not hear about a club accepting working-class members. The endless world of possibilities some people see in neoliberal capitalism seems not to have materialized completely, at least not with regard to class, gender, and racialized dynamics, in the world of golf in Mexico City.

Conclusion

The present chapter offers an overview of the history of golf to illustrate the long-term power dynamics that have characterized this sport in Mexico. The history of golf permits one to illustrate how modernity, with its constant desire to rationalize the world, was intimately connected with the expansion of capitalism. It was not a coincidence that golf attracted businessmen in large proportions. In a myriad of metaphorical and literal ways, golf replicated with great precision the circumstances, scenarios, dilemmas, challenges, and interpretations that modern businessmen faced on a daily basis. The desire of President Alemán to bring golf to every corner of the country seemed intimately connected to the same desire to transform Mexico into a modern capitalist nation. Golf, modernity, and capitalism were so closely linked together that the promotion of one of them would apparently lead to the promotion of the others.

As David Harvey argues, however, modernity was not a "tabula rasa, upon which the new can be inscribed without reference to the past" (2003:1). Modernity was inextricably associated to pre-modern ideas about race (Goldberg 2002; Robinson 2005). The distinction between a modern and non-modern individual, community, and nation was not simply a matter of technological improvements. At its core, the modern/non-modern dichotomy reflected deep-seated views about those left out of the racialized spirit of modernity. This process of racialization associated with the development of modernity and capitalism fulfilled the crucial role of finding a large group of righteously and justifiably exploitable workers. In other words, the racial inferiority of poor locals became the perfect excuse to turn them into exploitable labor to construct the new modern, rational, and capitalist world.

Drawing on the history of golf in Mexico, the following chapter offers an analysis of how class relations inform the organization of contemporary clubs in Mexico City. Using ethnographic and interview material, Chapter 2 demonstrates how golf is an invisible game when lived from the lower side of the class hierarchy but a highly visible one when experienced from the higher end of the class pyramid. Class, however, is not the only dynamic that determines relations of privilege and disadvantage, and therefore the following section also examines how class collides and intersects with gender dynamics to give shape to the highly privileged and (in)visible space of golf.

2

Invisibility and Hypervisibility

The notion of class entails the notion of historical relationship. [. . .] Class happens when some men [and women], as a result of common experiences (inherited or shared), feel and articulate the identity of their interests as between themselves, and as against other men [and women] whose interests are different from (and usually opposed to) theirs.

—E. P. THOMPSON (1963:9)

Introduction

The morning I met with Rafael, a 60-year-old golfer who owns a well-established advertising company in Mexico City, a business-related crisis delayed our interview for more than two hours, time I patiently spent reading several golf and business magazines in the waiting room at his company. At the end of the interview, Rafael apologized for the long wait by inviting me to play golf at his club, saying, "I'm really sorry for the delay. Golf prevents this sort of incident; when you meet someone at the club you can chat for a long time without interruptions and delays. Why don't you come play [golf] with me on the weekend, and we'll be able to chat without interruptions." I accepted Rafael's invitation and agreed to meet him at the club early Saturday morning. I borrowed one of the newer cars available to me through my close family circle and drove an hour to the other side of the city. Even on the weekends, Mexico City comes to life early in the morning—well before sunrise, the streets are full of neatly dressed workers, people hastily walking to bus stops, buses running in multiple directions, and street vendors selling several types of food, including local specialties such as *tamales* and *tacos de gusiados* (tacos stuffed with different fillings). These dynamics are the same across the city; from the noth side to the south side, similar scenes play out at every major intersection throughout the metropolis. This early morning ebb and flow of workers, vendors, and public buses, however, dwindles and then ends near the entrance gate of the residential area that surrounds Rafael's golf club.

As I traveled to the club on Saturday morning, when I was about five blocks from the private guardhouse that regulates incoming and outgoing traffic around the golf club, I could still see public buses, well-groomed workers walking swiftly to their destinations, and street vendors selling meals and snacks that, while not fast food in the meaning of the term in the United States, were certainly served and eaten rapidly. After passing the guardhouse checkpoint, however, the bustling urban dynamic dissipated. I saw only scattered figures—a few early morning runners, a handful of people walking dogs, and some gardeners with their tools strapped on the back of their bicycles. When I met up with Rafael and three of his friends at the clubhouse restaurant, they were eating fruit and bread and having coffee. We had a few minutes to relax before our 7:20 tee time (the assigned start time). As I introduced myself to Rafael's friends and joined the conversation, I could not stop thinking about the dramatic shift in the atmosphere between the world beyond the club, where people were swiftly trying to get to work, and the world within the club, where members were enjoying a slow-paced, relaxing morning among friends.

Four and a half hours later, the other golfers and I sat down at the bar for drinks and lunch after finishing a round of 18 holes. The site was a spacious place, with several tables and plenty of comfortable chairs. Behind a bar, a wide wall filled with shelves stocked a large collection of spirits, conveying the notion of abundance. Most of the tables offered a nice view of the end of the course, allowing people to see who was currently finishing a round. The place was almost half occupied at the time—midday. After we sat at a table, a waiter dressed in black pants and a white shirt promptly showed up and politely asked us about the game we just finished, "Gentlemen, how was your game?", adding, "Who is the winner today?" After hearing some comments about the finished game, he asked us, "What do you want to drink, we have . . ." and named a long list of alcoholic options, emphasizing the sense of opulence that the well-stocked shelves behind the bar visually offered. After the drinks and food were served, we engaged in a relaxed interaction.

The conversation first revolved around re-creating what had just transpired on the course. Golfers discussed great shots, errors, comebacks, poor skills, inconsistent performances, and any other elements that allowed them to memorialize the game we had just enjoyed. Sometimes the group's conversation became a communal interaction when club members at adjacent tables participated in the jokes or noted parallels between what just happened on the course and other moments or players.

As I made my way back home, I wondered whether the contrast between most city dwellers' hasty movements and the more tranquil pace of club members might be one element underlying how people think of themselves and situate their place in the local class hierarchy. As the opening quote suggests, maybe the nonchalant feeling that dominates interactions between club members helps to articulate notions of common identity and interests among wealthy golfers, in contrast to those individuals who hurriedly walk to reach their jobs.

The current chapter analyzes the class composition of golf clubs, demonstrating that class dynamics cannot be solely reduced to economic relations. The first part shows how players commonly framed the broader golf community in terms of similarities. This, however, does not mean that all golfers and golf clubs were regarded as equal. There are tensions and antagonism, particularly among players situated at the extreme ends of the internal socioeconomic hierarchy, i.e., between golfers belonging to the least expensive and most exclusive clubs. The second part examines how clubs erected firm social boundaries with the outside world, creating spaces that are invisible to the larger city but hypervisible to the internal group. This analysis demonstrates how class dynamics modified spatial perceptions. The chapter ends by illustrating how gender intertwines with the class system, creating a class- as much as gender-based privileged space.

Class is a Relationship

As the Introduction indicated, the cost of membership in the 13 private golf clubs in and around Mexico City varies greatly. The large gap between the "modest" clubs and the more elite clubs poses a conceptual problem: Is it possible to talk about all these clubs in similar terms? Do the "affordable" and the high-end clubs serve the same class category? Can all these clubs and golfers be studied as a single group? In purely economic terms, these clubs belong to different groups, each with its unique interests and positions. This purely economic understanding, however, reduces a multidimensional set of relations to solely economic aspects. While it can be tempting to envision class as a synonym of income brackets, in the real world class is not a thing that is possessed but rather a set of relations that are never neatly defined and that involve a myriad of contradictions and complex interactions.

The two clubs charging more than \$100,000 in membership fees cater exclusively to a small segment of the upper class. Most golfers describe these clubs as being for the "super-rich." The remaining clubs are home to a combination of upper-middle- and upper-class individuals in proportions that vary according to factors such as the cost of membership and location of the club. Despite these differences, however, golfers from both types of clubs talk about golf as a common space and describe the clubs as sites where they can find trustworthy and personable individuals and where they can easily make friends. The snowball technique I used to collect the sample of interviewees revealed connections between golfers at clubs with varying degrees of wealth: I met golfers in prestigious clubs who introduced me to golfers in less prestigious ones and vice versa.

Even though the significant variation in membership fees reveals clear economic differences between golf clubs, most golfers talked about fellow players in terms of similarities. Golfers did not describe golf clubs as being fully separate entities (in the way, for example, that churches differentiate between one another), but rather thought of most golf clubs as a set of spaces inhabited by people who share many things in common. Ruth, a golfer in her early sixties who started playing 40 years ago—after her husband became an avid player—and was a member of one of the more elite clubs in Mexico City, expressed the idea that golfers have many things in common and can easily relate to one another, noting how easy it was to connect with other players, both at her club and at other clubs:

> Golf allows you to share plenty of time with those who are playing with you; you may not know them beforehand, but you feel an affinity—how someone plays, which club he plays at, what he does for a living, where does he work—golf offers plenty of space and time to connect. You meet people playing golf and later you bump into them again in other spaces, a theater, a cinema, wherever, and we ask each other about the game, how was your game today? Have you played recently? [. . .] We invite each other to tournaments in different clubs in the city or outside the city. All these relations create a larger family of golfers, people you meet on the course; it is incredible, how many people you meet through golf. First, you start in your own club, you meet people, play with them, join the internal tournaments. Then, you start playing in tournaments in other clubs, where you see another environment and meet new people, and you end up making many new friends.

Many golfers emphasized the idea that it was easy to meet people and make friends among fellow golfers, who, as Ruth noted, shared other common spaces (e.g., workplaces, cultural events, schools, neighborhoods). As argued by Thompson in the passage quoted at the beginning of the chapter, class works as a set of relations based on common experiences that create social bonds, taking the form of friendship and camaraderie. The special bonding that class identity generates among golfers was also described by Gerardo, a corporate executive in his late fifties who learned how to play golf while studying for his bachelor's degree in the United States more than 30 years earlier. He maintained that golfers connect with one another easily:

> Yesterday, here [in the office], I was in the process of negotiating a contract [and] one of the lawyers working for the other client stared at me and said: "I know you, I know you." He had recently seen me at a golf tournament and, even before we started working on the contract, we chatted about golf for about half hour, at different levels, kids, junior players, because he is also involved in the sport, like me. [. . .] When we started working, I was negotiating with him as a friend, as someone familiar to me; golf generates solid trust.

Although economic differences do exist between these players, golf functions as a common social space in which people bring with them not only financial assets but also other forms of capital they possess. This is the case with social capital, which functions as a metaphorical credential that allows people to claim membership in a group. This form of capital generates a sense of belonging and forms ties of trust, which in turn allow people to obtain and trade a myriad of resources that circulate inside a community (Bourdieu 1986a). In the United States, there is extensive literature showing the value of social capital in multiple contexts, such as in ethnic communities (Nee, Sanders, and Sernau 1994; Portes 1987, 1995) as well as among the urban poor (Fernández-Kelly 2016; Stack 1975; Wacquant 2006). Social capital plays an important role in letting people obtain innumerable goods embedded in the social networks they belong to, from information about job openings to economic loans. The value of social capital, however, depends on the overall status of the group with which people can develop ties of camaraderie, friendship, and trust. The highly privileged condition of golf clubs in Mexico allows members to create social bonds that give people access to resources of great value, such as the trust of the corporate lawyer with whom Gerardo was negotiating a highly valuable contract. Class, therefore, is a set of relations influenced by economic as well as other forms of assets, such as social capital.

Class is also a Sour Relationship

There are exceptions to this pattern of social bonding based on class similarities, however. In some cases, the class differences between golfers, particularly those at the high and low ends of the spectrum, hinder interactions. Dario, a man in his late fifties who had started playing golf more than 30 years earlier, described the fault lines created by class. Two golfers, each of whom had met Dario at interclub tournaments, gave me his contact information. I had difficulty setting up a time to talk with him—he was busy and seemed uninterested in my research about business and golf (I discuss this point in more detail in the Appendix)—but after several phone calls, he lukewarmly agreed to be interviewed. The meeting took place in his office, located in an old building, moderately renovated, in an industrial area near the center of the city. Dario explained that he first tried the sport when a relative and some friends who worked as caddies had invited him to play golf. On the slower days of the week, the group would sneak into the course very early, before any members arrived, and play nine holes (half a round); their short game and early arrival meant they were able to pass unnoticed and played for free. At the beginning of the interview, Dario claimed to be unaware of the relation between business and golf because he was not a businessperson, but a civil servant who enjoyed golf. At the time of the interview, he played at the less expensive clubs in the city. He described his club in the following way:

> People joke about it, saying, if you play at "Club X" and can no longer afford the costs, you can sell your membership and move to a less expensive club such as "Club A" or "Club B," but if you have trouble paying the fees at my club, then you go to hell [laughing] because there isn't any cheaper option.

On one occasion, members of one of the most expensive clubs in the city invited members of Dario's club to play an interclub tournament. Recalling the event, Dario focused on the class differences between members of his club and the upscale players, which was illustrated by the other group's possession of expensive objects. He recounted:

We looked ragged next to them, and, the caddies, you could tell, ok, the caddies were very well dressed, [and] the players used only new balls. We, instead, played with our used balls; they had Pro balls, you see, those are expensive balls. We used Pinnacle [inexpensive balls]; you could tell the difference, ok.

Despite their less expensive equipment, Dario and his friend defeated the two wealthier players. At the end of the game, however, their opponents accused the pair of violating the handicap rules and convinced the organizers to disqualify Dario and his friend for not revealing that one of them had previously participated in a category of better players.[1] "One of the guys took out his phone and did a search on us on the Internet and found that my friend had competed years back in another category [of better players]." Notably irritated, Dario continued:

We lost the game. Why? Because those golfers are used to always doing what they please. So, in that club, members are like that, they are super wealthy. It is not easy to keep up a conversation, except with those members who are like me, who have similar types of interests. You can feel the difference [the class gap]. But, not in other clubs, no, no, no, no, you don't feel a difference in other clubs. People are friendly, I have played with ambassadors, governors, with, with, important people in multiple clubs and they are fine, but people at that club, they act aloof.

Dario's experience shows the role that economic assets play in how golfers develop class identities. However, this type of ill will also emerges among members of the same club (i.e., people who have paid similar amounts of money for their membership), which indicates that wealth alone does not constitute class identity or determine class interests. Miguel's interview provided an example of within-club animosity. Five different golfers from three different clubs suggested that I contact him, describing him as someone who "knows a lot about golf." Miguel was a charming player in his late sixties who had extensive knowledge of the game and was clearly at ease at golf. Miguel's father and grandfather were also golfers, and therefore Miguel had played the sport since

---

1. The handicap is a numerical representation of a golfer's playing potential, which is used to group players in different competing categories.

childhood. His strong playing skills, deep knowledge of the game, and amiable personality had made him a popular figure in the community; at the time of the conversation, Miguel was an executive at a technology corporation.

We had a long conversation while sitting in the bar at his golf club, which is a highly respectable club—upscale, but not the most expensive club. After describing the recent transformations he had observed in the world of golf, Miguel complained about some of the newer members who had taken up the sport, saying:

> Sometimes you get surprises, some of them very bad. Unfortunately . . . even here, there is a saying among some golfers here that goes, "The course in this club is hard because of the rough, which goes all the way to the changing rooms" [laughter]. There are very nice people, but there are also vulgar members, and sometimes you end up playing with unpleasant people.

Miguel's comment hints at a certain level of disapproval of other members. Players in Mexico City discuss golf clubs primarily regarding the characteristics and difficulty of the courses—fast, slow, easy, hard, and so on. The "rough" is the thicker, unmowed grass along the perimeter of the holes, designed to punish players whose balls land there. It is considerably more difficult to play from the rough than from the fairway (the well-maintained, short grass at the center of the playing field). Thus, saying that the course is hard because of the rough can be interpreted technically as saying that the swath of taller grass at the perimeter is wider than normal. The added clarification that the "rough goes all the way to the changing room," however, shifts the focus to the golfers, implying that some members have a less-than-ideal class background (i.e., are "rough").

This was not the only sarcastic comment I heard from a golfer describing fellow club members. Interviewees often made this type of comment after I had stopped the tape recorder. In a few cases, however, golfers openly belittled their fellow club members during the formal interview. For example, Horacio, a golfer in his late forties and member of a higher-end club—who learned the sport in his mid-twenties when he spent the summers in a house at a golf community his family owned in the southern United States—criticized other members when

I asked him to elaborate on how similar or different the members of his club were:

> Here [in my club] there are people who . . . I think of them as social climbers, ok, as gate crashers . . . but there are also many people who, on the other hand, they just want to play for fun, to enjoy the game with their buddies and no, no, they are not looking for anything else, they don't want anything else, ok.

During the interview, Horacio indicated that most people play golf for the sake of it. There is a minority of golfers, however, who join the sport aiming to increase their prestige and build their careers; in Horacio's words, they are "gate crashers." These types of comments and jokes raise the question of the relationship between class and economic assets. If wealth is the sole basis for class belonging, why do golfers belittle other members with relatively similar amounts of financial resources, placing these "social climbers" outside (and beneath) their own "more desirable" class group? If money determines class position in a straightforward manner, why is it that some people with similar levels of economic assets do not immediately feel connected to and identify with one another? The answer is that while class identity is certainly connected to the possession of wealth, class cannot be reduced to income brackets (Elias 1983). Although access to golf requires the possession of considerable economic assets, golfers' interactions with one another are based not only on monetary resources but also on the possession of other forms of assets, for instance, cultural capital.

Cultural capital refers to the set of dispositions deeply internalized by individuals that make them talk and dress, among other traits, in ways that are considered preferable. This form of capital originates from people's exposure to formal schooling, either directly or indirectly by socializing among people who have attended school. This concept does not suggest that people "act" as if they were professional actors, simulating their actions. Instead, the argument goes, we are socialized since early childhood to follow certain patterns that are regarded as desirable by those around us, such as speaking in forms that are viewed as appropriate by our family circle and immediate social interactions (Bourdieu 1986b). Therefore, cultural capital is related to the amount of formal education people have, the fashion sense individuals demonstrate, people's hobbies, the type of conversation someone feels comfortable having, and how people express themselves. Although never in a straightforward way, a similar amount of cultural capital allows people to connect and develop friendships with others, which in turn helps establish ties of trust (allowing people to exchange and increase their social capital).

The case of Dario illustrates this argument. Whereas his limited possession of economic assets and cultural capital in relation to his wealthier opponents prevented the development of camaraderie, this has not been Dario's experience in most other clubs. In his own words, "No, you don't feel a difference in other clubs. People are friendly, I have played with ambassadors, governors, with, with, important people in multiple clubs and they are fine, but people at that club, they act aloof." Within golf clubs, class interactions between members are strongly influenced by non-economic factors. The social distance between golfers is not necessarily the same as the physical distance—after all, golfers in the northern part of the city introduced me to golfers in the southern part. Rather, social distance is determined by the type and quantity of assets (both material and symbolic) people possess. Some people have enough economic capital to both pay for a membership and buy a house in the nearby residential area but do not have the same level of cultural or social capital that most of their fellow golfers have (or the other way around).

Uneven distribution of multiple forms of capital creates tensions inside the golf community (a point extensively analyzed in the following chapter). Yet class dynamics are complex and sometimes contradictory. Not having as much education or economic resources as other members does not always block the possibility of friendship; people may bond over other commonalities. For example, I heard many people praising fellow golfers based on their high level of golf skills. Likewise, golfers who have similar assets sometimes compete rather than develop amicable relations. Class, therefore, is never a thing that people possess, but rather a set of relations that are spatially organized.

A Spatial Relationship

Despite the tension and animosity that sometimes emerged between individuals at the economic extremes (i.e., the high- and low-end clubs) and the differences that existed between people inside clubs, most interviewees agreed that there was something special about the sport of golf that made it relatively easy for golfers to connect with each other (in Thompson's 1963 words, to find common class interests). Golf clubs in Mexico function as stable and durable communities because upper-middle- and upper-class individuals come together in a shared space. The considerable accumulation of assets (foremost but not exclusively economic), even in "affordable clubs," creates a privileged space in which class commonalities translate into camaraderie and fellowship. Access to this space grants an entire set of benefits that sometimes are consciously perceived but more often are unconsciously assumed by those inside the community.

A Reclusive Space

The spatial distribution of golf clubs in Mexico City followed a historical pattern of class self-segregation. There are three courses that were originally located in isolated areas on the farthest peripheries of Mexico City but are now within the contemporary boundaries of the city; two were built in the early twentieth century, and another was established during the 1950s (the last one was built over communal land, which could not be legally turned private at the time of its construction). Over time, the clubs' surroundings changed radically. The small, planned, and modern residential areas near these clubs were slowly engulfed by an expanding and not-so-well-planned metropolis. In recent years, these areas have used gates, walls, and other barriers to block outsiders from crossing, driving, or walking through the modern and well-organized residential spaces that surround golf clubs.

A recent body of research on Latin America has analyzed the rise of gated communities and other forms of secluded spaces in the region (Caldeira 2000; Coy 2006; Janoschka and Borsdorf 2004; Low 2004). One of the key factors underpinning the expansion of these types of urban spaces is affluent groups' concerns about crime, based on both real and perceived dangers (Dinzey-Flores 2013; Low 2001). This fear of criminal activity might have influenced the members of Mexico City golf clubs as well, motivating them to erect architectural barriers that completely block outsiders from coming into, or even seeing, the clubs. However, golf clubs' long history of class segregation suggests that factors beyond contemporary concerns about crime led to these clubs being hidden from public view. Indeed, the historical analysis in Chapter 1 indicates that the reclusive nature of courses reflects a long history of class and racialized self-segregation.[2]

---

2. During the sportification of golf in nineteenth-century Britain, upper-middle-class golfers shifted the golf course from an open-public site to an open-enclosed site. This shift

The enclosure of golf clubs predates the contemporary trend of building gated communities for the upper strata to allay their concerns about criminality and safety. The creation of a vast enclosed athletic space is the result of the nineteenth-century embrace of modernity (and its interrelated process of class and racial exclusion), not twenty-first-century urban malaise. The historical development of golf clubs suggests that the isolation of these athletic sites was a political statement about who should and should not be allowed to access these modern landscapes rather than a response to concerns about security. These clubs are now surrounded by a combination of residential areas (originally developed for members) and arteries with high-speed traffic moving in multiple directions. Whyte (1980) and Sennett (1996) argued that expanding urban areas in the United States and England (respectively) developed high-speed arteries as a mechanism to maintain class distinctions. Similar systems were at play in Mexico City—the main arteries around these prestigious clubs were designed to facilitate the rapid transportation of residents rather than social interaction.

In all my visits to these golf clubs, I never saw anyone resting against the outside walls of club buildings (other than someone waiting for a bus) or friends and families gathering to spend time together next to the foliage-covered fences that surrounded some of these clubs. I did, however, see people walking quickly, paying little attention to either the walls of the clubs or the tree branches that extended over these walls. Whyte explained that "if a place is attractive to people it might be attractive to undesirable people. So it is made unattractive. There is to be no loitering, no eating, no sitting" (1980:60). This explanation certainly applied to the areas surrounding the golf clubs in Mexico City, where the spatial division mirrors the social division existing between those inside and those outside. Unsurprisingly, passersby did not congregate outside the golf clubs, even though they were green oases in the middle of a metropolis characterized by its lack of green space.

Besides these three clubs in the city, there are 10 additional clubs in the larger metropolitan area (which is only distinct from Mexico City for bureaucratic and other legal purposes). Seven of these clubs were constructed during the era of the Mexicanization of golf between 1960 and 1980, and the other three were erected between 1994 and 2002 (Horta 1989;

---

replicated the noble tradition of enclosing athletic spaces to reinforce social distance from the lower classes (see Eichberg 1986).

Morales y Favela 1996). Each of these clubs followed the pattern of class isolation that characterized the early development of clubs in Mexico City. At the time of their founding, these clubs were situated in new residential developments that catered to upper-middle- and upper-class groups and were far from densely populated areas of the city. Yet the city has slowly engulfed most of these clubs, just as it happened with the oldest clubs. The persistence of this pattern is due in part to the lack of land inside the city but is also the result of a desire to enact social differences through the urban landscape (Dinzey-Flores 2013, 2017; Iturriaga Acevedo 2016).

These 10 clubs are well connected to high-end residential areas in other parts of the city's periphery by modern toll roads but are not very well linked to any of the heavily populated areas of the city. When I visited one of the newest clubs to conduct interviews, I was surprised by the notable absence of public buses or bus stops in the area. The lack of public transportation was particularly striking in a city where most primary, secondary, and even tertiary avenues host a constant flow of inexpensive public buses carrying people in all directions. I did notice several taxi stands, where a line of taxis waited for clients. The on-demand nature of taxi services allows for less crowded streets and convenient rides, but taxis are considerably more expensive and likely not economically viable for many in the middle and working classes. I asked a young caddy who worked in one of these clubs how he usually comes to work; he answered, "I don't have a car and it would take me a lot to walk here [from where the bus leaves him], some of us [caddies] meet at a taxi stand and ride together."

The area was also home to ultra-modern apartment buildings, U.S.-based chain coffee shops, small eateries with neatly arranged outdoor tables, restaurants offering a wide range of dining options, small boutiques, and expensive imported cars moving through the streets, including several convertibles, which are seldom seen without the retractable top in the rest of the city. The urban setting was more reminiscent of a neighborhood in another country than a typical Mexico City neighborhood. As Whyte argued, "the way people use a place mirrors [their social] expectations" (1980:63). The lack of public transportation in this relatively new area of the city made it economically unviable for "undesirable" people to gather and spend time in the vicinity. In today's Mexico City, all golf clubs follow class-based self-segregation. The most centrally located ones do it by hiding their presence behind tall fences, thick bushes, and discreet entrances, while the newer ones have kept "undesirable" people at bay by being located in areas that limit the flow of inexpensive public transportation. Therefore, following Whyte (1980), "there is to be no loitering, no eating, no sitting" for working-class people.

This class-based pattern implicitly creates a racialized separation, in which darker skinned subjects are almost only present as subordinated workers. This is not to say than an open color-line system operates in Mexico (Knight 1990; Navarrete 2016). In fact, U.S. understandings of race lack currency in Mexico. In this nation, people believe in the idea of mestizaje (mixed race). According to this assumption, all Mexicans are the product of a long process of miscegenation that has given birth to a distinctive mestizo phenotype and culture (Moreno Figueroa 2010; Moreno Figueroa and Saldívar Tanaka 2016; Sue 2013).[3] Terms such as *blanco* (white), *negro* (black), and *oriental* (Asian) lack the clear connotations and influence they have in the United States because Mexicans assume that these groups have been collapsed into a single Mexican mestizo group. People, hence, consider that traditional Western ideas about race have not influenced the concept of mestizaje at either the individual or national level (Knight 1990; Pitt-Rivers 1977; Sue 2013). Yet despite the deeply believed ideas that race (as a concept) does not exist in Mexico, because almost all Mexicans are part of a single racialized group, there is an insidious way in which racialized patterns appear everywhere and nowhere at the same time in the privileged space of golf and beyond. I will return to the point later in the book, in Chapter 4.

Visibility and Openness

Visibility and openness are what characterize the environment inside golf clubs. After crossing the architectural barriers created to keep the city outside, vast open-enclosed spaces fanned out like green sanctuaries. The feeling of being in an oasis was accentuated by the fact that there are very few green spaces in Mexico City outside of golf clubs. Nowhere else in the city will residents find a large site with meticulously kept vegetation evoking a generic Anglo-American landscape. While the city's upscale malls and expensive private universities were also designed to evoke the

---

3. By phenotype, I understand a set of visual cues about people's appearance (e.g., nose shape, skin color, hair texture, lip size, and body fat) which are strongly influenced by cultural ideas. Frantz Fanon referred to these perceptions as the "epidermal schema" (2008:84), emphasizing how ideas of race and social belonging are firmly based on these principles. I will return to the point in Chapter 4.

aesthetic of an undefined Anglo-American space, the sheer size of the spaces and the lushness of the vegetation were unique to golf.[4]

In all the clubs I visited, the architectural organization was designed around open spaces. For example, the club's driveway always led to a majestic clubhouse door. The door opened to an entryway with an elegant desk where a receptionist, usually a woman, greeted members and guests in a friendly and smiling manner. The recurrent presence of these female workers marked a spatial transition between the city and the club. The courteous aides reassured prosperous golfers of their uniqueness and distinction by welcoming them in an individualized manner. In all the cases I witnessed, the receptionist clearly knew the name or last name of the members. These workers, however, did not greet golfers in a manner suggesting personal friendship. Instead, a combination of reverential terms—such as courtesy titles (i.e., *señor* [Mr.] or *señora* [Mrs.])—where included before welcoming golfers. After the salutation, the worker asked courteous questions aimed to make members feel at home (i.e., how are you today?). These interactions calmed and uplifted members by centering social attention from external concerns to their immediate needs and emotions (for a parallel analysis about affluent men in Australia see Donaldson and Poynting [2007]).

After crossing the entrance, the internal space of the clubhouse exudes a sense of openness. For example, when I met people at a club, they could easily spot me entering the clubhouse even if they were seated on one of the sofas or wide chairs located on the other side of the main hall. There are no obstacles blocking the view from the entrance to the far end of the large hall. The club restaurant is usually near the main hall and is also an open site—patrons can easily see the entire room. A vast entry point leads members into a large room full of tables that ends at a wall filled with large windows offering views of the golf course or a spacious garden. The openness of the space allows people to chat with one another easily. This spatial characteristic was evident in the recordings of the interviews that occurred inside the clubhouse. My conversations with members were constantly

---

4. Mexico City is home to the largest urban park in the entire continent, Parque de Chapultepec (Chapultepec Park). There is a museum of contemporary art in one section of this park. Interestingly, the surrounding green space around the museum possesses a feeling distinct from most other parts of this vast park. It was a golf course in the very early twentieth century, called the Aztec Club. It disappeared when another club was erected in a more reclusive area by the 1920s. An old journalist and two different golfers let me know about the existence of this club.

interrupted by people greeting other members or chatting briefly with someone passing by. In one case, an interviewee suggested that we sit on a sofa in a corridor leading to the pool because it was a quiet spot during weekdays, and yet the conversation was still interrupted on two occasions when the interviewee greeted and chatted with other members passing through the hallway.

Paradoxically, the golf course itself—a vast open space—offers a high degree of privacy. The hilly and zigzagging layout of the course and the lines of trees that separate fairways from one another obstruct players' views on the course. Unlike other sports in which groups of athletes can play close to each other (e.g., tennis, where there are usually multiple courts side by side), golf requires plenty of distance between groups of players. The real danger of a small, hard, fast-moving ball hitting another player means that groups of golfers must keep distance between them to prevent accidents. Other than the changing rooms, the course is the only area of the club in which space is arranged so that a player's view of others is constantly blocked.

Only the small group of golfers playing together and the caddies following them can see and hear what transpires on the course. I did not record the four interviews I conducted while playing golf because of the difficulty involved in carrying a recording device and holding a club at the same time (especially given that I was a novice at the sport). I memorized, as much as possible, my observations and the issues discussed on the course. Once in my car, I wrote down everything I remembered about the conversation and interactions. Reviewing my notes later reminded me that, despite my anxiety about my poor golf skills, the course offered the best conditions for interviewing people: four and a half hours of uninterrupted time with a group of people about whom I wanted to learn in detail.

The paradoxical privacy offered by the golf course contrasts with the public nature of the bar. The bar is commonly known as the "19th hole" because the standard design for a golf course situates the bar next to the 18th hole (the final hole of the game). The bars I visited had distinctive aesthetic elements but shared certain essential characteristics, such as being spacious and comfortable sites offering attentive service and a beautiful view of the course. The 19th hole was a place in which I never felt rushed or cramped. In one occasion, for example, even when the site was occupied at about 60 percent of its capacity, I still could easily walk between the tables to reach the restroom. The interaction between members also followed a consistent pattern in all the bars I visited. After a group sat down at a table, a waiter arrived promptly to take their order (always dressed in black pants and a white shirt, sometimes combined with a black vest). Waiters commonly repeated a long list of beers, spirits, and wines that were available. Players often ordered something to eat, either individual plates or an appetizer to share with the group. The drinks and food arrived swiftly, and players engaged in an undisturbed interaction.

The carefree attitude of the 19th hole stands in stark contrast to the hectic atmosphere of most working-class, and even some middle-class, restaurants in the city, in which clients are served, eat, and leave in rapid succession. At every club, players regarded the 19th hole as the quintessential site for socializing. Horacio, a club member in his late forties who learned to play golf in the United States, described the bar as the place where "you can see real camaraderie, it is where you can meet new people." All the male interviewees emphasized the importance of the bar as a space for players to socialize. For example, Fernando, a man in his early thirties, who began playing golf as a child because his family owned a membership in a high-end club, argued:

> The bar is like having a circle of friends, it is like if you enter into a bar and there is a table with 20 dudes, having fun, and you only know five of those guys but don't know the other 15, you can still comfortably sit at the table without feeling like you are crashing [the party] . . . you know . . . because after all, you are part of the same circle, you are a member of the club, all of them are in the same socioeconomic situation, which creates a feeling of friendship.

As pointed out in the introduction, the early part of the conversation turned around the just-completed game. Players praised one another on outstanding shots, made jokes about lousy decisions, and remembered other games played together. In some cases, the group's conversation included golfers at adjacent tables who participated in the jokes or who were asked to comment on related topics. While waiters sometimes added bits of information about past events, I never saw them joking with members—some laughed at the members' jokes, but none made humorous remarks to members. The "19th hole" served as a site where the skills, attitudes, and character of players, which were witnessed by only a few fellow members on the course, were orally re-created for the community via witty accounts. In doing so, the bar extended the visibility of club members all the way back to the course by making other members' scores, jokes, and abilities public to the rest of the group.

Before starting the fieldwork, I was familiar with the U.S. literature about the exclusion women commonly face at golf clubs and particularly at the 19th hole (Chambers 1990, 1995; Crosset 1995). However, I was unsure about the gender policies in Mexico City. While seated in the 19th hole, I brought up the point of gender exclusion during an interview with Ruben, a club member in his late fifties who owned a mid-sized factory producing autoparts, to which he answered, "Look, the 19th hole is forbidden for women in 99 percent of the clubs [in Mexico]. I don't know if you notice it, but in this club, the 19th hole's entrance is right next to the men's changing rooms. Women and men occupy separate spaces [in this club]."

In Ruben's club, there were two corridors on opposite ends of the main hall. One of them led to women's changing rooms, while the other led to men's and also to the interior door to the 19th hole (the bar also had another entrance facing the course). It seemed that if an inattentive woman walks into the bar without knowing that by customary rules women do not enter this site, the organization of space itself will remind her that she is in the "wrong place." When I brought up the point with male golfers in other clubs, they immediately recognized the gender segregation present in golf but did not think of it in detrimental terms. Ivan, for example, a club member in his late thirties and owner of a consulting firm, said, "women cannot enter the bar in my club," and, after a pause, added, "in golf, everything is designed for men, but women have other spaces." It was not uncommon for interviewees to think of the gender division of space almost as a natural condition.

For example, Daniel, a golfer in his late thirties who was a junior executive in a U.S. corporation, indicated, "I don't think that the feeling of the 19th hole [bar] would be the same if women could access it. At least, I wouldn't make the same jokes, would you?" Interestingly, Mercedes, a female golfer in her mid-fifties, who worked in an outsourcing company and also actively promoted the sport among female club members, argued that women are banned from the main bar because "men love to be vulgar and behave boorishly, that's it, there no other reason." Coincidentally, the institutional history of one of the oldest and most important golf clubs outside of Mexico City described the 19th hole in a similar fashion. "Women cannot enter the 19th hole. They cannot drink nor eat there; it is exclusively for men. The reason is that male members talk tough, say things that women should not hear" (Castellanos 1999:123). Besides rude jokes, the conversation at the bar among men also commonly included discussion about technology (such as cars) and financial issues, elements that seemed to be essential in the construction of a privileged sense of masculinity.

Privileged Space

The openness that characterized almost every area of these golf clubs, at least for men, seemed a conducive feature to let them socialize as much as observe one another. The high level of visibility facilitated by the spatial arrangements at the clubs allows members to interact with one another as well as gather a great deal of information about each other, which they can then use to identify the social origins and class position of fellow members. In *The Court Society* (1983), a book on the life of the aristocracy in Europe, Norbert Elias argued that the royal court played a key role in the organization of the noble class. The court was the space in which people identified one another's social origins and upbringing, primarily by observing behavior, manners, and attitudes.

> [The] courtly art of human observation is all the closer to reality be-cause it never attempts to consider the individual person in isolation. [. . .] Rather, the individual is always observed in court society in his social context, as a person in relation to others. (Elias 1983:104)

Similarly, the open spatial organization of golf clubs permits upper-middle- and upper-class individuals to engage in the game of class observa-tion. The spacious hall, the open restaurant, and the bar, which allow male members to "see" the skills and abilities of other members, are the sites where people observe one another to determine their hierarchical position in relation to the broader community. Of course, most club members do not know every other member. Some interviewees recognized that they only knew small groups of members in their club. Even when they do not know one another, however, members reported feeling comfortable with players based on the commonalities they discovered when they interacted and observed one another. Similarly, when members spoke poorly about other members, they offered concrete details of the less-than-ideal behav-ior those club members had exhibited. The openness of the sites allows club members to observe one another in detail.

The 19th hole, for example, was the best place to observe other men in the club. It was the space where men heard about another male member's impressive golf skills (a form of athletic capital that generates respect among other golfers), learned who liked to bet but remained composed when he lost (a sign of detachment from material objects), found out that a fellow player was quite funny (I discuss the meaning of humor in detail in the following chapter), or discovered who cheats (which is regarded as a sign of moral failure, a point also discussed in the next section). The fact that women were excluded from this process of observation at the bar limited their ability to be considered as serious golfers. Most of the women interviewed complained that men belittled their golf skills even before seeing them play.

Further information on the importance of the "art of observation" in golf clubs, following Elias's argument, came from interviews I conducted with four golf journalists as part of the fieldwork. All four worked for specialized magazines, and two also freelanced for national newspapers. They knew a lot about golf but were not golfers themselves. Most could talk for hours about the characteristics of this or that course but either rarely played the sport or had never played at all. Thus, the journalists were insiders in some ways but outsiders in others. While they sometimes repeated almost religiously golfers' common beliefs about the sport, at other moments they were quite critical of golf and golfers. In short, these journalists both corroborated some of the common mantras in the sport and offered some of the sharpest insights into the game. One of them, a man in his mid-forties who had written about the sport for more than 15 years, observed,

> A lot of people talk about golf as a sport, and it is, yes, it's a sport, but most golfers play to be in the right place, to be seen because this is what golf is for—this is a game of seeing and being seen. This is the essence of the game.

The organization of space inside golf clubs corroborated the observation: these clubs are hypervisible spaces in which members observe one another in relation to the rest of the community. Based on the many situations they follow each other, people develop feelings of association. Building on Thompson's quote at the beginning of the chapter, people develop stronger connections with those who are perceived as having common experiences and similar interests because trust is a class-based feeling.

Conclusion

I began this chapter with a description of the contrast between the sense of urgency that imbues most large intersections in Mexico City on weekend mornings and the relaxed ambience that characterizes golf clubs at the same time. As suggested in E. P. Thompson's quote, this distinctive experience reveals how class is a set of relations that situate individuals and groups in contrasting positions. The first part of the chapter offered empirical evidence to show how golf is the preserve of dominant classes in Mexico. This section also showed that despite the economic differences that exist between clubs and among individuals within clubs, most players think of golf as a space inhabited primarily by people who share common characteristics based on their privileged background. The fact that the city dwellers who pass by the clubs are utterly oblivious to their existence limits social contact, reinforcing the differences that exist between members of the upper strata and the rest of the city's population.

The second part of the chapter shifted to a focus on the interior of the clubs, showing how the organization of space changes radically beyond the threshold of the golf club. Inside the clubs, space is organized in a way that offers a hypervisible experience in which people regularly interact and see one another. The golf course is the only part of the club where players have a significant amount of privacy. However, when male players leave the course and enter the bar, they are once again made visible, and even the events that transpired on the course become public knowledge. The hypervisible dynamic that permeates the internal spaces in these golf clubs is linked to the fact that class distinctions not only produce groups based on shared interests but also engender internal struggles over status and honor. All these elements are based on the "art of human observation," a game that allows people to situate others in relation to the broader community. The discussions about the reclusive external condition and the open internal characteristic of golf clubs illustrate how space and spatial dynamics play an essential role in the articulation of class differences and similarities.

The analysis of class relations in the present chapter turns into a more "intimate" account about daily interactions, such as people's sense of humor, linguistic relations, and perceptions of honor in the following section. Chapter 3 offers a detailed analysis of the relation between the spatial openness of the clubs and the internal class organization of the community, showing the specific class-based dynamics that form, or block, relations of trust among affluent golf players. The analysis also demonstrates how class collides with other social forces to form a privileged space.

3

Inside the Community

Different classes construct their sense of territory and community in radically different ways.
—DAVID HARVEY (1989:265)

Introduction

In his early thirties, Fernando was one of the youngest players I interviewed for this study. His father had acquired a membership in a highly respectable golf club more than 30 years before, and thus Fernando had been a member of the club his entire life. He assured me that it was far from being an exclusive club, even though it cost more than $40,000 to become a member. I first contacted Fernando through a mutual acquaintance I had met when both of us were studying for graduate degrees in Britain. His interview was one of the easiest to arrange: when I called him and introduced myself, he responded that his friend had already told him about my project. After we chatted briefly about London and other places he had been in Europe, Fernando eagerly agreed to talk with me about golf, suggesting that we meet in a cafeteria near his office one afternoon the following week. Fernando was the co-owner of a software firm, and his office was located in a middle-class neighborhood. The area was easily accessible by public transportation, so I took the Metro to our meeting.

For just over an hour, Fernando elaborated extensively as he answered my questions, offering plenty of concrete examples to illustrate his comments. He repeatedly stressed that the game of golf generates a sense of congeniality. It was he who, as described in the previous chapter, claimed that the "19th hole" (the club's bar) was a welcoming site full of friends, "because after all [the people at the bar] are part of the same circle, are members of the club, they are in the same socioeconomic situation." He offered several examples that showed how playing golf could transform unequal social relations into quasi-democratic interactions. For example, he said that during golf tournaments the existing inequalities among players are temporarily forgotten. He explained: "Golf tournaments generate relations among equals, because everybody plays golf, you see, on the course you speak with others as your peers, OK. Who knows, in the future I may sell you something or you may hire me, [. . .] but at this moment, we are equals."

In addition, Fernando emphasized that golf allows players to further develop the trust that already exists between people who share many commonalities. When we had been talking for just over an hour, there was a pause in the conversation as I momentarily reviewed my notes and scanned the list of topics I wanted to cover. Fernando wondered aloud how the traffic would be when he drove home and asked me how heavy the traffic normally was on my own route home. It was obvious that Fernando had assumed that I had driven to the meeting. I replied that I did not have a car and normally traveled by public transportation and noted that there was a Metro station near our meeting spot. Fernando did not comment on my answer, but the dynamic of the interview changed noticeably; while he was never rude, he no longer elaborated on his answers as he had done during the first hour of the interview. His replies became short, and the interview lasted for only about 10 more minutes.

Before we parted ways, I asked Fernando to help me contact other golfers to interview for the project. He agreed and asked that I call him sometime in the following weeks. Given his offer to help me find additional interviewees, I thought maybe his demeanor had shifted simply because he was tired and just wanted to go home after a long day. However, when I tried to contact Fernando in the following weeks he did not answer my phone calls and never returned my messages. This response was very different from our first contact, which was a very friendly phone conversation. I left seven or eight messages in the following weeks, but all went unanswered, and I eventually stopped calling him. Given that in Mexico, car ownership is a strong indicator of membership in the middle or upper class while public transportation is commonly associated with working-class people, I began to wonder if my candid answer to Fernando's question had conveyed a class message—one that, unlike interactions on the golf course, situated me as someone unequal and therefore untrustworthy.

This chapter elaborates on the analysis of class, demonstrating how a multitude of mundane and ordinary actions reproduced class inequalities. The first part reflects on the connection between everyday language and the reproduction of social hierarchies inside clubs. Then follows a discussion of how perceptions of honor, honesty, intelligence, and civility informed a narrative that situates golf far away from popular sports, associating the latter with negative traits. This account allows club members to claim a form of athletic exceptionalism for golf, justifying exclusionary practices on arguments that transcended wealth. The second part of the chapter explores the internal class divisions within the golf community, including the internal struggle between old-timers and newer club members. The former insisted on the importance of non-monetary forms of capital to determine the boundaries of the community, whereas the latter put more weight on financial assets to set up the limits of the group.

The Manifestation of Class

All the interviewees agreed that class was a key influence on the world of golf. In most cases, interviewees immediately associated class with financial assets. For example, Diego, a player in his early sixties who worked for a transnational corporation—and who suggested that golf has not helped him to improve his social relations yet proudly shows me a picture of himself with a former U.S. Ambassador in Mexico, with whom Diego used to play golf when the U.S. delegate was attending functions in Mexico— connected golf and class by noting the high cost of playing the sport. He explained, "In Mexico, people strongly believe that golf is an elitist sport, very expensive, OK. It is debatable whether it is elitist or not, OK, but it is true that very few people have the resources to afford it: membership, monthly fees, food, drinks, caddies, etcetera, [golf] is not cheap." While the high cost of the game was the most common way people connected class and golf, interviewees also articulated other dynamics linked to, but not entirely subsumed by, economic elements.

We All Are Equals

After I waited for two hours to interview him while he took care of a business matter, Rafael, a golf player in his early sixties and the owner of a well-established advertising company, was very helpful during our conversation, offering protracted answers to my questions. When I asked him to describe the average golf player in Mexico City, he said:

> Generally speaking, people in golf are personable, friendly—first, as a rule, people never use their last names, [and] when introducing

themselves everyone uses the informal "you." It doesn't matter the age, social condition, nor your job, if someone has a golf club in his hands and stands at the tee [the starting point of the game] that person should have class, OK, and class is not based only on money, is it?

The first part of Rafael's comment illustrates the unintentional way class dynamics were expressed in day-to-day speech interactions at the club. He suggested that golfers should never use last names but rather should always address one another with only first names, regardless of the age difference between them or their respective social positions. After I interviewed Rafael, I began to pay more attention to the way golfers talked to each other, and my observations confirmed his description. Club members rarely used last names when they introduced other golfers to me, nor did they use my last name when introducing me to other golfers. In fact, on one occasion a male golfer and I were talking at the snack bar of a club when a woman (a club member) passed us as she was playing on the course. Knowing I was looking for more women to interview, the male member asked her to come over so he could introduce her to me. After a 23-minute conversation, the woman walked away to finish her round. The interviewee apologized for not knowing her last name, saying: "She is Claudia and her husband is Raul; I don't remember their last name." In a society deeply concerned about class hierarchies and notions of status (Alder Lomnitz and Pérez Lizaur 1987; Iturriaga 2016; Nutini 2008), the dynamic of using only first names among members is an expression of how privileged the golf community is in relation to the larger society.

In contrast to Rafael's argument above, Mexico is a country where class hierarchies are continuously acknowledge through language. For example, speakers can express recognition of high social status by using the formal version of the second-person pronoun (i.e., *usted*, which does not have an English translation), by using a courtesy title (i.e., *Señor* or *Don* [Mr.] and *Señora* [Mrs.]), or by including a professional title before a person's last name (e.g., *doctor* [physician], *ingeniero* [engineer], *arquitecto* [architect], *maestro* [professor]). The last example is a clear illustration of how class is embedded into language. Despite recent increases in educational attainment, the average Mexican citizen has completed only 9.2 years of schooling (INEGI 2015)—the equivalent of elementary, junior-high, and one year of high school in the United States. Higher education is simply out of the reach of most of the population. Including an academic degree or occupational category before a last name is a colloquial way of referencing educational disparities and its related class outcomes in daily speech. In this case, class is not expressed by referring directly to the possession of economic assets but rather by noting the possession of a large amount of formal education—cultural capital (Bourdieu 1986).

The privileged position of players allowed them to completely disregard the customary rules of acknowledging class disparities via language, meanwhile workers expressed the highest forms of linguistic respect (and subordination) when talking to members. When referring to golfers, workers most often used the titles *Señor* [Mr.] or *Señora* [Mrs.], the honorific Don [Mr.], and/or the member's professional title before his first name or last name, regardless of the age difference between the two or gender identity. On one occasion, an interviewee invited me to the restaurant at his club to conduct the interview while we had breakfast. Almost immediately after we sat down, a waiter approached us and asked, "*Patrón* [master], what do you want to order?" I was amazed at hearing this linguistic form of submission in a restaurant. The term *patrón* [master] is commonly used by street vendors as they approach possible clients. The term implies a large hierarchical gap between the person speaking and the person being addressed.

Rafael's observation that golfers always call one another by their first names regardless of social condition illustrates one way that class privilege informs the social relations in golf clubs on a day-to-day basis. The use of first names among golfers, combined with the fact that workers never called golfers by their first names, situates club members in one category and workers in another. The former can call one another by first name because they are equals, while the latter must show respect when talking to golfers because they are not equals. After elaborating on the importance of the use of the informal "you" among golfers, Rafael brought up another topic when he asserted: "Obviously, the golden rule of golf is honesty." His statement highlights another set of mundane actions that reproduce class privilege among club members in Mexico City: these actions center on the importance of honesty, integrity, morality, and ethics in golf.

Civility and Honor

The golfers I spoke with repeatedly stressed that golf is a game of honor and civility. The interviewees often backed up these statements by noting that golf is the only sport in which people call penalties on themselves (e.g., if they move a ball by mistake), that no other athletes record their own scores with no help from an external authority, and that most golfers are well mannered and courteous. These practices have been associated with golf since the gentrification of the sport in the late nineteenth century (Cerón-Anaya 2010), when players used these actions to establish an apparent moral boundary between those who played golf, who were assumed to be righteous, self-disciplined, honest, and polite, and those who played other popular sports, who were assumed to be dishonest, unruly, and rude (Collinson and Hoskin 1994). The contemporary emphasis on honor and gentlemanly behavior in Mexico's golf clubs maintains this moral boundary between golfers and those who engage in other popular games that condone and even celebrate dishonesty.

In her comparative study of upper-middle-class people in the United States and France, Michele Lamont (1992) argued that upper-middle-class individuals recreate class distinctions based on economic as well as moral elements. The latter is "centered around such qualities as honesty, work ethic, personal integrity, and consideration for others" (1992:4). The narrative of honor and civility that pervaded the interviews embraced these same qualities and shows that the golf community imagines itself as morally different from the lower classes and, therefore, deserving of a place at this privileged site. Fernando, the younger player featured in the chapter's opening vignette, captured the moral boundary that golfers imagine exists between golf and other popular games by emphasizing the gentlemanly nature of the sport. He explained:

> I learned that golf is, since I was little, that it is a sport for gentleman. We could be betting a lot of money, but this is still a sport for gentleman—money does not matter here, what it matters is how gentlemanly I am with you and you with me. See, you can't play golf like you play soccer. I don't know, maybe soccer once was a sport for gentlemen and it degenerated because of popularity. [. . .] I learned it this way . . . with my friends, with the people whom I've played golf with since we were little, all of them have this philosophy. It is something very important, I don't know if it is even sacred, but it is very important, and you know what . . . it isn't that someone taught me, nor that someone constantly repeated the issue, I don't even recall if someone told me that, but in golf, in golf you need to be a gentleman even if you don't like the guy who is playing next to you.

Fernando continued by elaborating on what he considered gentlemanly behavior, explaining that golfers should never take advantage of
their opponents or trick them in order to win. In his own words,

> Using your opponent's errors to win is for cowards; golf is a
> gentleman's game. It's like, if you have a duel fought with swords
> and your opponent drops it by mistake and you kill him at that
> moment—a gentleman would never do that, he would wait until
> the opponent picks up the sword to continue the fight, isn't it?

Fernando was not the only interviewee to offer this type of explanation, but his description was the most succinct and fully articulated.
Interviewees indicated that, unlike players of other popular sports, golfers
learn to behave honorably against their opponents. In contrast, athletes
and teams in many popular sports often win precisely by tricking their
opponents or using their mistakes to defeat them. Boxers, for example,
constantly try to infuriate their opponents in the ring by tricking them,
knowing that when a fighter becomes angry he is more likely to make
mistakes (Wacquant 2006). Further, dishonorable conduct (e.g., using
deflated balls in football, scoring with one's hand in soccer, and improving
grip by using sticky substances in baseball) is common in many sports,
and although it is against the official rules, when such conduct is revealed it is not always condemned unanimously and in some cases is even
celebrated.

The claimed moral superiority of golfers over other athletes, however,
is best understood in terms of class boundary-making rather than any conclusive evidence about the moral condition of certain athletes and sports.
That is, golfers understand their upper-middle-class and upper-class status
as being based on not only the hefty fees they pay to join a club but also the
way they think about golf and use their bodies as they play. In Fernando's
explanation, a true golfer wants to win but not at any cost, unlike popular
sports where victory at all costs is a common mantra. A true golfer wants
to win, but only if he or she can do it in an honorable manner, because a
true golfer is defined not by victories or the material rewards that may result from winning but rather by honor.

This reduced emphasis on victory highlights the idea that a proper
golfer distinguishes between the person (playing golf) and the role they
are playing (as a golfer). The former do not need to be victorious at any
cost because being a golfer is only one aspect of their identity. Erving

Goffman (1961) identified this type of discrepancy, which he called role distance. Role distancing refers to the way people sometimes convey limited enthusiasm or even detachment in their actions and attitudes to remind others that they are distinct from the role they are playing. People with vast resources are more prone to use role distancing because they have multiple highly valuable roles through which they can express their identity (e.g., owner of a company, owner of a house in a highly respected neighborhood, member of prestigious associations, alumna/us of distinguished schools). In contrast, poor people have a limited number of roles that confer prestige, and therefore their identities and the roles they play are sometimes collapsed into a single unity.

The golfers I spoke with embodied role distancing when they (implicitly) defined golf as an end in itself—an athletic game that they practiced not necessarily to increase their chances of winning, although they certainly welcomed victories, but primarily to improve themselves, develop analytical skills, and meet like-minded people. While popular sports are strongly linked to "submission to collective discipline" (Bourdieu 1999:535), golf is a sport of individuals in which people never forget that they are playing a game. Authentic golfers are clear about their role on the course: they are not there to win at all costs, but rather to demonstrate that honor and civility are intrinsic characteristics of their personality, and therefore their right to inhabit this privileged space goes beyond their possession of economic assets. This idea was nicely captured by Horacio, a club member in his late forties who learned the sport in his twenties in the United States. Horacio explained:

> I am a very disciplined guy, I cannot stand the wise guys, OK. I cannot stand people trying to cheat, I cannot stand those players who are paying more attention to my score than to theirs. I hate it, because I am not competing all the time. I do want to play better than my opponent [and win]—it's in our nature—but, if someone else wins, that's it. But there are people who cheat in order to win, I hate that.

The interviewees indicated that a true golfer understands that victory is not the ultimate goal among amateur players because affluent individuals do not subsume their identity to golf; it is just a game and only one aspect of their identity. In Horacio's words, "*Si me ganó me ganó y ya* [If someone else wins, that's it]," there is no need to cheat.

Horacio's description shows that class is not a clear-cut distinction: some of those who are included within class boundaries based on their economic status (an externally constructed boundary) are excluded by other golfers based on their moral behavior (an internally constructed boundary). Horacio is arguing that there are some rotten apples inside the community who do not belong there and that they reveal their true "nature" by cheating.

Most participants agreed that it was more honorable to lose a game or even a tournament than to win via deception, by not counting all their strokes or by moving the ball to a better spot. Cheating was widely perceived as a behavior that exposed not a great desire to win but rather an untrustworthy character. Further, cheating revealed that a golfer did not comprehend the role distancing that occurred inside the community. Interviewees repeatedly expressed the view that cheaters were intrinsically dishonest individuals through stories about golfers who broke the rules in order to win. Laura's assessment provides a good description of the moral condition golfers associated with the act of cheating. Laura, a player in her late fifties who was a long-time member at an upscale club—and who was a competitive tennis player in her teenage years— emphasized the importance of honor in golf by associating the game with the idea of ethics and decency:

Golf teaches you ethics, decency. If you do not have ethics, you break the rules, in golf and in life. OK, golf teaches you ethics, to be focused in life, because by deceiving others, you really hurt yourself, you know that you did something wrong and feel guilty about it, you lose self-respect.

In Laura's explanation, ethics and honor are not abstract concepts but rather the foundation for honest and civil behavior (the opposites of cheating and deception). Later in the conversation, she provided a very specific example of the way in which moral elements draw lines between members inside the golf club. She recounted the story of another woman at her club, someone she initially liked and admired but lost respect and affection for when the woman condoned cheating at a friendly tournament. Laura explained: "Once I played with another woman whom I really admired. She was super nice, we were friends. We went to play a tournament at Club X. We went with other two women, but the two of us were a team." She continued, offering a detailed description of the tournament and saying how much she liked the course at the other club, and then described the act of cheating and her reaction:

> We were playing and suddenly my ball was closer to the green than where I thought it had landed, and later in the game it happened again, and again. I thought, "Something is going on." I started to pay more attention and noticed that the caddy was moving the ball [leaving it in a better spot, closer to the green]. I called to him and said, "What's going on? Why are you moving the ball?" He said that he didn't move it; that the ball landed there, but I saw him doing it. I told him, "Don't do it again, that's not my style. Don't do it. People know me, you are going to ruin my reputation for nothing." I told my playing partner what the caddy was doing [and] she said, "Who cares? It's a friendly tournament." I said: "No, I am sorry, we are playing for a crystal trophy of this size [she put one hand on her waist and another on her chest, indicating approximately 20 inches] and I don't like cheating." I was very angry and decided that if we won I would give the trophy back.

Laura looked angry as she described the incident, and when she finished she asked, "Do you know how I saw her, do you know how my perception of her changed? I really admired her, but I lost all respect for her. I never played with her again."

Laura's sentiments were not unique; many interviewees expressed a belief that cheating to win was not simply a minor violation of the rules but rather the manifestation of a fundamental character flaw. Thus, most of the golfers agreed that if someone cheats on the course they are more likely to cheat in life. Ernesto, a golfer in his late fifties who played in one of the newest clubs on the outskirts of Mexico City—and who was introduced to the game by a relative, with whom Ernesto frequently used to travel to the United States—held this view. After repeating the mantra that honor is an essential aspect of golf, he described his thoughts about cheating: "If I notice that someone is cheating on the course, I lose all trust in him. I don't do any business with him and if we are already doing business together, I keep close track of my money. He who cheats in golf cheats in real life." Golfers argued that only a small percentage of fellow club members commonly cheat, while caddies indicated that the behavior was more common than golfers recognized.

When I asked caddies what constitutes a good caddy, most interviewees offered a list of the tasks a skillful caddy needs to do: among them was to keep a close eye on the score of the golfers they are caddying for as well as the rest of the group (up to three more players). One of the caddies emphasized the importance of keeping track of everybody's score, saying "in that way we [caddies] prevent other players from cheating on the golfer we are working for, we [caddies] need to constantly remind people the spots from where they hit the ball [proving the exact number of strokes a golfer hit]." I followed up the question asking this caddy whether golfers commonly cheat on each other. He said, "I wouldn't say that it's widespread but it happens." More than an assessment of the accurate character of club members, the contrast between honest and cheating behaviors is linked to the way class influenced people's everyday perceptions.

A comparison of golfers' attitudes about cheating and the parallel act of purposely letting another player win reveals the influential role of class. Several golfers stated that there are times that golfers should lower their own playing potential or deliberately inflate their stroke count to let another player win. While this is also a form of dishonesty, the interviewees did not perceive it as such. They considered inflating their stroke counts or playing poorly on purpose as ways of being kind to others rather than dishonest or unfair practices. Carlos, a golfer in his early fifties who owns a construction company and had a membership in a highly reputable club, was very candid about this point during the interview. He elaborated at length on how important golf had been for his career. As he explained how to successfully meet and connect with people in golf clubs, he first stated that "you need to be a good player." He followed this statement by showing me a set of exercises he said would improve my swing and even describing how I could incorporate them into my daily work routine (stretching his arms one side to another of his chair and asking me to follow him). Next, he suggested that golfers must always be "*amables* [kind]" to other players. He observed:

> In golf, you form so many new relationships, you can connect with so many people through golf, it is amazing, but sometimes you need to let others defeat you, you need to let others win. If you are always winning, you end up losing, even among friends. You need to be kind in relation to winning, you don't always play to win, win, win, because if you do that, people will slowly exclude you. You need to let others win sometimes, one day, two days, and then you

win again. You see, you need to think of golf as a game, as a place to have fun and share, rather than a sport or a competition.

Other players repeated variations of this idea, adding more specific suggestions. For example, Rafael, the 60-year-old golfer who owns an advertising company, suggested that if I wanted to meet someone to discuss business matters, "it's better to select an easy course to play—everyone will have a good game, and you might let someone win." Rafael noted that following this advice would increase the likelihood that everyone playing would be happy and excited when they sat down to talk about business matters after the game. Ruben, a player in his late fifties who early in the interview claimed that his club was "truly a middle-class golf club," recommended a similar strategy. He suggested that if a playing partner was having a really bad day and becoming angry or frustrated, "you better tear up your scorecard and throw it in the trash," to show the other player that you care about camaraderie and friendship rather than competition. A few players offered explicit examples of how I could graciously let other players win, but in most cases when I raised the point, participants responded with a short phrase affirming the practice, saying, for example, "It happens" or "Yes, it's nice to be kind." Notably, not a single participant challenged this practice or regarded it as a manifestation of an unethical character.

Golfers' unwitting assumptions about class created a moral distinction between deceiving other golfers to win and deceiving other golfers to let someone else win. Players welcomed and celebrated victory only if it was achieved in an honorable manner, within the rules of the game, because they believed that honor, civility, morality, decency, and integrity are the truest markers of a golfer and triumph is relegated to a secondary role. Further, golfers believed that when victory is linked to material benefits (for example, in tournaments), cheating reveals an excessive interest in material objects.

Golfers believed that while the desire to win at all costs, even via cheating, characterized a few "bad apples," this outlook did not guide social relations within the clubs. However, golfers felt that deceiving someone to let them win was not an act of cheating but rather a form of kindness. This belief was a form of role distancing based on golfers' unconscious ideas about honor and civility—players distanced themselves from the need to always win, reassuring themselves that golf is just a game, and their main goal was self-improvement. Being courteous and letting others win was a way for affluent players to express detachment. Those who cheated were perceived as untrustworthy because they did not demonstrate a deep-seated understanding of the role distancing that was common among most members of the community but instead exhibited an excessive desire to win, something golfers associated with lower-class athletic games. Notably, in the world of popular sports, purposely lowering one's own athletic performance to let others win is one of the most unscrupulous things an amateur athlete can do. In the world of boxing, for example, a fighter who lets an opponent win will lose the respect of his fellow boxers (Wacquant 2006). In golf, class principles manifest in practical ways: increasing the importance of honor and civility and decreasing the emphasis on winning.

The weight put on the idea of civility however is also a reminder of the colonial roots of the sport (Stoddart 1999), as argued in Chapter 1. The critical distinction golf players make between unruly, dishonest, and uncivil popular sports and the honest, tidy, and restrained world of golf draws from the old colonial differentiation between civility and barbarism. Throughout the nineteenth and early-twentieth century, colonialism situated civility "as a value and ideal that only a few highly educated natives could aspire to when fully acculturated into European culture" (Hansen 2018:296–297). European civility functioned as a central justification to promote the spatial separation between white settlers and non-white locals, who lacked control and civility. The latter was perceived as an intrinsic quality of Western European people, and, by extension, with whiteness (Thiranagama, Kelly, and Forment 2018; Goldberg 2009). In today's Mexico, the association between incivility and popular activities, on the one hand, and civility and golf, on the other, is a narrative that openly articulates a class argument and covertly expresses racialized perceptions. In a powerful manner, the idea of civility symbolically reinforces the multiple barriers that separate these clubs from the rest of the city. In addition to this type of perceptions, many of the golfers I spoke with also linked the game to the notion of intelligence, asserting that golf promotes analytical skills.

Intelligence

Rafael, the player in his early sixties who owned an advertising firm, found my project amusing and intriguing, deciding to actively help me (point that I discussed in more detail in the Appendix). When I asked him for the contact information of other golfers at the end of the interview, he immediately picked up the phone and started calling his friends in front of me. One of the people Rafael called was Victor, who, after hearing that I was doing a research on business and golf, invited me to play in his club. Victor's club was located in the northern part of the city. As most other invitations, we met on a weekend morning at 7:30 a.m. After finishing a round of 18 holes, the group of four players and I sat down in the bar for drinks and lunch. As part of the conversation, one of Victor's friends extensively elaborated on the relationship between intelligence and golf. He explained that golf was a sport for people who used their intellect in their daily activities. According to him, golf players expanded their analytical skills when they played this game. His statement implied that critical thinking was not a primary characteristic of other sports or their players.

This was not the first time I had heard this type of statement. During my fieldwork I was constantly lectured about the relationship between golf and intelligence. People noted that each shot is different, and thus players must use an analytical process to determine how to approach their shots. For example, the ball can land in short grass or tall grass, between the roots of a tree, or in a sand trap; a windy day requires low-flying shots, whereas on a calm day players can make high-flying shots; the ball performs differently on dry versus wet surfaces; and the ball moves much faster on the green (the scoring area) than on the fairway (the main course) because they have different types of grass. Interviewees explained that players must consider all these variables as they quickly determine which one of the 14 clubs included in a regular set of golf clubs they would use to hit the ball on a particular shot, while also evaluating how hard to hit the ball. Further, golfers must make these assessments and calculations while maintaining a steady conversation with their fellow players. Therefore, the interviewees concluded, golf requires strong thinking and analytical skills. In contrast, many interviewees associated lower mental capacities with caddies (see Chapter 5 for an extended discussion).

It was rare that a single golfer articulated this relationship between intelligence and golf in its full form. In most cases, participants explained shorter versions of the link between intelligence and the sport. This was what happened with I spoke with Ricardo, a golfer in his early sixties who learned the sport as a kid because his family owned a membership in a reputable club. Ricardo was one of the golfers present when another golfer invited me to play at his club. After the game, when we were seated in the snack bar, Ricardo argued that "golf is a sport that is played with the mind.

This sport is for smart people, it requires a lot of concentration, nerves of steel, it implies a whole attitude in life." To validate his argument, Ricardo noted that after a "bad hole" (a phrase commonly used to indicate that someone played very poorly on one of the 18 holes), golfers had to have a high level of concentration to move beyond their mistakes and frustration and play the next hole with a fresh mind and positive attitude.

Almost all the golfers I spoke with touched upon the mental aspect of golf in one way or another during their interviews. For example, Gerardo, a corporate executive in his late fifties who played in a different club than Ricardo, also described golf in terms of mental capacity. He said, "Golf is a mental sport—it is a game of pressure." Carlos, the golfer who showed me a set of exercises to improve my swing and described how to incorporate them into my daily work routine, offered the most elaborate explanation of the relationship between golf and intelligence. When I asked why golf was commonly played by people associated with business activities, he explained:

Golf helps people to mature. Here [on the course] people's mental capacities change in a way that does not happen in other sports, because in golf, hit by hit, you force your body and mind to become better, and that impacts your job. If executives start playing golf, I assure you that in a year they will increase their confidence. [. . .] The Japanese and Americans are not fools, these are the two countries where there are the most golf courses, why? Because in one way, although there is no research on it, they have seen how golf improves people's intellectual capacity, improves physical abilities, and also concentration.

The argument that golf is a game for smart people because players must assess a large number of variables at every step of the game assumes that this is not the case in most other sports; however, when played at a competitive level, all sports require participants to have strong analytical skills. For example, such skills are necessary for runners (Collinson 2008), boxers (Wacquant 1995), and soccer players (Nelson et al. 2013).

The assumption that "golfers are smart" portrays the distinction between golfers and other athletes as a natural condition and thus helps players justify their presence in this privileged space in terms of their innate mental capacity rather than in terms of economic assets—a distinction that is too ordinary and might raise uncomfortable questions about the unfair distribution of wealth. The anecdotal evidence interviewees used to support their claims that golfers were intelligent, rendered class hierarchies and racialized perceptions into a seemingly logical and natural social order. The latter, however, is never completely coherent because it includes a permanent dimension of tension.

Class as (an Internal) Struggle

Class is generally perceived as a structure that brings people together by fostering particular types of relationships within and between class groups based on the specific interests of each of these groups. The narratives of civility, honor, and intelligence, for example, are mechanisms through which dominant classes articulate their interests and justify their presence (based on something other than money) in this privileged social space. However, a second aspect of class also surfaced in the interviews—one based not on the within-group unity but on the multiple divisions, conflicts, and tense relations within a class group. This aspect of class was present, for example, in a joke Miguel told about his club—"The course in this club is hard, because of the rough, which goes all the way to the changing rooms"—and the way Horacio described some of his fellow club members—"like gate crashers" (both instances discussed in Chapter 2). Class as an internal conflict also appeared in Fernando's and Laura's disappointment in fellow club members who (in their opinion) did not embody the civility and honor (i.e., role distance) they considered the core of the community.

This internal class animosity was also present in sarcastic and cautionary remarks club members sometimes made about other members of their own clubs whom I had interviewed or planned to interview. For example, after hearing that I had interviewed Carlos, the member who suggested it was important to let others win, an older golfer warned me about his ideas, saying: "Take his ideas with a grain of salt, Carlos has a very commercial view of golf." Another time, a player belittled the president of his club, who was also a board member of the Mexican Golf Federation (MGF), because the president and the MGF had blocked all attempts to promote the sport outside small circles of highly affluent individuals. In some cases, these internal conflicts were the result of personality differences or individual attitudes; however, there was a consistent pattern in the jokes, comments, and disrespectful observations, which suggested that rather than being personal troubles, these verbal fights were part of public issues, to use C. Wright Mills's famous phrase.[1] Specifically, these struggles were the result of the structural transformations generated by neoliberalism in Mexico in the late 1980s.

Old Money Versus Nouveau Riche

In her history of one of the most important golf clubs in the Mexico, Castellanos used the example of an important regional tournament played at the club to describe the nostalgia that characterized club members' discussions of the past (1999). During this annual event, golfers competed to win a cup that had no financial worth but great symbolic value, because it was a source of great honor and respect. The trophy was showcased in the most elegant shopping mall in the city for weeks before the tournament. Anyone who visited the mall, either shoppers or workers, could catch a glimpse of the cup. While the trophy was exhibited publicly, the contest to win it was a private affair—the tournament was open only to members of the club and selected guests. The winner gained honor in the form of both a highly valued trophy and the respect of the larger public, which learned about the tournament's outcome in articles published in the most prominent local newspapers. The trophy and the tournament were almost like sacred objects in that their value was measured in cultural and symbolic, rather than material, terms. The cup represented distinction, which may or may not ever translate into any type of economic gain.

During my fieldwork, I met the editor-in-chief of a specialized golf magazine who had both played golf and covered the sport for many years. His comments about recent transformations in the world of golf in Mexico City coincided with Castellanos's (1999) account. For example, the editor indicated:

Years back, people competed for, even in big national tournaments, a prize that was a trophy, something that had value but not commercially. The prizes were first, second, and third place medals, and that was it. [Nowadays], unfortunately some tournaments offer

---

1. In *The Sociological Imagination* (2000 [1959]), C. Wright Mills argued that the main objective of sociology, as a discipline, is to demonstrate how experiences or life situations which are commonly regarded as personal troubles (such as unemployment, poverty, or racism) are inextricably linked to broader economic, social, and political processes (i.e., public issues).

stratospheric [economic] prizes. You see, people do not care about honor anymore.

According to the editor, until the early 1990s there were only two national-level tournaments and a handful of important regional events. By the 2010s, however, "There are about 200 tournaments in the country and all of them offer big economic prizes." Many long-time players shared this dim view of the large economic rewards offered in today's tournaments. For example, Mercedes, a woman in her mid-fifties who had played at a respectable club for more than 20 years—and who was deeply involved in promoting the sport among female club members at the time of the interview—expressed disdain for the way tournaments had changed. She lamented: "Tournaments have changed a lot; it is sad. Nowadays people only want to play because of the economic prizes. We have polluted the game with so much money." Remarkably, no golfer ever indicated the role neoliberalism has played in the transformation of golf and society at large (I will discuss the point later).

In all my visits to golf clubs, I never saw an advertisement or any other type of publicity for specific companies or services. On one occasion, however, I attended a tournament held at one of the most important clubs outside of Mexico City. The tournament was sponsored by a global corporation and was open to any golfer who was able and willing to pay a hefty entry fee, which provided access to the tournament and club facilities for a day. During the tournament, banners of different sizes and shapes were displayed throughout the course. The logos of the main sponsors were visible at each tee (the starting point of each hole), each green (the end of each hole), the snack bar, the driving range (warm-up area), and the clubhouse entrance. At the center of the course, five large tents and three small ones promoted a variety of services and products linked to the sponsors, including insurance services, airline tickets, luxury cars, and brands of upscale alcohol. All the companies present that day gave away free prizes such as caps, golf balls, shirts, drinks, and discount coupons. At midday, a stall cooking "garnachas," a type of food usually considered "street food," was set up in front of the main sponsor's tent, allowing golfers to eat a popular street dish in a highly sanitized environment.

While the marketing director of one of the main sponsors was excited about the event when I interviewed him weeks later, assuring me that these types of events were a great success, some long-time golfers disliked the level of commercialization that characterized these type of tournaments. Horacio, a golfer in his late forties who had played since his mid-twenties, expressed disdain for this specific tournament, saying:

> What do you find in this tournament? You find a lot of hostesses with tight outfits, which lowers the status, it cheapens the tournaments, OK. They promote this and that other brand, it is presented as [making quotation marks with his fingers] "the experience," and stuff like that. This is a backward form of commercialization. They want to sell you everything, the whole thing is cheap.

Complaints about the hypercommercialization of golf were commonly accompanied by another set of objections focused on the large number of people who have recently taken up the sport despite not being "golfers." The editor of the golf magazine, for example, estimated that around 30 percent of the people who currently play golf in Mexico City are newcomers to the sport. He claimed it was possible to identify these novices because they are not familiar with the etiquette of the sport. He said: "You can immediately tell, they don't dress well, OK. In order to be a golfer, you need to dress like one and they don't dress well. Bermuda shorts and untucked T-shirts are not part of golfers' etiquette. They are not traditional golfers."

Patricia, who was in her early thirties but had played golf since childhood because her family owned memberships in two different clubs, exemplified the long-time golfers who disliked the transformations the world of golf had undergone in recent decades. She indicated that in recent years, multiple acquaintances had asked her for "golf lessons," either because they had been invited to play in a corporate event or because they wanted to participate in a tournament in the very near future. Patricia complained: "I am not an instructor and one cannot become a golfer in two weeks." Later in our interview, she added:

> Mexico's problem is that golf has grown really fast because of companies [corporations], but there isn't a golf culture [among the new players], it's money that has promoted the current growth. People who have never played golf before are invited to participate. That isn't OK.

She concluded by saying: "Here, golf has become popular; there are many novices on the course." I also discussed golf's recent transformation with Miguel, a golfer in his late sixties who had played all his life. His answer mirrored the nostalgic narrative in Castellanos's book (1999), suggesting that in the "good old days" money alone was not enough to gain access to the world of golf. He explained:

> Look, I have noticed this, golf has always been linked to money, but lately it is also a snobbish activity, OK, the fact that I can tell others that I am a golfer or that I am a member of this or that club seems to make me better. This is sad, because for many years memberships were only inherited; for instance, I play with the membership that my father once owned, and I am going to give it to my son, and more than likely he will give to . . . and so on, OK.

After a long digression, Miguel returned to this point, adding that while golf has always been an expensive sport, "Nowadays, anyone can buy a membership." He suggested that in the past, people had to have both money and pedigree and now people only have to have money. Many golfers romanticized the past in similar ways, and long-time club members made a distinction between an earlier era when people could only gain access to clubs by having large amounts of multiple forms of capital (educational, social, financial) and the current period, in which significant financial assets, even in the absence of other types of capital, could procure entrance into respectable clubs. This complaint, however, does not fully reflect the empirical data. While some established clubs have relaxed their policies to increase their cash flow, others, including some of the most prestigious clubs in the city, have retained their strict admission policies.

Diego, a player in his early sixties who belonged to a mid-status club, described the continued focus on non-financial criteria at one Mexico City golf club: "At 'Club High Class,' I know that the applicant's file is circulated among current members, [and] if 5 percent of the current members vote against [it], the candidate is rejected, no matter what, and I know this because I know people who have been rejected." At the same time, Carlos, the golfer who had advised me to let others win, noted: "You need letters [of recommendation] to gain access to some of the most prestigious clubs, but you can get these letters if you deal directly with a member interested in selling his membership. He can get you the letter; it has happened, OK." The comments of these two players as well as the complaints of several long-time golfers suggest that class dynamics have changed over time, but the direction, pace, and extent of this change has varied across clubs.

One source of these transformations was the neoliberal turn that occurred in the 1980s at a global scale (Harvey 2007). Neoliberalism reshaped the organization of traditional class dynamics by emphasizing the value of financial assets. For example, in the 1990s a luxury carmaker sponsored an extravagant golf tournament in Mexico City in which, rather than competing for trophies representing honor and distinction, golfers fought to win one of the 18 expensive cars the sponsor awarded to the golfer with the best approach shot at each hole. These types of corporate-backed tournaments, which were open to "anyone" with enough money to pay the large entry fee, marked a notable shift from past tournaments, in which a select group of players were invited to compete for an object of revered status but limited economic value.

These events gradually modified the role of honor in the world of golf. Over time, economic assets gained prominence over other forms of capital, thus depreciating the value of certain assets possessed by long-time golfers, such as social capital. While many long-time members lamented this shift, some newcomers proudly chronicled their role in the transformation and commercialization of the sport. Carlos, the golfer who showed me a set of exercises to improve my swing, for example, described his participation in a group of players who had organized a series of highly commercial and very successful tournaments in recent years. He recalled the experience fondly,

> People really liked the tournaments that we organized. We gave away very good [expensive] prizes. [. . .] I met many people there; today, I can call the CEOs of some corporations and they pick up the call. They met me organizing tournaments and they trust me now.

In a similar vein, Martin, a man in his mid-forties who co-owned a company which organized international sporting events and who had only recently begun playing golf, described his role in the expansion of the sport in Mexico. He enthusiastically claimed that his company had brought more media attention to golf, which, he argued, would attract more sponsors and increase the sport's exposure to new audiences. With satisfaction, Martin concluded, "We are contributing to the expansion of the sport." Carlos and Martin are examples of golfers who have similar amounts of economic assets as others in the golf community but whose views about the world of golf are strikingly different because they have different amounts of other forms of capital (e.g., social capital). These two interviewees were part of a group of newcomers who were interested in transforming, rather than preserving, class relations and interests within the community because such a change would likely increase their own prestige in the privileged space of golf in Mexico.

Conclusion

The notion that class represents a set of interests and relations that place two class groups in opposition to one another helps to explain why people who have similar life trajectories bond with one another. These bonds go beyond notions of friendship or camaraderie, entailing a broader sense of community. This sense of community is present, for example, in the moral boundary established between golfers, who are perceived as honest, polite, and chivalrous, and athletes in most other popular sports, who are perceived as condoning and, in some instances, even celebrating dishonesty and chicanery. This broader sense of community also appears in the way language colloquially marks the distinction between those who can call one another by their first name and those who must include indicators of deference in their linguistic interactions with others. The perception of golf as a mental sport, and by extension of golfers as highly intelligent, is another element that reinforces class boundaries. This narrative conveys that golfers are defined not only by the possession of economic capital but also by a high degree of intelligence (a characteristic commonly assumed to be a biological trait). The idea that golf requires and promotes strong analytical skills generates the illusion that money is not a prerequisite for being a golfer but rather a coincidental commonality among golfers.

The idea that class exclusively represents interests and relations that place different groups in opposition fails to capture one important aspect of class relations: a set of internal battles over the conditions that define one's own position in the group and the boundaries of the group itself. Banning someone from joining a golf club is the most obvious way in which club members enforce class boundaries, but members also bolster these boundaries in more subtle and nuanced ways in their everyday actions, including sarcastic comments, jokes, disrespectful remarks, and cautionary suggestions. As one interviewee explained, although "golf has always been linked to money," golfers have witnessed a recent shift, and "nowadays, anyone can buy a membership." Given that the player's comment referred to a club that charged a membership fee of about $40,000, the term "anyone" was obviously not used in literal sense but rather to refer to people who have amassed considerable fortunes in recent years but lack the manners, attitudes, and deeply internalized worldview that make someone a "true" golfer.

Although class relations seemed the most obvious force articulating social interactions and spatial dynamics inside affluent golf clubs, I also noticed a myriad of elements suggesting that racialized ideas also influence the organization of these upscale sites. Drawing on the discussion of class presented in the previous two chapters, the following section advances the idea that class cannot be fully understood if racialized patterns are not taken into consideration in the analysis of privileged spaces. Therefore, Chapter 4 maintains that class and racial ideas are two elements so deeply intertwined that one cannot speak about the former without referring to the latter in contemporary Mexico.

4

An Ostensibly Raceless Nation

Race is an instrument in establishing exploitable labor.

—DAVID GOLDBERG (2002:51)

Introduction

I was introduced to Ruben by another golfer and first talked to him via phone. After I had described my work and asked to interview him, Ruben posed the question that prospective interviewees invariably asked: "Do you play golf?" The question did not have a straightforward answer. While I had taken a short course and had played a few times before, I was not a golfer in the customary sense; however, for the sake of the research I answered yes (I address this point in further detail in the Appendix). Ruben then asked, "Why don't you come to play at my club and we can talk there?" We agreed to meet the following Sunday in the warm-up area (the driving range) at 6:50 a.m. for a 7:10 a.m. tee time (starting time). The club was situated in the northern part of Mexico City and was considered an "accessible club"; in fact, Ruben described it as a "middle class club." I arrived on time and met Ruben and his two playing partners at the driving range. As described in Chapter 4, golfers use only their first names when introducing one another and do not discuss business matters during their initial interactions. This pattern held true at Ruben's club; he introduced me to the group (and them to me) using only first names. The three golfers were courteous and friendly, making jokes and asking questions about my research. In the four and a half hours we spent together, they never discussed business issues and offered only basic information about their careers, although I was able to make inferences about their work based on comments they made about their daily lives. Even in this "accessible club" the privileged condition of golf and its players was constantly hidden.

After we finished a round of 18 holes, the four of us headed to the 19th hole (the bar). As discussed in Chapter 2, the bar represents the quintessential male-bonding space in the world of golf. This club's bar was not as elegant as some of the others I had visited, but it was spacious and had all the elements needed to make golfers feel pampered: there were several tables and plenty of comfortable chairs, a wide wall behind the bar was filled with shelves stocked with a large collection of spirits (suggesting abundance), the waiters, dressed in the universal white shirt and black pants, were prompt and attentive, and our table featured a picturesque view of the course. The bar was busy when we entered. Ruben and his friends were greeted by other golfers who were already drinking and chatting, and two of these acquaintances joined our group. The early conversation revolved around the game we had just finished, with the players recalling outstanding and terrible shots and discussing one another's strategies. When the discussion of the game waned, the conversation turned to other topics, including news about other members.

One of the golfers Ruben and I had played with that morning began to talk excitedly about rumors that new clubs might be built in the region. Another player asked, "Does anyone know what happened with the motherfuckers who protested against the construction of the [golf] club in Morelos?" and someone else replied, "Police beat them up." The person who had asked the question swiftly replied, "That's good; someone needs to teach these *indios* their place [in society],[1] otherwise we won't be able to stop them, they will start asking for more." The golfers erupted in laughs after this comment, and although I was uncomfortable and annoyed, I mirrored their reaction in order to build rapport and facilitate further interaction. The conversation then turned to other topics, such as cars, money, and jokes about the players' golf skills.

On my way home from the course, I began to think about this exchange, and it continued to occupy my thoughts for a long time. The events these golfers referenced occurred in a town 50 miles outside Mexico City. The area is surrounded by beautiful landscapes and is quite comfortable, with high temperatures averaging 71 degrees Fahrenheit (21 Celsius) in the summer months and 64 degrees Fahrenheit (17 Celsius)

---

1. In Mexico indigenous communities are commonly referred as *indios*. Despite being a descriptive term, the latter is commonly used in common language as an insult. I elaborate on this topic in the following pages.

in the winter months. The local community traces its origins to pre-colonial times and retains a strong indigenous identity, expressed in ceremonies, the use of traditional farming methods, and respect for the environment. Since the 1960s, an increasing number of upper-middle- and upper-class city dwellers have built or purchased weekend homes in the region. In the last few decades, several developers have attempted to build a golf club in the area, but the local community has opposed each of these projects (Rosas 1997). For example, when a club was proposed in the mid-1990s, powerful developers and state and local politicians supported the project (over the argument that it will create jobs), whereas most locals opposed it. The initiative was halted after violent clashes between protestors and state police resulted in the deaths of one protester and many more were injured (Rosas 1997).

The way the golfers at Ruben's club talked about this event and the possibility of future resistance to the construction of new clubs revealed their beliefs about both class and racialized notions. The class-related implications of the comments (i.e., that working-class people cannot make decisions for themselves) were quite clear to me and probably all those involved in the conversation. In contrast, I found the racial implications of the comments (specifically, players referring to the protesters as *indios*) somewhat ambiguous due to the broadly accepted idea among Mexicans that race (as a concept) and racial differences (as the manifestation of this concept) do not exist in this country. Instead, most Mexicans believe that a long-term process of interracial marriage has created a racial and cultural "melting pot" described by the term *mestizaje* (miscegenation or mixed race); variations of this idea are also present in other Latin American societies (Godreau 2008; Ochoa 2014; Weinstein 2015). The concept of mestizaje assumes that racial distinctions cannot exist in a society in which everyone has mixed racial origins (I will return to the point later).

The conversation I witnessed at the 19th hole (along with other evidence I will present), however, suggests that the concept of race and its manifestations persist in modern Mexican society, albeit in a different and ambiguous form. The present chapter outlines a twofold argument refuting the widespread idea that the notion of race does not exist in Mexico. First, I show that people in Mexico view society through racial lenses. Second, I illustrate that race and class are inseparable because people's understandings of race are relational, situational, and contextual, and thus deeply affected by class principles. However, the relationship between the two is not necessarily as straightforward as the "money whitens" thesis suggests,[2] a point I return to later. These two arguments demonstrate that despite popular belief, both the concept of race and its manifestations do exist in Mexico.

Notably, I do not argue that race exists as a biological reality. A growing number of studies have demonstrated that contemporary understandings of race, both biological (as in, e.g., the United States) and cultural (as in, e.g., Latin America) perspectives, are based on unscientific assumptions (Desmond and Emirbayer 2010; Gall 2007; Goldberg 2002; Guimarães 2012; Hartigan 2013; Loveman 2009, 2014; Nemser 2017; Omi and Winant 2014; Pitt-Rivers 1977; Roberts 2012; López Beltran, Wade, Restrepo, and Santos 2017). To paraphrase Lipsitz (2006), race is, of course, a delusion, a scientific and cultural fiction that has no valid foundation in biology or anthropology. Yet race is a social fact, a set of identities that have been created and maintained with very real consequences for the distribution of wealth, status, and life chances.

The chapter presents the thesis of the racialization of class, arguing that racial understandings are deeply interconnected to class principles. The analysis starts by showing how despite the assumption that mestizaje eradicated all racial ideas, people employ a wide range of racialized notions in everyday interactions. Second, it shows how the class system profoundly influences these racial ideas. This argument does not assume that the wealthier a person is, the whiter they are considered to be. Instead, it is explored how racial notions change from more fluid cultural assumptions at the bottom and middle part of the class hierarchy to more rigid biological views at the top of the socioeconomic order. The transformation is linked to both the changing nature of capital and the phenotypical composition of the upper classes. The chapter ends using a series of concrete ethnographic examples to illustrate the argument of the racialization of class.

An Ostensibly Racelless Nation

In Mexico, the term *mestizaje* has two meanings. First, it refers to the set of phenotypical and cultural characteristics that define the condition of being Mexican; second, it invokes a narrative about the nation-state and

---

2. In Latin America people commonly believe that money determines how white someone is considered to be, regardless of skin color. In other words, the "money whitens" thesis argues that racial understandings are exclusively determined by class dynamics. For a discussion of the topic in relation to Brazil see Schwartzman (2007).

its symbolic boundaries—who belongs and who does not belong to this nation (Moreno Figueroa 2010; Wade 2005). Most Mexicans assume that traditional Western ideas about race have not influenced the concept of mestizaje at either the individual or national level (Knight 1990; Pitt-Rivers 1977; Sue 2013) and, thus, interpret any negative or positive references to someone else's phenotypical features or cultural behavior as class-based rather than race-based assertions (González Casanova 1965; Rosas 2014). A 2014 *New York Times* op-ed article titled "Latin America's Talent for Tolerance" by Enrique Krauze, one of the most well-known Mexican public intellectuals today, epitomized this perspective. Krauze claimed that "Mexico's enduring problem is one of acute class differences, classism, rather than racism." To support his argument, he noted that Mexicans do not use the term *mestizo* in daily speech and while there is a certain degree of animosity toward *indios* (indigenous), overall, Mexico embraces a tolerant racial model in which the idea of race has no currency (and, as a result, critiques of racism have less traction).[3]

Krauze correctly asserts that the term *race* lacks currency in everyday interactions in Mexico. For example, members of the urban mestizo population in most parts of the country would not be able to answer the question "What race are you?" (this statement is also true in other Latin American nations; see Godreau 2008; Guimarães 2012; Ochoa 2014). The question would seem nonsensical because the presumption is that Mexicans are, by definition, mestizos, and mestizos are the product of racial mixture. In sum, Mexicans assume that because they are mestizos (mixed race) they do not belong to any racial category. Indeed, the idea of mestizaje has diluted most racial categories (Doremus 2001; Knight 1990; Saldívar and Walsh 2014).[4] Terms such as *blanco* (white), *negro* (black), and *oriental*

---

3. Krauze's argument echoes the ideas developed by José Vasconcelos in the early twentieth century in his seminal book, *The Cosmic Race*, published in 1925. Vasconcelos argued that Mexico and Latin America were in the process of creating a "fifth" racial category as the result of a thorough process of miscegenation, both cultural and biological, involving native Indians, white Europeans, blacks, and Asians. He predicted that the individuals in this new race would embody the best cultural and biological traits of all earlier racial groups. Further, due to its mixed nature, the "fifth" racial category would not only render structural and interpersonal racism irrelevant but would also allow nation states to transcend racial categories.

4. A small number of studies have suggested that racial perceptions in Mexico vary notably by geographical context. Pitt-Rivers (1977), for example, concluded that in the southern state of Chiapas, where most residents self-identify as indigenous or *indios*, the term *white* has a degree of currency. More recently, Tellez and Flores (2013) found that 17 percent of people in Mexico self-identify as white, and Tellez (2014) argued that the racial concept of "white" has different meanings in the northern, central, and southern parts of the country, suggesting

(Asian) lack the clear connotations and influence they have in the United States because, with the exception of people whose phenotype does not "seem mixed," Mexicans assume that these groups have been collapsed into a single mestizo group.

This non-racial discourse is not only embraced by individuals but also permeates the language and activities of the Mexican nation-state. The state's administrative apparatus does not use race-based classifications in key bureaucratic interactions such as issuing identification or other legal documents (Goldberg 2009). Until the early 2010s, the Mexican census "does not include questions regarding individuals' skin color" or "ask respondents to identify their ancestry" (Villarreal 2010:655). In 2015, the National Institute of Geography and Statistics (the entity in charge of producing the census) included a question on black self-identification in the 2015 intercensal census, and, in 2016, the same institute added questions about self-identified skin color in a study of social mobility. The results of the 2016 questionnaire suggest a strong correlation between skin color and socioeconomic status (INEGI 2016). Although the Mexican press treated these results as a novelty, this information was neither new nor groundbreaking.

Scholars have documented the correlation between racialized bodies and socioeconomic status in Mexico (Colby and Van Den Berghe 1961; Iturriaga Acevedo 2016; Moreno Figueroa 2010; Nutini 1997, 2008; Sue 2013; Vaugh 2005; Villarreal 2010). As Colby and Van den Berghe argued, "the genetic continuum [of phenotypes] overlaps greatly with the social continuum" (1961:772). Thus, the apparent absence of race in Mexico is not an absence in the form of *not existing, not being available,* or *a lack of,* but rather is an absence in the form of *not being recognized* by the institutional apparatus and *not being acknowledged* in the most visible aspects of daily life.

Paraphrasing Wade (2010), the categories and concepts related to race and racial dynamics have been removed from specific institutional practices and governmental organizations and yet remain present (though obscured) in everyday relations across the class spectrum. The dichotomy between the *invisibility* of race at the institutional level and

---

that rather than the whole country adopting a homogeneous mestizo identity, each region has developed its own distinctive pattern of racial perceptions. I argue that among Mexicans, identifying as white is linked to socioeconomic status (i.e., "money whitens"). I elaborate on this topic in the following pages.

its *obscured visibility* in popular discourse and imagery (which are not subject to institutional regulations) explains why Mexicans often perceive racialized comments (e.g., the insensitive comment included in the vignette) as non-racial, class-based remarks. In addition, the combination of institutional *invisibility* and popular *visibility* sheds light on a series of patterns I encountered during the fieldwork. These included the correlation between "epidermal schema" and status,[5] the use of certain terms to simultaneously describe brown/black skin color and lower-class status, countless jokes and sayings that subtly conveyed a racial hierarchy, and the interweaving of class-based and race-based comments in the ambiguous arguments golfers commonly used to explain social differences.

The (Institutional) Invisibility and (Everyday) Visibility of Race

As asserted above, racial terms and references are absent from institutional practices and government documents in Mexico, and yet the concept of race persists in popular discourse and everyday interactions, illustrating the inaccuracy of the claim that race, as a category, does not exist in this nation. I open this section by exploring the usual way in which race is perceived in Mexico.

The Absence of Racial Categories

In most of Latin America, race and racial boundaries have been historically associated with fluidity (Godreau 2008; Harris 1970; Ochoa 2014; Sanjek 1971; Sheriff 2000) because race has been defined on the basis of cultural, rather than phenotypical, characteristics. The cultural basis of race offers the possibility of flexibility (at least theoretically), with the assumption being that people can adopt cultural patterns at will (Pitt-Rivers 1968, 1977). In the mid-twentieth century, for example, census pollsters in Mexico were asked to classify interviewees' racialized identities as either mestizo or *indio* (the only two categories recognized by the state) based on their clothing, food preferences, and the language used at home

---

5. Frantz Fanon (2008) coined the term epidermal schema to capture how the most obvious external features humans possess (skin color, hair texture, nose shape, lip size, and body fat) are used to determine racial categories and social belonging.

(Saldívar and Walsh 2014). It was widely assumed that mestizos spoke Spanish; wore a vaguely defined urban fashion style; and regularly ate bread, meat, and dairy. Indigenous people, in contrast, supposedly preferred traditional clothing (for men, a white shirt and white pants made with coarse cloth—similar to the attired depicted in the headed paper of the Mexico Golf Association, see Chapter 1; for women, a long skirt and an embroidered blouse), spoke a native language, and ate a corn-based diet. Because people could change their racialized identity by changing the cultural characteristics they embodied, the size of the indigenous population fluctuated from one census to the next throughout the twentieth century (Saldívar and Walsh 2014). In this context, racialized identities were considered malleable and, to a certain extent, subject to personal choice. Most Mexicans believed that mestizaje had created a highly fluid and inclusive racial model—an idea that was embraced in many other Latin American nations (Freyre 1938; Godreau 2008; Roitman 2009; Stutzman 1981; Wade 2009).

While the belief in the fluidity of race and the ability of anyone to become mestizo—and therefore Mexican—by adopting certain cultural traits persists in present-day Mexico (Krauze 2014; Rosas 2014), in everyday life both material conditions and phenotype constrain the malleability of racialized identities. Mestizo identity is more easily claimed by those with greater wealth, while those with less money find that others often question their claims to mestizo identity (I return to this point later in the chapter). In addition, mestizo identity is likely secure and assumed for someone with light brown skin and a more European phenotype and is more likely to be called into question for those with physical features nearer to those of native Indians or blacks (i.e., darker brown skin and black/afro-textured hair) (Grecko 2017; Manzo 2017; Vaugh 2005). Hence, despite the popular assumption that anyone can become mestizo by adopting certain cultural markers (such as speaking Spanish and dressing in a "urban" fashion), in everyday life the possibility of becoming a "legitimate" Mexican is smaller for blacks, indios, and Asians than for those with European ancestry (Moreno Figueroa 2010; Navarrete 2017; Sue 2013; Vaugh 2005). However, in the mestizo framework, phenotype is not a conclusive marker of racial belonging, as it is in biology-based racial ideologies (e.g., in the United States) (Wade 2005). Rather, phenotype serves as one clue to a person's identity (Moreno Figueroa 2010), and even for those with little money or a non-European phenotype, a performative command of mestizo cultural traits (e.g., language, clothing, and an urban lifestyle) reduces doubts about their racial identity (Vaugh 2005).[6] In sum, although the idea of phenotype in Mexico does not hold the power in has in nations that have adopted biology-based ideologies, its influence still persists.

The effect of ancestry parallels that of phenotype. The European roots of Mexican identity are frequently highlighted and emphasized. Middle-class people commonly reference a family member who came from Europe or emphasize the European "origin" of their last names. A real or imaginary connection with Europe serves as a marker of status and legitimacy among contemporary Mexicans (as Martínez [2008] demonstrated, such allusions have been common in Mexico since the colonial era). In contrast, the African roots of Mexican identity are portrayed as insignificant and obsolete, having dissipated via the process of mestizaje in the early colonial period (Vaugh 2005).[7] Until very recently, only those in academic circles and a small group of social activists recognized the existence of an Afro-Mexican category (sometimes referred to as Afro-mestizo or black Mexican).

In 2015, however, the nation-state decided to include the Afro-Mexican category in an inter-census project—activists and academics expect that the category will appear in the 2020 census questionnaire.[8] Notwithstanding the state initiative, asking Mexican respondents if they were Afro-Mexican or black caused significant confusion because people understood the question as asking "Are you a foreigner?" (Pérez Moreno 2017). The confusion rested on the apparent contradictory nature of the enquiry. Mexicans

---

6. There is a similarity between this argument and the way performative whiteness operates in the United States (see Crichlow 2013).

7. People of African origin have lived in Mexico since the sixteenth century (see Aguirre Beltran 1946).

8. At a recent conference on race and ethnicity in Latin America (held in Mexico), academics and people involved in the development of the Afro-Mexican question included in the inter-census questionnaire discussed the difficulty of capturing people's understandings about race and racial inequalities. The audience, composed of academics from the region and the United States, engaged in a heated debate about the meaning of the concept of race in Mexico. The discussion lasted well beyond the formal conversation, continuing in several informal meetings over the following days. Most of the scholars who had been trained and were working in the United States argued in favor of using the term *race* in order to allow researchers to explain inequalities based on phenotypical perceptions. In contrast, most of the academics who had been trained and were working in Mexico disagreed with the idea of using the word *race*, arguing that the concept lacks currency in Mexico and its use is a neocolonial conceptual imposition. This is not the first time this debate about race in Latin America has transpired. For parallel discussions about Brazil, see Bourdieu and Wacquant (1999) and French (2000), and for discussions of Puerto Rico, see Carrion (1993), Duany (2002), and Seda-Bonilla (1968).

think of themselves as mestizos and mestizos by definition are mixed-race subjects. Therefore, the idea of being Afro-Mexican seemed an absurd question because all Mexicans are mestizos (i.e., mixed race). The possibility of embodying a particular racial identity (Afro-Mexican) goes against the very idea of mestizaje—variations of this homogenizing idea are present in other Latin American contexts as well (Godreau 2008; Ochoa 2014; Skidmore 1993).

Most Mexicans perceive mestizaje as the opposite of the U.S. racial model: the former is understood as flexible, benign, inclusive, and fair, whereas the latter is viewed as fixed, violent, exclusionary, and discriminatory. This benevolent view of mestizaje, however, overlooks the fact that outside the institutional narrative in which all Mexicans are proud descendants of ancient Aztecs and Mayans, everyday interactions situate brown and black phenotypes, and non-European ancestry and culture, at the lower end of a hierarchy and place a form of whiteness at the higher end of the same hierarchy. This racial hierarchy becomes seemingly logical and obvious when partnered with the class system, a point I explore in detail later in the chapter.

In everyday interactions, common Mexican sayings, jokes, and adages constantly convey this racial hierarchy. For example, the popular phrase *"el prietito en el arroz* [the dark spot in the rice]" is used to describe someone or something that has tarnished a positive context or object. Because the term *prieto* [dark] and its diminutive *prietito* can refer to both a negative element and someone with a dark brown or black skin tone, the saying is highly ambiguous—it can refer to either a negative element in a positive environment or someone with dark brown/black skin who is out of (racial) place. Therefore, the adage simultaneously expresses a type of racial admonition and links the ideas of "darkness" and "badness." In the book *Tepoztlán, Cronica de Desacatos y Resistencia* (1997), which chronicles the conflict surrounding the construction of the golf club referenced in the opening vignette, María Rosas illustrated the racial usage of the term *prieto* when she quoted a poor peasant of indigenous origin who expressed serious doubt about the possibility of being hired if the golf club materialized. The resident used the term *prieto* to describe himself and others with dark skin, who he predicted would be excluded from jobs at the club: "[At the nearby golf club] even the doorman are *güeros* [fair-skinned]. Do they really want to hire *prietos* like us [at this club?]" (Rosas 1997:21).

As Sue and Golash-Boza (2013) showed, most Mexicans view sayings and jokes with racial undertones as inoffensive because they belong to the world of language and humor. The common belief is that these widespread expressions are not at all racist because they do not aim to hurt people but rather to highlight the humor in life (at the expense of some people). When someone is offended by these sayings or jokes, people often argue that the apparent racialization implicit in the remarks is simply the product of a local culture prone to laughing about everything (similarly, in Puerto Rico, a person who is offended by a racial joke is described as *acomplejado* [having an inferiority complex]). However, humor requires a degree of social agreement. Humor reveals deep-seated themes in people's understanding of reality. The existence and common usage of a large body of sayings and humorous remarks that ambiguously allude to a racialized hierarchy suggests that racial categories in Mexico are present in a wide range of ordinary interactions, even though they are absent at the institutional level (Wade 2010).

The absent/present and visible/invisible dynamics that characterize racial understandings in Mexico suggest a highly ambivalent system. Unlike the famous Mexican public intellectual Enrique Krauze (2014), I do not view this ambiguity as a sign that tolerance and flexibility are highly valued. Rather, in alignment with Godreau's (2008) analysis of Puerto Rico, I argue that the Mexican racial order is a slippery model that simultaneously reflects both a binary distinction between brownness and whiteness and a Latin American racial order that is elastic and class dependent. The confluence of these two racial understandings as well as class principles creates a relational, situational, and contextual racial model that is unavoidably slippery and usually perceived as "not racial at all." The ethnographic evidence I obtained while attending a one-day tournament at a prominent golf club in northwest Mexico illustrates this scenario.

The Persistence of Racial Categories

Through one of the networks of golfers I tapped into, I met the owner of a company that had organized a prestigious yearlong amateur golf tournament played in several extremely prominent clubs across the country. When the company owner invited me to attend the next event in the tournament, I accepted. The club was five hours from Mexico City, in the northwest part of the country. On the day of the event, I took a taxi from my hotel to the club. At the entrance gate, a private security guard asked for my ID and then talked to the tournament organizers through a walkie-talkie to confirm I was an expected guest. Once he had confirmed my status, the guard politely gave me instructions to meet up with the organizing team by walking along the outside perimeter of the club-house, even though there was a shorter route through the building. Once I reached the organizing team, the manager welcomed me kindly but then quickly excused himself and apologized for not being able to talk at the moment because he was frantically supervising several groups of people who were making last-minute preparations, including hanging banners with the names of tournament sponsors, erecting large tents in the middle of the course, setting up the registration stand, and directing the arriving golfers to the continental breakfast being served in the bar.

Another member of the team suggested that I should go to the bar and have breakfast with the participating golfers. As in all the other clubs I visited, the 19th hole (the bar) was a spacious room with lots of tables and plenty of comfortable chairs. One wall was filled with large windows, offering patrons a nice view of the golf course. The organization of space inside the bar on that day, however, did not follow the pattern I observed in other clubs. The bar was divided into two sections. On one side, several tables were set up in an "L" shape near two walls. The tables were covered with platters full of fruit, bread, and individual servings of assorted cereals as well as large urns of coffee and tea. In the narrow space between the tables and the walls, harried workers moved swiftly, refilling food platters, picking up used plates and cups, and cleaning up spills. In the other section of the room, there were several large round tables where about 30 people sat in groups. Unlike the workers bustling behind the food service tables, those seated at the round tables were unhurried as they chatted with each other, read the newspaper, looked at their phones, or enjoyed breakfast by themselves. As I hung my jacket and a small bag on a chair at one of the round tables, I noticed that most of the people who were sitting by themselves at the table were staring at me. I smiled at them and then noticed that some of the people sitting in groups had also begun to stare. Many of the golfers continued to watch me closely as I walked over to the food service tables. Their curiosity waned when I grabbed a cup of coffee, filled two plates with fruit and bread, and asked one of the servers for help bringing my food to the table. Most of the golfers ignored me for the next half hour as I ate and read.

I grabbed the newspaper at the center of the table and began to skim it. One section was entitled "*Con Clase* [With Class]." The front-page article in the section was entitled "*Ganadores* [Winners]" and was dedicated to the boys and girls who had won a children's golf tournament at the club the week before. Twelve pictures of smiling children of different ages and two adults (the general manager and the golf instructor) accompanied the text describing the event. Each picture included a caption with the full name of the child, regardless of their age. Only the instructor, Luis, was referred to by solely his first name; I later learned that Luis started his career as a caddy at the club. All the children in the pictures had a similar epidermal schema: blond or light brown hair, light-colored eyes, and white skin (all would be identified as white by U.S. standards). Meanwhile, the club manager and golf instructor had brown skin, black hair, and dark eyes. The pattern reflected in the newspaper photos—a fair epidermal schema among club members and darker coloring among club workers—was replicated almost without exception in the spatial organization of the bar at that moment. The workers at the food service tables had a range of brown skin tones, black hair, and dark eyes, whereas all those seated at the round tables, except me, had lighter skin and more European phenotypes. The pattern that was repeated in the newspaper pictures and in the bar where I was seated suggested a strong connection between epidermal schema and economic status (Villarreal 2010), which made me wonder if the curiosity my presence had generated among some of the golfers when I entered the bar was related to this correlation (INEGI 2016).

I spent most of the day near the sponsors' tents, chatting with the representatives of the companies that were giving away gifts and observing the constant flow of participants passing through the area. Most of the representatives of the sponsoring companies were quite friendly and talked to me for long periods of time. These individuals had multiple gradations of brown skin, especially lighter brown; sported outfits reflecting a broadly defined urban sense of fashion (e.g., khaki pants or jeans and T-shirts or polo shirts); and spoke urban Spanish with the accent of a middle-class native speaker. The main sponsor's stand was the only one that included women, three female hostesses dressed in tight one-piece outfits who also had lighter brown skin. Two of the hostesses had dyed hair, one blond and the other red. Almost all the golfers who passed in front of the area, however, had fair complexions, or, in the local terminology, were *güeros* (a word that always implies a degree of whiteness). These racialized dynamics made me reconsider the way in which racial and class principles operate in tandem in Mexico (a relation pointed out in recent statistical studies; see INEGI 2016; Villarreal 2010).

The Racialization of Class

In Mexico—and most parts of Latin America—popular knowledge assumes that racial dynamics are subordinate to class principles; in other words, money can transform the perception of brownness/blackness into a symbolic form of whiteness (this notion is expressed by the perception "money whitens," which is implicitly connected to the opposite idea that "poverty darkens").[9] The popular belief is that there is a direct proportional relationship between race and class, with the perceived degree of whiteness increasing or decreasing in accordance with greater or lesser degrees of wealth. In this view, the entire socioeconomic hierarchy operates under a single logic in which both impoverished and wealthy people have similar understandings of the effects of race and class. In other words, a janitor and a banker make the same assumption—that the accumulation/loss of capital modifies the way others racialize them. While some scholars have expressed doubts about the validity of the money whitens thesis (Telles and Flores 2013), my ethnographic data suggest the need for a more nuanced understanding of the phenomenon: the data support the existence of a "whitening" effect of money but imply that this effect is not as broad or homogeneous as previously assumed.

The data I gathered among golfers show that the money whitens thesis accurately describes class and race dynamics among lower- and middle-class sectors of the Mexican population, such that people with a darker epidermal schema can change the way others racialize them by increasing their wealth and consumption power. This accumulation of economic resources also allows people to modify their bodies via permanent or temporary cosmetic options such as plastic surgery or dying their hair a lighter shade. There is, however, a social location at which the whitening effect of money stops. This limit, which is never explicit, is located at the boundary between the upper-middle class and the upper class. Two factors drive the fading of money's whitening effect in the upper echelons of society: the lower value of economic capital among wealthy individuals and the distinctive epidermal schema of the upper-middle and upper classes in Mexico (Colby and Van Den Berghe 1961; Nutini 1997, 2008).

---

9. For example, in his current study of peasants in the highlands of Peru, Orin Starn reports that the locals commonly describe fair-skinned poor peasants as dark-skinned individuals (personal correspondence with the author June 2017).

Money Whitens (but Not Always)

In Chapter 3, I introduced the argument that capital operates in a variety of forms (Bourdieu 1986) and that the value of each form of capital shifts according to the specific historical conditions (Bourdieu 1983; Elias 1987). In this chapter I extend this understanding of capital and its various forms by adding racial components to the analysis; specifically, I argue that the ability of capital to whiten its owner varies by the form of capital and the socioeconomic location of the individual. Traditionally, the popular notion that money whitens has included an assumption that the more money someone has, the more likely other people are to change their racial perceptions of that person. However, this postulate fails to consider that while financial assets have a constant economic value across all class groups (i.e., money can buy the same amounts of goods regardless the class position of the buyer), the status that emanates from the possession of a certain amount of money varies across the socioeconomic hierarchy. Whereas an expensive car is a rare object among members of the working class and, therefore, a source of very high status for its owner, the same car is likely a fairly standard possession among wealthy individuals and, therefore, not a particularly significant source of distinction for its owner.

For example, a golfer from the least expensive club in Mexico City mentioned that the parking lot of the most expensive club in the city, which he had visited for a tournament, looked like a luxury car dealership, explaining that the lot was "full of Land Rovers, Jaguars, and so on." In this context, a very expensive car signifies belonging to the elite group that forms the club's membership base. However, because such cars are common possessions rather than rare objects, owning one does not whiten the golfer in the eyes of fellow club members. In other words, the possibility of converting wealth and its associated status into a white racial identification decreases when economic assets are plentiful and normal.

When wealth is the norm, other forms of capital, such as cultural capital, take precedence over economic resources. Thus, manners, perceptions, and behaviors are as important as one's bank account balance. Cultural capital is a resource that requires long periods of time for people to enact it in a "natural" and "effortless" way, convincing others of the authenticity of the behavior. As described in Chapter 3, for example, Fernando rejected other golfers based on their lack of manners when he complained that some of the more recent (nouveau riche) members were impolite and played golf as if they were playing soccer. As he discussed how he had learned to behave in a gentlemanly manner, Fernando indicated that no one had "taught" him this attitude, but rather he had "just learned" by observing those around him as a child. The natural display of appropriate behaviors requires social "training" over an extended period of time (Elias 1983). In other words, Fernando learned how to play like a gentleman by being exposed to a certain set of attitudes, ideas, and actions throughout his childhood and teenage years. Therefore, unlike material objects, such as a car, that can be acquired and exhibited in a fairly straightforward manner, attitudes, manners, and behaviors are time-consuming forms of capital because they require long period of time to be acquired and exhibited in a "natural" way.

In addition to the changing nature of capital at the top of the socioeconomic hierarchy, a second factor that weakens the whitening effect of money among the upper-middle and upper classes is the "phenotypically European" appearance of the majority of Mexicans in these sectors (Nutini 1997:231; see also INEGI 2016; Iturriaga 2016; Villarreal 2010). I argue that, together, these two aspects create the structural conditions that prevent those with darker skin and non-European phenotypes from immediately "whitening" via the accumulation of large amounts of money. In the following pages I use four examples to illustrate this pattern. First, I examine reactions to a golfer who wanted to include more middle-class people in the sport. Next, I discuss perceptions of private and public golf clubs in Mexico. Third, I present the case of a club member whom fellow members called a *naco* and *frijolito* (bean). Finally, I use my own experience interviewing an upper-class female golfer to demonstrate how class and race unavoidably operate in tandem in Mexico.

Example One: Race in the Cloak of Class. Bruno is a golfer in his midforties who worked for a technology corporation and had played golf since his early childhood years because his family owned a membership in a prestigious club. When we met, he played at a slightly less prominent but still important club, yet, based on his familiarity and knowledge of the environment, he had access to a large number of clubs in the Mexico City and its greater metropolitan area. "I have played [golf] since I was a kid, [and therefore] I have friends in almost all clubs," Bruno pointed out. However, he believed that to ensure the future of the sport, Mexico's golf clubs and the Mexican Golf Federation (FMG) needed to find ways to incorporate middle-class people into the world of golf. At his own club, he had suggested allowing non-members to pay a reduced fee to play on Mondays—the day the club was closed for general maintenance, thereby unwittingly guaranteeing that non-members would not interact with members—or offering golf workshops for lower-middle-class children. Bruno explained, "These projects will expand the fan base of the sport, creating a large number of players who will demand public courses, and, who knows, maybe creating the possibility of having a Mexican Tiger Woods [an outstanding U.S. golfer] in the future." At the federation level, Bruno had suggested that golfers who did not belong to a club should be allowed to maintain a record of their scores on the FMG's website to establish an official handicap, which is not allowed under the current rules (as of 2015). An official handicap would allow players without a club affiliation to participate in official tournaments and, if they won, to represent their city or country at national and international tournaments.

Bruno had discussed these possibilities with his fellow golfers and FMG board members, but none of them were willing to entertain these ideas. The last time he had presented a project to the FMG board, the president of one of the most prestigious clubs in the city responded, "This idea is unfeasible, it will flood the clubs; the clubs will be invaded with those guys from the Zapatista Army." The "Zapatista Army" refers to the EZLN, or *Ejército Zapatista de Liberación Nacional*, a revolutionary but non-violent group based in Chiapas, one of the poorest states in Mexico. The primary social base of this organization is indigenous people who embrace a discourse that is stridently anti-capitalist, pro-democracy, and, more importantly, strongly promotes Indian pride.[10] However, it is very unlikely that members of the EZLN would take up golf even if they could. The president's comment is not a literal reference to Zapatistas. Instead, the reference works as a class and racial metaphor. In the eyes of the European-looking upper classes (Nutini 2008), a Zapatista is phenotypically indistinguishable from members of the lower and middle classes, groups who are poorer and browner in relation to those at the top of the socioeconomic pyramid (Villarreal 2010).

It is worth noting that the term "white" does not possess the immediate recognition that it has in the United States (Lipsitz 2006), because, after all, the ideology of mestizaje obscured most racial categories. Instead, whiteness is expressed through words denoting country of origin

---

10. The EZLN took its name from one of the most progressive revolutionary factions during the Mexican Revolution (1910–1921). As it happens, the original Zapatista Army occupied and destroyed the clubhouse of one of the oldest and most prestigious Mexican golf clubs in 1914 (Wright 1938), see Chapter 1.

(i.e., *gringo* [U.S. citizen], European, Spaniard, British)[11] or a combination of phenotypical and class characteristics (i.e., *güero* [light-skinned] and *mirrey* [high-class young men]). In the same way, non-whiteness is rarely conveyed by calling someone "brown" but more commonly by using terms that simultaneously and implicitly express class and phenotypical elements, such as the remark about Zapatistas.

Thus, while the hypothetical expansion of golf to the middle class would most likely not attract Zapatistas to the clubs, it would bring brown-skinned individuals, who despite any amount of wealth they attain, are still viewed with distrust by some members of the upper class. The use of this image—an EZLN member playing golf—shows how upper-class Mexicans invoke racialized ideas in everyday speech without explicitly naming them. This type of ambiguity precludes the possibility of the speaker being accused of racism. As such, a complaint can be easily dismissed as a mischaracterization of a classist remark, which is tolerable in Mexico. After reiterating the president's comment, Bruno said, "This guy is not my friend, I cannot put you in contact with him, but it would be great if you could talk to him. You will then see the narrow mentality many golfers have."

Example Two: Perceptions of Private and Public Space. The absence of public golf courses in Mexico City, a metropolis of around 20 million inhabitants, limits the development of the game to a small affluent minority. Most interviewees explained the lack of public courses by invoking economic arguments ("There are no public courses because there is no demand for them"). Few players suggested any other reasons. Alejandro and Hector, both golfers in their early fifties who had learned the sport in their early teenage years, offered typical explanations. Alejandro and Hector were old-time friends and each owned companies selling golf services, such as organizing private tournaments and arranging golf workshops for executives, to corporations. I interviewed them in the bar of an upscale hotel in the financial district of Mexico City, after the three of us had attended an FMG press conference (remarkably, at the beginning of the press conference I greeted a member of the Mexican Golf Federation, who, after hearing that I was going to interview Alejandro and Hector at the end of the conference, warned me about their comments,

---

11. Despite a large number of non-white communities, the idea of blackness is never equated with Western European nations or the United States in popular views. These countries are perceived as white nations.

saying: "they are the type of people who're more interested in selling rather than promoting golf"). When I asked the two men about the lack of public courses in Mexico, they gave the following explanations:

ALEJANDRO: There are public courses on the outskirts of Mexico City, and I can even think of one in the city, but almost as a rule people deny their existence; it is an unwritten rule. When you ask the general managers of some of these courses: "Is this a public course?" they swiftly answer, "No, no, no, this is a private club.

HECTOR: The word public is like a bad word, ok, it's a label that nobody wants. Nobody says it, but golf courses on beach resorts are public; anyone who pays the fee can access them. But, if someone with a bad look or who's badly dressed shows up, he is kicked out because these are run as if they were private clubs. There is a degree of elitism.

ALEJANDRO: There is a lot of elitism. I think that even though it's a good idea to have a public course, I cannot imagine anyone who works in golf, ourselves included, openly saying, "This is a public course. Carpenters, cabinetmakers, and construction workers, all are welcomed." I doubt it will happen.

Just as the club president's reference to Zapatistas evoked both class and racial hierarchies, Hector's reference to someone with "a bad look" or who was "badly dressed" simultaneously conjured beliefs about both race and class (Navarrete 2016). In his study about the Mexican aristocracy, Nutini (2008) found that noble people used expressions about appearance to convey racialized perceptions. "There is a high degree of preoccupation among aristocrats about phenotypes, or as several informants euphemistically put it, 'por tener buena facha'—to have a good appearance; that is, to look European" (Nutini 2008:60). In Mexico, whiteness, brownness, and blackness are rarely expressed in direct forms, as if people were afraid of conjuring racial inequalities. Instead, racialized ideas are communicated through notions that openly imply class and discreetly convey race. In this fashion, Hector's comment about the exclusion from golf clubs of people who are "poorly dressed" or with a "bad look" allowed him to express the undesirable condition of non-white lower-class customers without the need to say so openly.

Following on Alejandro and Hector's argument, carpenters (carpinteros), cabinetmakers (ebanistas), and construction workers (albañiles) occupy the bottom part of the socioeconomic hierarchy, and thus even a public course would be financially out of reach for them (a situation that occurs in the United States, where despite the large number of public courses, golf is a sport played primarily by members of the upper middle class; Gibson 1998; Sherwood 2012). Therefore, these interviewees were not literally talking about *albañiles*, *ebanistas*, and *carpinteros* as potential golfers but rather used these groups metaphorically to evoke a set of phenotypical and class characteristics (i.e., brown skin and limited resources) that link certain sectors of the working and lower-middle classes in the eyes of the upper class.

Example Three: Not Fully Mexican. Two golfers from the same club (who were not friends with one another) used pejorative terms that evoke both class-based and racialized insults to describe a fellow club member. In the first case, one golfer called this player a *naco* (a pejorative term with a somewhat ambivalent meaning I discuss in detail below) and in the second a club member called him a *frijolito* (bean). Laura, a golfer in her late fifties who had played at a prominent club for about 30 years—and who was a competitive tennis player in her teenage years—explained that this new member had begun to spend time with the same group of people with whom her husband, a very well-known member of the club, commonly played and socialized. She described the group as "fantastic," saying they were all "first-class people." After elaborating on the playing skills of these golfers, she added, "All were first class but this guy, a good man but still a *naco*."

Laura then explained her reasons for disliking this player. First, she indicated that it was unclear how he had amassed his fortune (suggesting by the move of his hand and fingers grabbing things on the air the possibility of embezzlement). In addition, she thought his behavior revealed a stingy attitude (as mentioned above, attitudes are a more expensive asset, because they require long periods of time and plenty of economic resources to be acquired and authentically demonstrated)—in other words, she thought he was cheap. On one occasion, the group of golfers, including Laura and the wives of the other golfers, had dinner at a very exclusive restaurant. As the golfers were dividing the check, the so-called *naco* complained about the amount of money the group planned to tip the waiter, arguing for a lower gratuity. Laura complained, "The place was really nice, we were already paying a lot of money for the food. Who cares about the tip? The guy was cheap." Most of Laura's critiques of her fellow member, such as being greedy and cheap, could be interpreted as expressions of class dynamics—tensions between old and new money. Nevertheless, her use of the term *naco* implies both class and racial elements. In fact, "since the 1970s, the word *naco* has become one of the most offensive terms in Mexican Spanish; primarily due to its ambivalence. It simultaneously implies a racist, classist, and aesthetic meaning" (Serna 1996:747).[12]

The *Dictionary of Mexican Spanish* offers three meanings for the term *naco*: "1. Indian or Indigenous of Mexico. 2. Of someone who is ignorant, clumsy, and lacks education. 3. Of someone who lacks taste or class" (DEM 2017). According to Zentella (2007:30), the word is a truncation of the term Totonaco, which is the name of a specific indigenous group in Mexico; at some point during the early twentieth century, the term became a generic way to refer to any individual of indigenous origin in Mexico. Pitt-Rivers defines *naco* in more abstract terms, as "one with whom there is no community" (1977:330)—this definition is similar to Simmel's figure of the "stranger" as an inassimilable alien (Simmel 1950). The lack of commonality implied by the term is based on the supposed native phenotype and lower-class origins of the subject of the insult (Monsiváis 1976), which is viewed in opposition to a more mestizo/European phenotype and wealthier background. Thus, *naco* is strongly associated with the idea of indigenous and by extension brownness, which are the opposite of whiteness. As Navarrete (2016:71) explained, "*Naco*, and its antonym *güero* [a person with a whiter epidermal schema], mixed with great malice class and racial prejudices. Being a *naco* is associated with inadequate behaviors, lack of fashion taste, poor manners, Indian origins, brown skin, and ultimately ugliness."

In everyday interactions, *naco* works as a symbolic assault on someone's class and racial identity, suggesting that the insulted person is not a true mestizo, but rather an *indio*, and therefore not fully Mexican. The word is used to publicly identify and call out certain people as racial and class imposters. The term incorporates ambivalence about and overlap between class-based and racialized perceptions. Although *naco* can also be used to insult a person with a whiter epidermal schema who is perceived as unsophisticated, the plural form *la naquiza* (the wider population of *nacos*) is never used to refer to affluent groups or upscale neighborhoods inhabited primarily by light-skinned individuals. Thus, while I heard golfers describing recent fair-skinned members as *nacos*, I never heard the term

---

12. The word *naco* can be used as both a noun (a *naco*) and an adjective (a *naco* golfer).

used to refer to an entire golf club. Rather, *la naquiza* always refers to activities, sites, and groups populated by lower- and middle-class individuals, who, in general, have a greater range of brown skin tones (INEGI 2016; Nutini 1997; Villarreal 2010).

Gerardo, a corporate executive in his late fifties who learned how to play golf while studying for his bachelor's degree in the United States more than 30 years earlier, also made a disrespectful comment about the so-called *naco* golfer. Gerardo recalled his fellow player complaining aggressively about being defeated in an internal tournament: "In short, the *frijolito* [bean] kept complaining, he didn't want to lose." Like Laura's comments, Gerardo's criticism (including his association of lower-class origins with aggressiveness, anger, and lack of emotional self-control) can be interpreted as conveying a clash between old and new money. Notably however, beans, mostly brown and black varieties, are a staple crop in Mexico and are strongly associated with indigenous groups and working-class households. Calling someone a bean fits well into a racialized logic that assumes a strong link between certain phenotypical features (darker hair and skin) and socioeconomic condition (working class) without any further explanation of the association.[13]

This case illustrates how money whitens, but not always. A large amount of economic capital signifies access to the spaces of dominant classes, but it is not an immediate source of whitening within the privileged community. As explained above, the reasons are connected to the value of financial assets among affluent individuals and the phenotypical composition of the group. One the one hand, when economic assets are plentiful and normal, other forms of capital, such as cultural capital, i.e., manners, perceptions, and behaviors, become as important as wealth. The abundant economic resources of the "naco" player helped him to gain access, but money by itself did not translate into a racialized higher status and social acceptance. The supposedly cheap and aggressive attitudes he exhibited made other club members think of him as someone lacking civility, and, hence, as someone with whom "there is no community."

On the other hand, the marginalized golfer could not easily convert his substantial economic capital into a form of perceived whiteness because phenotype plays a greater role among members of the dominant classes. The reason is that "the overwhelming majority of the lower classes

---

13. The expression *frijolito* uses the same racialized logic present in the pejorative term "beaner," used in the United States to insult Mexicans and Mexican Americans.

are phenotypically Indian, while the great majority of the upper classes are phenotypically European" (Nutini 2008:54). The supposedly cultural and fluid nature of the ideology of mestizaje becomes more rigid at the top of the socioeconomic pyramid, where a white(r) epidermal schema becomes a salient feature when people try to claim membership among these groups.

Example Four: Class Assumptions Based on Racialized Appearances. The final example focuses on the "confusion" that occurred before I interviewed Laura, the golfer who complained about the *naco* player. Laura was one of the few interviewees (all of them women) who invited me to conduct the interview at their home instead of asking me to have lunch together or meet at a bar. Laura's house is in a traditional upper-class neighborhood in Mexico City. I arrived on time for our meeting and parked the car I had borrowed outside her house. After I announced myself through the out-door intercom, explaining the motives of my visit, a domestic worker in uniform came to open the door and asked me to follow her. Instead of walking up the wide and sumptuous limestone stairs directly in front of us (which led up to an elegantly carved large wooden door), she began walking toward a small ordinary aluminum door at the end of an underground garage.

When we were about halfway to the service door, Laura came out of the wooden front door and loudly said, "Don't take him that way, come this way," as she pointed to the limestone stairs. Once I arrived at the main door, Laura apologized for the confusion. The unwitting reaction of the domestic worker—asking me to follow her through the service door—as well as Laura's timely "correction" of the confusion shows that class and race cannot be disentangled in Mexico. To the domestic worker, I phenotypically looked like a worker or service person, and thus the "legitimate" place for me to enter was the unimpressive service door. In contrast, Laura's racialized perception of me, and therefore, of the door I should use, was based on the fact that we had met inside a prestigious golf club while I was interviewing another member.

A "bad look," as well as its constituting opposite "good appearance," are some of the labels people used to articulate racialized distinctions. My experience with the domestic worker at Laura's home illustrates how racialized hierarchies are so deeply ingrained in members of Mexican society that they are unwittingly enacted in a multitude of everyday dynamics. Despite Laura's apology and the pleasant and friendly interaction we had during the interview, Laura never again answered my phone calls or messages asking if she could put me in contact with her upper-class friends. After all, as explained in the opening vignette in Chapter 3, I might have not exhibited enough cultural and social capital to show that Laura and I were equals, and therefore I was not a member of the group.

Conclusion

This chapter shows how race (as a concept) and racial inequalities (the manifestation of this concept) exist in Mexico despite the broad assumption that neither are present. This double invisibility of race relies on the fact that racial differentiations are absent from the most obvious institutional forms. Mexicans use terms such as white, black, or brown as descriptiors—*negro, negrita, blanquito, guera, morenito*—but these are not assumed to be racial identities. Further, no one uses the term *mestizo* to identify themselves or others. In the same fashion, the nation-state does not ask for or record the racial condition of individuals beyond the categories of *mestizo* (mixed race) and *indio* (indigenous). These two terms are understood as flexible categories that can be modified at will, although embracing the indigenous category is rarely viewed as desirable in urban contexts.[14] The assumed flexibility of the system is based on the belief that anyone can become mestizo.

In addition, the mestizo and Indian categories are assumed to be ethnic rather than racial descriptions. Whereas the popular understanding presumes that the former encompasses cultural elements while the latter is based on biological markers, in everyday life people reference both culture and biology when talking about *indios* and mestizos. Godreau's argument about Puerto Rico (2008) also applies to Mexico: the language used to talk about race in Mexico is semantically slippery to the extent that ethnicity seems like a euphemism for the idea of race. Despite the evidence that racialized ideas do play an important role in Mexico (Moreno Figueroa 2010; Nutini 1997; Nutini and Isaac 2010; Telles 2014; Villarreal 2010), however, whenever someone insists on using the term "racial" to describe the mestizo order, collective knowledge is mobilized to remind the transgressor that the idea of race has no currency in Mexico.

In contrast to the absence of racial categories in institutional spaces, a whole range of racial categories emerges in the popular sphere. Here,

---

14. However, in the 2000 and 2010 census the number of people self-identifying as *indigena* (indigenous) increased steadily (see Saldivar and Walsh 2014).

a hierarchical order that situates blackness and brownness at the bottom and whiteness at the top materializes via jokes, sayings, and metaphors. This racial gradation strongly mirrors the class hierarchy, and thus racial ideas are strongly linked to class principles. The influence of class on race does not produce a system defined by the former, as assumed by the popular belief that "money whitens." While money does have a whitening effect among those with lower socioeconomic status (the working and middle classes), its power to whiten fades away among those with high levels of socioeconomic status for two reasons: wealth becomes a normal condition and most wealthy Mexicans have a European phenotype.

Notably, in all the cases described above, space plays an important role in conveying the racial hierarchy without explicitly referring to it. Golfers' fears that exclusive clubs might be "flooded" by members of the EZLN (rebel Indians), *albañiles* (construction workers), *ebanistas* (cabinetmakers), and those who are badly dressed become metaphors used to express the potentially undesirable consequences of breaking down the spatial barriers that separate *indios* and their phenotypical peers in the working and middle classes. In this hypothetical scenario, the world of golf would be swamped by racial and class "imposters," which would subvert the upscale and racialized legacy of golf clubs.

As Chapter 3 discussed, golfers used a multitude of everyday interactions to mark the limits of the community. One of these strategies was linked to common speech. Whereas club members commonly referred to each other by first name, regardless of age or gender differences, workers always included all forms of linguistic subordination when talking to golfers. The relation between caddies and golfers epitomizes this pattern. The former constantly used words of utmost respect when talking to members, such as including the professional titles of golfers before addressing them. In contrast, club members talked to caddies using nicknames and other terms expressing a combination of affection, domination, recognition, and condescension at the same time. In fact, as Chapter 5 will demonstrate, the interaction between caddies and golfers is one of the most enlightening ways to further analyze the relationship between class, race, and space in Mexico.

5

Caddies

Race is traditionally thought about in terms of people, but ultimately (and originally) its politics becomes comprehensible only when it is contemplated in territorial terms: race is always, more or less explicitly, the racialization of space, the naturalization of segregation. Race orders space, social space, from the common to the private.

—LUND (2012:75)

Introduction

During the first stage of fieldwork, my only contact with caddies occurred during the rounds I played with the golfers I interviewed. My conversations with caddies were brief and constrained by the presence of club members. On one occasion, a caddy who was about 60 years old gently pulled me aside and waited until the other golfers and caddies had walked several feet away to talk to me "in private." In a soft voice he said, "If you want to do business with these dudes [the golf players], you must play fuckin' great," and then proceeded to give me some technical advice. I interpreted his comment as a sign that my inexperience with the sport was obvious to him and that he empathized with me. However, I did not know whether the caddy engaged in this empathic act as a strategy to gain a larger tip or because he perceived (class and racial) similarities between us. I was unable to answer this question and most other questions about caddies because at this point I had neither talked to caddies for any significant length of time nor spent time at the caddies' house, the site where they waited to be assigned to work with golfers.

As I began to grapple with the idea of privilege, I realized my knowledge of the world of golf in Mexico was incomplete. The more I talked with club members and reviewed my field notes, the more I appreciated the fundamental role caddies played in golfers' narratives about identity and belonging. The golfers I interviewed commonly described what constitutes a golfer not by referring to a set of characteristics that club members possess but rather by listing characteristics that *are not* representative of golfers. The figure of the caddy was fundamental to this inverted description. Caddies were a sort of photographic negative of golfers—they represented the opposite of everything golfers embodied. Thus, to round out my fieldwork I conducted a second stage of data collection focused almost exclusively on the figure of the caddy and the spaces caddies inhabited. Notably, the process of interviewing caddies was considerably easier than the time-consuming process of arranging meetings with club members (I discuss this approach in detail in the Appendix).

One of the journalists I interviewed during the first stage of fieldwork gave me the contact information for Luis Peralta, a caddy in his mid-fifties. The journalist told me that Luis has worked at the same upscale golf club for the last 20 years and "has friends in other clubs as well." I called Luis, told him who had given me his contact information, explained that I was conducting a study of the history of golf, and asked if I could interview him about the transformations in the sport during his lifetime. Luis immediately agreed to be interviewed, telling me that we could meet the following day at the caddies' house at the club where he worked, adding "I'm always there."

As in most other clubs, the main entrance was quite modest, and could even be described as insignificant. The principal gate was located directly over a main traffic artery, giving club members immediate access to a central road. In contrast, it was a 10-minute walk from the same artery to the workers' entrance door, which was immediately recognizable because it mirrored the almost universal arrangement of urban workers' entries to their sites of labor: a metal door with a large tinted window. In a panoptic fashion,[1] the window allowed the guards behind the door to see who was ringing the bell without being seen themselves, creating a sensation for those at the door of being scrutinized. At the bottom of the window frame there was a thin slot that allowed those requesting entry to pass through documents. When I rang the bell, a voice inside said, "yes." I told the hidden guard my name, explained that I was looking for Luis Peralta, and simultaneously passed my national ID through the narrow slot to show that I was indeed who I said I was.

---

1. French philosopher Michael Foucault (1995) coined the term "panopticism" to refer to the expanding surveillance techniques that capitalistic nation-states have developed and deployed to regulate people's behavior.

A guard dressed in a blue uniform opened the door and, as he returned my ID card, once again asked who I was looking for. I repeated myself, explaining that I was looking for Luis Peralta and he was waiting for me. With a puzzled expression, the guard told me that no "Luis Peralta" worked there. I insisted that Luis was a caddy and when we had talked by phone the previous day he had invited me to visit the caddies' house. Hesitantly, the guard turned his head toward the patio behind him where caddies were waiting to be called to work and shouted, "Does anyone know Luis Peralta?" After repeating the question two or three more times, someone shouted back, "That's *Pollo* [Chicken]. Luis Peralta is his name." The guard apologized, explaining, "You see, I only know him by *Pollo*" and then let me inside. When I shook hands with Luis, he said, "I'm sorry, I forgot to tell you that everybody knows me here as *Pollo*."

This experience immediately brought to mind a story included in the official history of one of the most prestigious golf clubs outside Mexico City, about a caddy who dreamed that he had won the lottery. In his dream, the caddy used his newfound fortune to buy a membership in the club where he worked. When he went to the bar to celebrate and have a drink, members greeted him by his caddy nickname, saying "Hello Mocho," but the caddy-turned-golfer demanded that they no longer use his nickname, commanding, "Stop with that Mocho, now I am Mr. José." Unfortunately for Mr. José, the experience was only a dream (Castellanos 1999:154). As illustrated by Mr. José's dream, being a caddy entailed being called by a nickname. Only those who had just started working in the profession, commonly young men, did not have nicknames. In contrast, no golfer was ever introduced to me by a nickname, nor did I ever hear one golfer refer to another with a nickname.

Nicknames are a humorous way of describing a person's identity. They capture the ways in which others see someone's personality, character, or physique, highlighting, for example, whether someone has a big or small nose, limps or has an energetic manner, laughs too much or not at all, looks like someone famous, or reminds others of an animal. The fact that none of the other caddies knew a Luis Peralta and that Mocho demanded others call him Mr. José after he became a member, at least in his dreams, reveals how nicknames express class hierarchies through the ordinary act of naming (perceived as humor).[2] In both the story of

---

2. The power imbalance present in the act of nicknaming others is also illustrated by the actions of former U.S. president George W. Bush, who publicly nicknamed all members of his cabinet, yet they could not nickname him, at least not in public.

Mr. José's dream and my experience of meeting Luis Peralta, space played a fundamental role in conveying social status: the club bar is a space populated by subjects who control their own destinies and identities and therefore are never nicknamed, whereas the caddies' house is inhabited by people whose fate and sense of self are determined by external forces, and thus *as a matter of course* are nicknamed. The way in which caddies imagined and regarded the spaces meant for club members and the way the space for caddies imposed an external identity on these workers both corroborate geographers' long-held argument that the social world is inexorably spatial and the spatial is always political (Harvey 1989:261; Lefebvre 1991:47; Massey 1992:10). The political dimension of space refers to the way in which power is distributed in society.

The current chapter uses the racialization-of-class thesis to demonstrate how the exclusion of caddies is based on class and racial dynamics, which are commonly conveyed through spatial arrangements. The analysis starts by showing how caddies' low status is linked to their working-class origins as much as a narrative that justifies their impoverished condition on racialized grounds. The analysis then explains that although caddying offers a higher salary than most other working-class jobs, there are still multiple mechanisms that perpetuate caddies' economic subordination. Interviewed club members constantly articulated a racialized discourse to speak about the spaces that caddies occupied. The chapter reveals how in a country that assumes that race (as a concept) and racism (as its manifestation) do not exist, space and spatial dynamics are highly effective ways to convey racialized hierarchies without the need to openly verbalize them.

Caddies

In all the clubs I visited, caddies were contingent workers who received payment only when they were called onto the course and hence do not receive a steady salary, a point I return to later in the chapter. The caddies described themselves as members of the working class. Three of the most common terms caddies used to define themselves and their colleagues were humble, underprivileged, and poor. Bolillo, a caddy in his late fifties whose nickname referred to a type of traditional savory bread, told me that when he started caddying in his late teens, he had only one pair of shoes in good shape and could not afford to replace them. He explained, "I took care of them as if they were made of gold. On one occasion, it was raining so heavily that I took them off, put them in a plastic bag, and caddied the 18 holes shoeless." *Pollo* also referenced his humble socioeconomic background when he said that he started caddying as a teenager because "we didn't have money in my family and I needed to contribute, that is how I became a caddy."

When I asked the caddies I interviewed why only a few Mexican caddies have tried to become professional players even though a handful were scratch golfers (i.e., they can play any course with a handicap of zero, which means that they play in the ideal number of strokes), all the answers touched on caddies' class backgrounds in one way or another. In their responses, the workers spoke about their humble origins and explained how expensive it is to start a career as a professional golf player. Costa, a caddy in his late thirties whose nickname refers to his birthplace near the sea, was an outstanding player. He said that he considered becoming a professional when he was in his late twenties but abandoned the idea when he realized what an expensive enterprise it was. For example, to qualify for tournaments in the United States, which have larger economic rewards, players must first win several national tournaments in Mexico. These contests take place in different regions, which means players incur significant travel and lodging expenses in addition to inscription fees and caddy fees. Further, cost-saving measures would entail physical exertion that would lower a player's opportunity to win. As Costa explained:

> You cannot save money by traveling by bus or staying in a cheap hotel far away from the area where the tournament is being played [usually the most affluent area in town], because you need to be rested and refreshed, and, because you need to be where the networking events are being held. [. . .] You cannot carry your own clubs [to save the caddy's fee], because you will be tired by the second part of the tournament, [. . .] it is not possible to compete in those conditions.

Costa summarized his decision to abandon a possible professional career by noting, "This is the problem all caddies [who are good players] face: we don't have the means to support ourselves while [we are] starting to make money."

A journalist I interviewed told me about a caddy who was so talented that he had earned the right to play in the European professional league's season (second in importance only to the PGA tournament season in the

United States). However, the caddy had lost the first two tournaments of the season by default because he did not have the funds to travel to the games. The journalist added, "The next tournament is in two weeks and he still has no funds to travel. Nobody wants to support him, neither the club [where he works], the [golf] federation, a company, nor a [club] member." Costa explained the end of his own dream of becoming a professional player by noting that he accepted a job offer from a club member who owned a car dealership, combining a part-time maintenance position at the dealership with caddying at the club. This combination offered him a secure working class position but did not allow him to play as a professional.

Money Matters

Multiple caddies said they were pleased with the amount of money they earned at their jobs. Mike, a caddy in his early twenties who had recently joined the profession and thus did not yet have a nickname, said, "The money you earn here is quite good. It's true that we don't have a steady salary, but sometimes I can make more money in one weekend than my friends make *a la quincena* working in factories" (in Mexico salaries are commonly paid on a biweekly basis; this two-week paycheck is referred to as *la quincena*). Many caddies emphasized this point, stating that on certain days, particularly weekends, they made good money. The likelihood of making a lot of money is connected to the number of members who show up to play (the more members playing, the more likely it is that a caddy can make extramoney) and how generously the golfers tip. When conditions are good, caddies can sometimes make more money in one or two days than their acquaintances and relatives who work in formal jobs can make in two weeks. Notably, caddies always used working-class positions, such as factory jobs, as the comparison point, illustrating that these were the other jobs they could imagine themselves having.

Despite the widespread agreement that caddying offered a good income, many caddies, particularly those with families, complained that the main problem with the profession was that their earnings were unreliable. *Gonzo* (Schnoz), a caddy in his mid-forties whose nickname referred to his large nose, noted,

> There are weeks in which I make good money [to which, someone at the back of the patio shouted in response, "Those days you'll find

him at the cantina"], but there are also bad ones. School holidays are bad for us, because club members take their families on holidays and don't come to the club. There are times when you don't earn any money for a whole week. In those cases, you need to borrow money from friends or relatives [notably, no other caddies made a joke about the latter comment, which may have been too unsettling to laugh about].

Some caddies argued that being very organized with their personal finances could remedy the highly variable nature of their earnings. For example, Vicente, a caddy in his early fifties whose nickname refers to his resemblance to a popular actor, noted that he always tried to save money to prepare for the less profitable days: "We all know how this is [the income is unsteady]. We need to save money to avoid getting into [financial] troubles. Some [caddies] spend the money fast, I always try to save part of it." Vicente was one of the few caddies who referenced this type of middle-class/neoliberal argument, identifying economic discipline as an antidote to the marginal economic position of the profession.

In contrast, this middle-class/neoliberal argument was the most common one golfers used to explain the lower class position of caddies. In the view of most club members, caddies' economically marginal status was linked to their poor management skills. For example, Arturo, a golfer in his mid-sixties who owned a consulting firm, concluded that "caddies make good money, I know some of them who have sent their kids to college and have small but well-built houses. The problem with most caddies is that they waste the money."

The assertion that caddies had poor financial management skills was commonly accompanied by two criticisms that implied that caddies had insurmountable moral shortcomings. First, some golfers argued that caddies loved to bet, either when they played against one another or bet on the golfers they worked for. Emilio, a man in his late fifties, who worked in a very well-known golf magazine, noted, "I can tell you that these dudes [caddies] love to bet; they even bet on the game of the golfers they're caddying for. If you pay attention, you'll see them doing it—I've seen them doing it." Some golfers claimed that caddies bet their weekend salaries during the rounds they played against one another on Mondays, when clubs are regularly closed for maintenance and caddies are the only ones allowed to access the course. While the caddies I interviewed did recognize that some of them enjoyed betting while playing against their coworkers, they refuted the idea that they bet on the skills of their patrons (the issue may be too sensitive to acknowledge, as a patron may complain to the administration, thereby jeopardizing the caddy's job). Golfers' accusation that caddies loved to bet implied that caddies made a good income but lost much of it to gambling.

The second moral criticism was that caddies spend all their money on alcohol. Arturo, the mid-sixties consulting firm owner who said that caddies waste their money, added, "The problem with caddies is that if you offer them training, schooling, and food, sooner or later they start drinking alcohol and that's the end. I've tried to help them, but it's impossible." This allegation was reiterated by Emilio, the late fifties, editor of a golf magazine, who concluded, "Caddies are the heaviest drinkers. Trust me, caddies are the ones who drink the most alcohol of all the people related to golf." Paradoxically, Emilio made this claim in an environment that strongly encouraged alcohol consumption. All clubs have the celebrated 19th hole (the main bar) at the end of the course. In addition, during a round of golf (18 holes), players pass two kiosks where they can purchase alcohol. During one round I played, we passed the first kiosk around 10:00 a.m. The player who had invited me asked if I wanted something to drink. My immediate thought was: Drink? At this time? Drink what? To build rapport and maintain a smooth interaction, I replied "What do they have?" My fellow player answered, "Whatever you want," and then added, "beer, tequila, whiskey, rum, or water, what do you want to drink?" We both ended up having a beer.

Diego, a golfer in his early sixties who was a senior executive at a transnational corporation, added a new layer to the common narrative that portrays caddies as morally dubious subjects. He indicated,

> It is sad what is going on with the youth at the clubs. The other day there was a fight between a bunch of teenagers in a nearby club. Half of them were drunk and the other half on drugs; they kicked and punched each other. Nowadays, many young members drink a lot [of alcohol] and do drugs. It's sad. And you know what, caddies are the ones introducing drugs to the clubs; they are the ones giving drugs to these rich kids. I have seen kids hiding in the bushes doing drugs, and caddies are promoting this problem.

Diego's assertion that caddies were responsible for introducing drugs to young people at the clubs reminded me of the common narrative in the

United States that links drugs with poor black and brown communities (Alexander 2012). In both Mexico and the United States, racialized poor individuals serve as the perfect scapegoat when individuals try to identify simple reasons for highly complex problems.

Golfers' assumption that caddies frequently engage in immoral behaviors and lack self-control encouraged the belief that caddies' impoverished condition was the result of their own moral flaws. Poverty, therefore, was viewed as a self-inflicted wound—it was caddies' own fault. This explanation did not, however, account for the consistent association between class position and epidermal schema. In other words, if class dynamics were the sole regulating factor in a society, it would be surprising to find a correlation between skin tone and socioeconomic position and yet the vast majority of caddies had darker brown skin, black hair, and dark eyes, whereas most club members had lighter skin tones, and many even perfectly fit the definition of "white" commonly accepted in the United States. The unexpected and unexplained relationship between class and racial dynamics, which has been observed by other researchers in the broader national context (Iturriaga 2016; Nutini 1997, 2008; Villarreal 2010), went unnoticed by almost all of the club members. Before elaborating on the issue, it is worth looking at caddies' job responsibilities.

Beyond Carrying Bags

In the United States, only exclusive private clubs have caddies (Sherwood 2012), but in Mexico caddies are ubiquitous, working in all types of golf clubs. Hiring a caddy was mandatory at all the clubs I visited. Several golfers informed me that there were only a couple of clubs near the city where hiring a caddy was optional. Even at those clubs, caddies were always available. The primary obligation of caddies is carrying the bag of the golfer who hired them and looking after that player. The caddies at the clubs I visited walked closely behind the group of golfers for whom they were working, paying close attention to the needs of the specific golfer who had requested their services (in some cases golfers request a specific caddy; more commonly, however, caddies are assigned to players as they start the game). If the golfers used a golf cart, the caddies kept pace by standing on the cart's platform for golf bags, grabbing the roof to steady themselves.

Caddies also cleaned the clubs and balls after they were used and tracked the trajectory of flying golf balls so they could tell the golfers where they had landed; if a ball got lost, they were expected to take the lead in finding it. In addition, caddies were responsible for recording the scores of their assigned players as well as remembering other golfers' scores to prevent cheating. Despite the commonly voiced argument that golf was about honesty and integrity, caddies reported that some golfers did cheat and therefore they had to pay close attention to all the players' scores. Finally, they fulfilled banal requests, such as fetching drinks or delivering messages between groups of players.

Yet caddies had a pejorative label for colleagues who limited themselves to the above responsibilities: *carga palos* [club chargers]. Most caddies reported that their job went beyond these duties. For example, a good caddy was expected to help the golfer assess the distance between the ball and the scoring area (known as the green). This distance is a key factor in the game because it determines both the strength with which a golfer should hit the ball and the selection of the club—a set of golf clubs contains 14 distinct clubs, each used for a slightly different purpose. Good caddies were also expected to offer players advice on technique. The caddies who worked for me, for example, identified the technical errors I made when hitting the ball. In addition, caddies suggested specific strategies, such as making risky or conservative moves (e.g., hitting the ball over a tall tree to save shots or approaching a hazard, like a lake, using several strokes to prevent the ball from landing on the hazard). Offering this type of advice and knowledge constituted the more advanced responsibilities that good caddies were expected to fulfill in their jobs.

I learned that caddies also offered emotional support in a less visible but highly effective way. For example, at the end of a hole, caddies often highlighted the good shots a player had made as a way to sustain the player's momentum. Even if most of the strokes at that hole were very bad (e.g., erratic shots, balls hitting trees, balls landing outside the playing area or in a lake), caddies pointed out the one or two good shots, as if attempting to convince the golfer that he was not that bad after all. I also noticed caddies making jokes after bad performances, in what seemed to be a subtle strategy to shift the player's attention away from his bad game and frustration and toward an external source of humor and relaxation. They frequently anticipated the golfers' needs, asking if anyone wanted another beer or water, just as female hostesses commonly do. Finally, caddies celebrated good shots and impressive performances in a way that suggested that the caddy and the player who had hired him were linked by more than just an economic bond.

This part of a caddy's job was strongly reminiscent of Arlie Russell Hochschild's (1983) concept of "emotional labor." Hochschild coined the term to describe a series of facial and bodily displays exhibited by female flight attendants and retail workers to express empathy with passengers and customers. Emotional labor, which is commonly associated with feminine professions, is a way to transform a solely economic transaction into a seemingly friendly interaction or relationship. In doing so, workers subordinate their own emotions, desires, and points of view to the feelings and expectations of the customer, allowing the latter to ignore the fact that workers may not be pleased to serve them but only doing it for economic rewards. A modified version of Hochschild's description of emotional labor serves as an accurate depiction of the relational aspect of caddies' work:

> The smiles [as well as the jokes and excitement] are part of [his] work, a part that requires [him] to coordinate self and feeling so that the work seems to be effortless. To show that the enjoyment takes effort is to do the job poorly. (1983:8)

Sociologist Ashley Mears (2015) argued that in the United States, emotional labor is a central component of the work experience for people offering services to affluent individuals. The experiences of caddies in Mexico reflect both Mears's findings and Hochschild's description of emotional labor. For example, Tino, a caddy in his mid-thirties whose nickname referred to his good playing skills (the Spanish term *tino* can be translated as precision when hitting the ball), described his job as follows:

> Many people think that a caddy just carries the bag, and that's it, but that isn't true. The role of a caddy implies a lot of responsibility, 70 or 80 percent of the reason that a boss [golfer] plays well rests on us. Because, we caddies need to help them, to help them improve, to make them feel happy. The better a golfer plays, the happier he becomes, and the more likely he will be back soon, OK. We need to support him, to stay there in his bad moments.

Despite Tino's assessment of the role of caddies, the emotional labor these workers offered was not always well received. Bruno, a golfer in his mid-forties who had learned to golf as a child because his father was an enthusiast golfer, for example, indicated that he felt annoyed when a caddy constantly offered suggestions about his swing or playing style. He noted, "There are caddies who feel the need to tell me what's wrong with my technique and game. There are days that I cannot stand it anymore and tell them to shut up." Carlos, a player in his early fifties who owns a consulting firm and had a membership in a highly reputable club, complained, "Some caddies act as if they know more about golf than the golfer themselves; they try to give you instructions on how to play." Emilio, the editor of a golf magazine, was emphatic that golfers should not develop close relationships with caddies because otherwise "caddies become too familiar with players, making caddies believe that they can become friends with players. That is wrong. Caddies are employees who should focus solely on carrying the bag and do no more." The significant class disparity between caddies and golfers made it difficult for both parties to understand and coordinate the manners and behavior expected from workers.

Despite the magazine editor's recommendation that caddies should only focus on menial tasks, some golfers candidly noted that some of their fellow club members were dependent on their caddies due to their own poor golf skills. Gerardo, a corporate executive in his late fifties who learned how to play golf while studying for his bachelor's degree in the United States, described traveling back to the United States many years later with other golfers and playing on courses where caddies were not available. He said,

> It is unbelievable to see how some players are so dependent on caddies [in Mexico]. If there are no caddies, some of these folks are unable to follow the trajectory of the ball [to see where it lands], they cannot calculate distance, cannot find their ball. All that slows down the pace of the game; it is annoying.

I heard a similar comment from Bruno, who, when talking about a famous old course in the seaside resort of Acapulco where there are no caddies,[3] remarked,

> I have played there with friends from my club. You won't believe it, but some of them cannot play without a caddy by their side. These

---

3. According to the participating golfers, this was the only course in Mexico that did not have caddies.

guys [the golfers], are not used to following the ball; I was the one telling them where it landed. One of them asked my opinion about the distance [to the green], he couldn't calculate it by himself!

Ruth, an accomplished golfer in her early sixties who was involved in the promotion of amateur tournaments for female club members, also mentioned the dependency of some male players on caddies, noting how she does not need caddies around her to determine a strategy or calculate the distance to the green (I return to this point in the following chapter). Most caddies had both the ability to carry out the necessary emotional labor and all the technical abilities needed to play golf. As described above, most could calculate the distance to the green and knew when and how to use the different golf clubs. They also knew the basic rules of the sport (which are quite detailed). Further, a handful of caddies were extremely talented players. However, while caddies had extensive knowledge of the sport, and frequently had impressive golf skills as well, not a single golfer suggested that caddies could be considered golfers. In fact, many suggested the opposite. Club members used multiple scenarios and metaphors to convey the absurdity of regarding caddies as golfers. Golfers' discussions of driving ranges and the role caddies played at these ranges revealed their opinion that caddies could not be golfers.

Caddies and Driving Ranges: Construction Workers in Disguise

Between the mid-2000s and early 2010s, Lorena Ochoa, a female Mexican professional golf player, became one of the top three players on the U.S. Ladies Professional Golf Association's (LPGA) tour. Ochoa's success transformed the media coverage of golf in Mexico from a game covered only in specialized magazines and newspapers targeting those in the highest income sectors to widespread reporting in mainstream newspapers and TV sports segments. In the span of a few years, golf became a highly fashionable sport in Mexico. While the increased popularity of golf did not lead to the development of public courses,[4] it did produce a proliferation of driving ranges—relatively inexpensive places where aspiring golfers can learn and practice their golf swing. It is difficult to determine the precise number of driving ranges operating in Mexico City because many operate

---

4. Several participating golfers reported that one of the wealthiest municipalities near Mexico City had considered a plan to build a public course in the mid-2000s. The idea was rapidly abandoned after social movements and politicians on the left portrayed the plan as a strategy to steal public resources for an elitist game; I will return to the case in Chapter 6.

informally, but by the early 2010s there were at least eight. While this might seem like a very small number in relation to the local population, even five years before there had not been a single driving range in the city.

I visited four driving ranges: two in athletic complexes used mainly by soccer and basketball players of all ages, one on the roof of a textile factory in downtown Mexico City (with a nice view of the area), and one in a residential neighborhood in the northern part of the city. The two ranges in athletic complexes catered to lower-middle- and some working-class individuals. They resembled large baseball cages about 10 feet tall, 25 feet wide, and 80 feet long. On one end of the cage were about four green square carpets, each with a flexible plastic golf tee (a small stand used to support the ball during the first strike at each hole in golf) affixed to one corner. Players stood on the green carpets to practice swinging a golf club and hitting balls off the tee (which is not as easy as it sounds). At one of these driving ranges, a banner with the phrase "learn how to play golf here" invited curious soccer and basketball players to try the newly in-vogue sport. At the other, a large banner at the entrance of the complex read, "golf lessons now available here." Both ranges closed within two years, although I heard that new ones had opened in other areas of the city.

The other two driving ranges were set up in buildings, where for about 60 to 80 pesos (between $3 and $5) visitors could rent a golf club and a bucket of 45 balls. The cost per bucket decreased considerably with the purchase of two or more buckets. The range, located on the roof of a six-story textile factory, offered a nice view of the area and aimed to convey an elegant atmosphere. The site was decorated with lots of plants and multiple posters of golf courses. It held about eight tees. The net that enclosed the space was about 120 to 140 feet from the tees, considerably farther away than those at the previous two sites. Behind the tees were tables where customers could rest, chat, and eat something. A waiter dressed in black pants, a black vest, and a white shirt offered soft drinks and a simple menu (e.g., hamburgers, hot dogs, French fries, fried tacos) to customers practicing their swing. The location was chosen to be easily accessible to the owners of the many factories located in the vicinity. On the three occasions I visited this range, most of the customers practicing their golf swings were in their mid-to-late thirties, and several were of Asian origin and appeared to be non-natives, based on their limited vocabulary in Spanish.

The final driving range differed from the one on top of the textile factory primarily in its décor and spatial layout. This range, which had plenty of plants, green walls, and an internal garden, seemed designed with the goal of more accurately recreating the lush vegetation that characterizes golf courses. Here, hopeful golfers could hit the ball to the other end of the internal garden, about 120 feet away, where a net prevented the ball from hitting a wall or flying toward the street. A waitress dressed in a black skirt and a white shirt offered customers soft drinks and a small selection of food. I visited this driving range five times. At both the factory-top range and this range, each time I visited, a person in a golfing outfit (i.e., khaki pants, T-shirt, vest, cap, and golf shoes, all from fancy golf brands) welcomed customers and offered his services as a golf instructor.

After chatting with the instructors, I learned that all of them were caddies at golf clubs and worked as instructors at the driving ranges on their days off. On more than one occasion, I saw people taking lessons or setting up meetings to start lessons with these caddies/instructors. In this (lower-middle-class/middle-class) context, fancy golf clothes allowed caddies to successfully replicate via their bodies the aesthetic taste linked with the affluent world of golf, including the subtle racial implications of this appearance, which transformed them from caddies into legitimate—white(r)—golf instructors. This transfiguration, however, only works in the eyes of the lower class and some members of the middle class, not among dominant groups.

During an informal interview with the owner of one of these driving ranges, he explained that the range's location in a residential area aimed to attract golfers who could not visit their club on weekdays due to traffic, weather, or work demands. As the conversation progressed, however, he began to complain bitterly that despite multiple attempts to advertise the business—he had purchased ads in specialized golf magazines, and on weekends he had spent several hours outside the doors of two nearby golf clubs, giving away flyers with coupons offering a free bucket of 45 balls and a hamburger for first-time customers—no more than a handful of golfers had ever visited the range and none had become regulars. The owner ended the conversation with a degree of frustration, saying, "I don't understand why golfers don't come, this is a nice place to practice." A year later when I returned to the range, it had a new owner. Both this driving range and the factory-top range went out of business within four years. Unlike the owner, who thought of his business as a nice place to practice golf, almost all the club members I asked about driving ranges viewed them with either disdain or suspicion.

For example, Miguel, the 60-year-old charming golfer who was a high-ranked executive in a technology corporation, humorously referred to driving ranges as *tiraderos*, a word that can be translated in three ways: a shooting site, as in shooting golf balls; a mess, a place that lacks order; and a dump, a site where trash has accumulated. Miguel alluded to all three meanings. First, he described the technical problems golfers face if they learn the sport at these sites:

> What has already happened in Japan could also happen in Mexico—there are people who've never gotten outside a driving range; they haven't been on a course. These *tiraderos* [driving ranges] are located in buildings, in which you hit the ball here [pointing to the floor next to him] and the end of the building is there [pointing to few feet away from him]. They don't have a clue where the ball is going, but they stubbornly keep hitting the ball. It's sad, but they aren't going anywhere.

The initial part of Miguel's comment alluded to the first two meanings of the word (a shooting site and a place that lacks order). Driving ranges are sites where potential golfers hit balls, but the act of hitting lacks order and meaning—it will not lead to improved skills, and they would not be able to play on a private course. After elaborating on the importance of knowing the average distance someone can hit the ball because that determines the type of club they should use, Miguel moved on to the third meaning of the word (a site where trash has accumulated). He proclaimed,

> If you go to a *tiradero* to shoot [golf] balls, to practice, you will find people like him [Miguel pointed toward a caddy walking in front of us]. The instructors are disguised construction workers, butchers. It is true, they are well dressed, no doubt about it, true, but they don't know anything about golf.

As I argued in the previous chapter, the jobs of construction worker and butcher are strongly associated with the working class as well as racialized ideas of who constitutes the working class. Miguel's remark that a caddy is a butcher or construction worker in disguise, concealing his true self by dressing in a genuine golfers' outfit, evokes both a set of negative tropes about the lower socioeconomic classes and a veiled racialized narrative. The disdain for construction workers who "pass" as golfers, at least in the eyes of the middle and lower classes, followed the same racialized logic embedded in the use of the word *naco* (described in detail in Chapter 4).

Mercedes, a women in her mid-fifties who had actively promoted amateur tournaments for female club members, also viewed driving ranges in a negative light. When I asked her what she thought of driving ranges, she said,

> I'm glad to hear that you're doing research on these issues, because it is very sad. There is a proliferation of driving ranges, but what is the purpose? Who is teaching there? If you don't have a membership in a club, it is meaningless to go and practice. People [who learn at a driving range] won't be able to play the sport. People are not learning how to play golf [there]. It's sad.

Ruth, a woman in her late fifties who was also involved in promoting amateur tournaments for women club members, adopted a less judgmental tone when talking about driving ranges. She said that ranges could be convenient practice sites for golfers who were too busy to get to the club. Yet, when I asked her if she had ever visited one, she emphatically replied, "No, no, no, I know that there is one around the club, but I have never been there."

The only golfers who expressed positive comments about driving ranges were those who, because of their marginal position in the world of golf, had benefited from visiting these sites. Agustin and Daniel fit this description. They were both junior executives in their early thirties who did not have enough disposable income to purchase a club membership but learned how to play golf by taking lessons at driving ranges and later made long trips to play at one of the semi-public courses just outside the city. Daniel played at least eight times a year with some of his primary clients, all of whom either owned a personal membership or could use a corporate one. Agustin, on the other hand, did not golf with clients but was aware that the owner of the consulting media firm where he worked was a golfer. While Agustin had never been invited to play golf with the owner, the instrumental way he talked about golf hinted that he thought it might happen in the future. For both Daniel and Agustin, golf was a "work tool" accessible only via the inexpensive spaces of driving ranges.

The way club members—at least the four described above—talked about these sites, especially their disinterest in visiting them, was inexorably linked to the class and racialized elements that characterize these inexpensive spaces. Interviewees' comments about the deficient quality of the golf instruction offered at driving ranges illustrate this point. In Mexico, golf instruction has historically been one of the few channels of social mobility and status achievement available to caddies. The suggestion that caddies/instructors are no more than disguised butchers and constructions workers evokes a common narrative among upper-middle- and upper-class individuals that entwines material and racial perceptions about the lower classes. The idea that it is inherently impossible for a "well-dressed butcher" to understand the game, re-creating the movements and strategies needed to play golf, and therefore to teach others how to play resembles the narrative discussed in Chapter 4 that views carpenters, cabinetmakers, and members of the EZLN as people who could not and should not gain access to the space of golf. Further, the way in which driving ranges were viewed as sites inhabited by impostors contained parallels to my experience meeting *Pollo* (Luis) and Mr. José's dream. Driving ranges were spaces disdained based on the class and racialized identities of the people who populated them.

The Distribution of Space

During the first stage of fieldwork, my interactions with caddies were "normal" from the perspective of a golfer. That is, caddies showed up just as we (the group of golfers) were about to start the game. The caddies then took care of my bag, cleaned my clubs and returned them to my bag, offered suggestions in terms of club selection, made jokes, helped me find my ball, explained how to improve my swing, celebrated my good shots, attempted to dissipate my frustration by recounting funny stories, and, finally, quickly disappeared when the game was over, leaving me and the other golfers to enjoy our lunch. In contrast, the second stage of fieldwork shed light on a much less visible aspect of caddies' experiences: how space works as a highly effective way to cement class and racial hierarchies without even naming them.

The Caddies' House

I visited three caddies' houses, two at more prestigious clubs and a third at a less exclusive club. At the wealthier clubs, the caddies' houses included changing rooms with cheap metal lockers, benches, and chairs;

private restrooms with showers, urinals, and toilets; and a "cafeteria"—a type of *cocina económica* or inexpensive eatery selling breakfast, lunch, and snacks. These "cafeterias" were simple but solidly built and included a covered shed with cheap tables and chairs and a TV (always on). At one of the clubs, an impressive altar to the Virgin of Guadalupe, paid for by one of only a few former caddies who had become a relatively successful professional player, completed the site.

At the less exclusive club, the caddies' house was much more basic. Caddies did not have their own changing rooms or restrooms but rather shared these facilities with the other workers at the club. In fact, the space reserved for caddies consisted of only a set of plastic tables and chairs set up on a cement floor shaded by a stand of trees and covered by a roughly 10 × 10 foot plastic canopy. There was no TV, but an old radio sitting on a plastic chair played popular music. These caddies had no "cafeteria." They had to either bring their own food or wait for street vendors to come through the area. All three caddies' houses were situated next to the street, which generated a feeling that the two areas (the caddies' house and the street) were extensions of one another. I interviewed Tom, a caddy in his early twenties who had not yet received a nickname, right next to the door of the caddies' house at his request. He agreed to the interview but explained, "We need to move over by the entrance because I'm waiting for someone who is going to pick me up and I need to see when he arrives." The door remained half open during our entire conversation (about 20 minutes), allowing Tom to see the street (and allowing the street atmosphere to creep inside when a street vendor stopped to sell tacos).

All three caddies' houses were secluded and set away from the rest of their respective clubs. At the most affluent clubs, the separation was maintained by fences, thick bushes, and other architectural barriers that almost completely prevented club members from seeing the caddies' house. At the third club, the caddies' space was hidden by trees and the hilly terrain that surrounded it. Only once in all the time I spent in the caddies' spaces did I see a club member in the area; in this case a female club member crossed the caddies' house briskly walking while taking a shortcut from her home—in the surrounding residential neighborhood—to the clubhouse. As she walked through the site she ignored everyone there, conveying the feeling that she wanted to leave the space as soon as possible. Interestingly, during the first stage of fieldwork, I saw a handful of caddies walking quickly through the clubhouses. Like the golfer taking a shortcut, they acted like they wanted to leave the space as soon as possible.

Beyond these exceptions, caddies never accessed the clubhouses and club members never accessed the caddies' houses.

At golf clubs, a worker known as the starter is in charge of controlling the pace of play on the course. They let waiting golfers know when they can start playing and they oversee the caddies' spatial movement onto the golf course. At the clubs I visited, the starter used a walkie-talkie, which was hanging from the fence or sitting on a table, to ask caddies to come to the warm-up area, usually located near the caddies' house. Caddies were called to the course based on a rotation system in which each one had an assigned number (on average, there were 60 caddies at each of these three clubs). The sequence was broken, however, if a golfer asked for a specific caddy or a caddy was not present when his number was called. Caddies argued that a close relation with one specific golfer was more common in the past but that nowadays golfers tend to develop less personal relations, which means more uncertainty for caddies. For example, while the weekends were almost always busy, the number of golfers playing during the week fluctuated significantly. Caddies could choose whether to be in the caddies' house on a given day. Norteño, a caddy in his late forties whose nickname referred to his northern Mexican origins, described the system:

> I worked today [Tuesday] at 6:30 a.m., but I'm not coming tomorrow because it's rare that my number is called again two consecutive days early in the week. I will be here on Thursday and maybe Friday, who knows, I may not caddy again until the weekend. We need to chase our turn.

Swing, a caddy in his mid-thirties whose nickname made fun of the way he played, reiterated this point when he explained, "It is common to stay here [at the caddies' house] one or two days waiting for your turn [but not being called]. [The] job is unreliable but we need to stay here taking care of it." Some caddies, like *Pollo*, stayed at the caddies' house even when they knew they wouldn't be called to work because they liked to spend time with their friends. Others estimated the chances of their number coming up and stayed at the caddies' house only if they thought they would be called. Usually, however, caddies had no choice but to spend long hours or even days waiting at the caddies' house because losing their turn meant losing their income for about a week. Bird, a caddy in his late twenties whose nickname made fun of his seemingly bird-like face, described the situation:

If I am not present when my number is called, I miss my turn and have to wait until the list starts again and my number is called. There are some weeks when even if I wait here all day, not enough golfers show up [so my number isn't called]. Rainy days are bad; people don't come. There are bad weeks, but on weekends there is always work, which helps bring money home. We need to be here no matter what, here, here.

Most caddies agreed that the waiting period was boring but was a necessary part of their job. During my time in the caddies' house, I saw caddies playing cards and dominoes, watching TV, playing on their smartphones, and chatting with other caddies. The individual interviews I conducted with caddies in these spaces also became moments of collective amusement and entertainment. Some caddies listened to what their colleagues were telling me and made loud jokes about their comments; if we were far enough away that other caddies couldn't overhear our conversation, they often shouted comments that questioned the validity of what their colleague was telling me or questioned his sexual preference or virility. Such comments were always met by the rowdy laughter of the community.

The act of waiting seemed like a natural condition of a job governed by external factors. Yet, as Javier Auyero (2012) argued, the act of waiting is not a neutral situation. Waiting is one way in which relations of domination (based on the lack of economic security among the poor) are reproduced on a daily basis. As Bird noted, caddies must wait patiently at the caddies' house or risk losing their income, a risk they literally cannot afford to take. Swing noted that the act of waiting is how caddies take care of their job: to be a caddy is to wait until you are called. As Auyero concluded, "To put it bluntly, everyday political domination is what happens when nothing apparently happens, when people 'just wait' " (2012:19).[5]

The long periods of time caddies spent waiting were invisible to club members because of the spatial seclusion of the caddies' houses. The "labor" that caddies invested in showing up on time and doing nothing but wait was not witnessed by golfers. Because other caddies were the only ones who observed the waiting, caddies' patience and commitment to their jobs never translated into positive comments about work ethic,

---

5. It is worth noting that a common formula used by enlisted personnel to describe life in the U.S. military, always being subject to the commands of one's superiors, is "Hurry up and wait."

responsibility, and dedication. Paradoxically, although caddies spent more time at the golf club than any other actor involved in the sport, golfers considered them impostors who were uninformed about the game. These negative opinions were reinforced among club members because golfers also never observed caddies' playing skills, one of the most valuable assets within golf clubs.

Caddies' Skills

Most golfers believe that the golf course is a site where one can assess the character, rectitude, perseverance, strategic thinking, patience, and strength of others with great precision.[6] According to the golfers I interviewed, this chance for objective assessment is the reason golf is so important for business matters. Golfers offered numerous concrete examples that emphasized this point. I heard multiple stories, in slightly different contexts, in which actions on the golf course served as a pre- dictor of business behavior—a player showed endurance in bad moments on the golf course and later replicated the same attitude in his business activities, or a golfer demonstrated great strategic thinking on the course and later revealed the same quality of strategic analysis in his professional life. Further, I heard several accounts of golfers deciding not to do busi- ness with fellow players who cheated on the course because they assumed these players would do the same in their professional lives.[7] In contrast, caddies had very limited chances to demonstrate their positive attributes on the course.

As mentioned earlier, most clubs were closed on Mondays. On this day, caddies were the only ones allowed to access the course and could play as many rounds as they wanted. When I asked caddies about their playing skills, they not only described their own abilities but also offered numerous stories illustrating the abilities of other caddies, just as club members had discussed the skills of their fellow golfers. Some caddies were quite talented, some loved to bet, others were fun playing partners, some cheated on the course, and others never showed up on Mondays be- cause they did not like the sport but caddied only for the money (the owner

---

6. Cock (2008) found the same narrative among golfers in South Africa.

7. This perception of an association between golf behavior and business behavior is also broadly accepted in the United States. See, for example, Alchian (1977), Andrisani (2002), and Norman (2006).

of a consulting company I interviewed, and who first introduced himself as a golfer, also admitted that he did not like to play golf that much, implying that he only played it for business purposes). Club members were barely aware of the caddies' personal traits because the spatial and temporal division of the course—closed to members but open to caddies on Mondays—made caddies' golf skills almost invisible to golfers.

Some golfers noted that the long-running tradition of closing clubs on Mondays was changing. In some clubs, for example, newer members had actively complained about the rule, arguing that memberships and annual maintenance fees were too expensive to restrict their playing time. The pressure from members had led some clubs to open seven days a week. Other clubs have tapped into the highly profitable practice of renting out their facilities for private corporate tournaments on Mondays. Two consulting firm owners noted that the private events they organized for corporations were held on Mondays. These two firms had access to three clubs and were hoping to reach agreements with others. These changes meant that caddies had more work opportunities but fewer chances to play golf.

Most caddies who become golf instructors entered the profession at a very young age (during their early teenage years, commonly because a family member was already a caddy) and used their Monday access to the course to improve their skills. The combination of observing players on the course and working to imitate their movements on Mondays allowed some caddies to become very good players. Dumbo, a caddy in his early forties whose nickname made fun of his large ears, told me that he learned how to play golf by watching golfers and then playing at the course every Monday when he was younger. He added,

> The [Golf] Federation used to bring American instructors to offer workshops quite often. We [caddies] weren't invited, but club members didn't say anything if we sneaked in. If it was here in the club I used to attend them. But I haven't seen that happen for a long time. I don't know why they don't bring American instructors anymore.

The possibility of caddies becoming instructors has been stalled by the growing professionalization of golf instruction. The consulting firm owners reported that there were already two U.S. golf academies operating in Mexico City. I called one of these academies to inquire about their services, and the employee who answered explained that they had a multilevel training program taught by certified instructors. When I said I did not have a club membership, the representative said I didn't need one. The academy had high-tech equipment, including cameras and simulators, which helped clients improve their swing on their premises. For an extra fee, the instructor would play a round of golf with me at one of the semipublic clubs on the outskirts of the city.

The technology the representative of the golf academy described was similar to what I had observed on an earlier visit to the offices of a consulting firm. Robin, a 60-year-old owner of the firm who was a competitive golfer in his youth, had given me a tour of the high-tech equipment his company used, including a type of baseball cage in which three cameras filmed a client's swing so an instructor could suggest a better posture. When I asked him who actually provided the instruction, Robin answered,

> In Mexico, there are no good professional instructors. If you really want to learn good golf [skills], you need to go to the U.S. In the workshops I organize [at corporate events], I bring an American instructor because nobody cares about the Mexican guys.

In Mexico, the term "American" is broadly understood as a synonym for white American. I then asked Robin if he could say more about why "Mexican guys" did not provide high-quality instruction, and he replied:

> Look, professional players, instructors, and caddies are part of the same story. A good caddy becomes the instructor in a club, he spends some time providing instruction, and then starts playing in some *torneitos* [small tournaments] because he is good, he has talent. But they [caddies-turned-golfers] do not have the preparation, or the pedagogy, or the emotional and mental strength needed to go and play against big names in the United States. They don't even have the right nutrition—look at what they eat, they're screwed. How can they possibly teach golf?

Robin's comments were based on discourses that upper-middle- and upper-class people often deployed when talking about the lower classes. In this case, caddies have talent—a natural (biological) condition that requires neither determination nor discipline—but their cultural background always hinders their ability to succeed. Robin's description of caddies parallels perceptions of African Americans in the United States, who are sometimes viewed as naturally (i.e., biologically) talented sportsmen but rarely associated with the qualities any outstanding athlete requires such as work ethic, self-control, will, discipline, and perseverance (Leonard and Richard 2010; Thangaraj 2012, 2015). Remarkably, Robin's comment about what caddies eat implied that these workers could not be considered legitimate golf instructors because of some "type" of internal anatomical difference produced by their deficient diet. The remark suggested that food created insurmountable distinctions in the bodies of golfers and caddies, as if each of them belonged to different biological—racialized—categories.

I asked most interviewees why, given the abundance of caddies in Mexico, only a handful had turned professional and none had succeeded in the most prestigious leagues in the world. I was less interested in hearing people's thoughts about professional golf and more interested in their views on lower-class workers. As mentioned above, caddies usually mentioned the lack of financial support to explain the situation. For example, Sope (pronounced so-pay), a caddy in his mid-forties whose nickname referred to a popular dish made of corn and beans, told me about his friend Mateo, who had competed for a year with relative success in the Mexican professional league but then decided to quit because, despite his accomplishments, he was making more money as a caddy and an instructor than as a professional player. Interestingly, two different golfers I spoke with talked specifically about Mateo, using him as an example of caddies' inherent lack of ambition.[8] Notably, these golfers never touched upon the financial consideration of Mateo's decision. Without pointing out the economic element, the choice of leaving behind a professional career to become an instructor/caddy again perfectly fit the notions that associate flawed, immoral, and inefficient characteristics with lower-class workers almost in a natural (i.e., racialized) way.

Not all golfers attributed caddies' limited success to a lack of ambition. Some recognized that certain caddies were both extremely talented and extremely driven and blamed the working-class origins of

---

8. For a similar account about black basketball players in the early years of the National Basketball Association (NBA), see Maharaj (1997).

these athletes for hindering their performance. Arturo, the golfer in his mid-sixties who owned a consulting firm, was very open about this fact. He explained, "Tournaments for caddies are unbelievable; indeed, it is amazing the level of skills that you see there, but these [events] are not appreciated because caddies are of a very low [socioeconomic] level." Golfers seemed to understand the distinction between caddies and golfers almost as a matter of "inherent" differences. For example, the journalist who complained about corporations' lack of interest in sponsoring the early careers of caddies as professional golfers fell back into this type of intrinsic (class-based) racialized distinction between golfers and caddies when he compared two professional golfers: Lorena Ochoa and Esteban Toledo. Ochoa reached the pinnacle of success in the LPGA in the 2000s, and Toledo, a former caddy, enjoyed a relatively successful career in a second-tier U.S. professional league during the 1990s. The journalist offered the following explanation for the disparity between the two:

> The differences between Esteban and Lorena are huge. Esteban is kind of rude, [he has] poor manners, he was a caddy and before that a boxer. Esteban is still a caddy. He has no charisma, no appeal; when you see him drinking water or grabbing a bottle of water, you don't connect with him, no, naaaahh. Instead, when you see Lorena [doing the same thing], she is cute, she is pretty. She has charisma [and] he doesn't; that has helped her open doors.

In the local context, Esteban has a darker skin tone than Lorena, although she would not necessarily be classified as white in the United States. However, the distinction between Esteban and Lorena is not based solely on skin color (as detailed in Chapter 4, the Mexican racial model does not focus exclusively on skin color). Rather, Lorena's perceived attractiveness emanates just as much from her manners, attitudes, and fashion sense as it does from her epidermal schema— both class and racialized dynamics place her into a white(r) position. It is not a coincidence that Lorena secured the largest sponsorship deal ever signed by a Mexican professional athlete (Lezcano 2005). In contrast, Esteban secured only relatively small sponsorship agreements. Interestingly, most of the golfers I talked to who mentioned Esteban during the interviews emphasized the fact that he had once been a caddy, and at least two interviewees referred to him as a caddy rather than a golfer.

The straightforward racialization of lower-class workers only became verbalized in one instance, when a golf player made off-the-record comments. A golf journalist I interviewed suggested that I should contact Juan, saying, "He'll be a good person to talk to; I know that he plays in multiple clubs around the city for his work." In his late thirties, Juan worked for a U.S. consulting firm, and as part of his job he commonly played golf with clients at their own clubs. The journalist was aware of this situation because he had written an article about Juan for a golf magazine some time ago. I interviewed Juan in a coffee shop in an upscale neighborhood in the northern part of the city. During the interview, I asked him why, given the large number of caddies in Mexico, only a few have attempted to become professional players. As the recorder documented our conversation, Juan argued that caddies lacked ambition and clubs provided limited support—a fairly neutral argument I heard several times during my fieldwork. When I had asked all my pre-planned questions, I stopped the recorder but kept chatting with Juan, having learned that some interviewees felt more comfortable speaking off the record (I discuss this point in detail in the Appendix). After about 10 minutes, Juan lowered his voice and said,

> You asked me before why clubs or the Federation did not support caddies [becoming professionals]. I will tell you what I think about it off the record. I think that most golfers do not support caddies, even though some are really good players, because caddies look like domestic workers. Caddies remind golfers of their maids and chauffeurs.

Juan was the only golfer who openly articulated a racialized argument to describe the impoverished position of caddies—no other golfer recognized (at least while speaking with me) how racial dynamics limited caddies' economic opportunities. The fact that Juan studied for his bachelor's degree in the United States and lived there for several years before returning to Mexico might have made him doubt the widely spread idea that racial categories do not exist in this country.

Although the lower-class position of caddies was commonly thought of as not racial in nature, the common trope upper-middle- and upper-class people used to lump together poverty and the body of darker-skinned workers speaks of a strongly racialized society. Paraphrasing Lancaster's (1991) analysis about Nicaraguan society, in contemporary Mexico, brownness and poverty have been considered abundant goods concentrated among the lower classes, whereas whiteness and wealth have been regarded as limited commodities condensed in elite spaces. Indeed, the spatial segregation of golf clubs allowed golfers to easily ignore the unpleasant fact that the underprivileged condition of caddies, and by extension the privileged condition of golfers, was based on obscured racism as much as class exclusion.

Conclusion

In this chapter I develop two interconnected ideas. First, I use the case of caddies to further the argument that class and racial dynamics cannot be separated in Mexico. The lower status assigned to caddies inside golf clubs is based on both their working-class origins and the racialized way affluent club members view these workers. The images and examples golfers used to describe caddies allowed them to communicate class and racial prejudices simultaneously, following the same logic that guides popular jokes, sayings, and insults. While class and racial boundaries are malleable in Mexico, golfers' arguments about caddies' morally dubious and unruly character solidified the boundaries that situate caddies as outsiders in the world of golf. In the perspective of most club members, caddies could never become golfers because they were non-golfers by their very (biological) "nature."

Most golfers blamed the marginal position of these workers on caddies' moral flaws, such as their irrepressible desire to bet or consume alcohol, or on the lack of affinity generated by their class position. For example, a journalist claimed that no one "connected" with Esteban Toledo, a former caddy, but most people felt a natural connection to Lorena Ochoa, a member of the upper middle class. These superficially class-based remarks, however, always contained racialized cues. The argument that neither the concept of race nor its manifestations exist in Mexico is only believable if one overlooks the difference in epidermal schema between caddies and golfers. When the economic and racialized dynamics that affect lower-class workers are examined, the disdain for caddies and the spaces they inhabit takes on a more explicitly racial meaning.

Second, I argue that spaces and spatial dynamics are central to the communication of racialized distinctions. Mexico is a country that regards race and racial inequalities as elements that barely influence social relations. Race is mainly seen as a foreign concept, and therefore racism plays a minimal role in today's society. Despite this widely believed assumption, racial notions and racist dynamics are constantly articulated in everyday life, although rarely in open and clear ways. Most of the time people conceal racialized arguments behind classist remarks. In this context, space offers the ideal conduit to effectively segregate people, justifying the separation by the "natural" otherness of lower-class workers.

Following Lund's argument at the beginning of this chapter, racial dynamics only become comprehensible when they are analyzed in spatial terms: "Race is always, more or less explicitly, the racialization of space, the naturalization of segregation" (2012:75). Spatial dynamics that operate along racialized lines—the seclusion of the caddies' house—allow golfers to replace openly racialized arguments with remarks about the natural (almost biological) deficiency of lower-class people. Hence, the distinction between a true golfer and disguised butcher is a matter of the space each one inhabits.

Circularly, the spatial exclusion of caddies reinforces a narrative that naturalizes the racialization of class dynamics, which concurrently turn the spatial distribution inside clubs into a logical and commonsensical way to separate people. Drawing on the arguments presented in chapters 1 and 3 regarding colonialism, the internal organization of space in these clubs strongly resonates with the justifications white colonial settlers used to distance themselves from the unruly and uncivil non-white locals. In both cases, the spatial segregation of locals and caddies based on alleged inherent moral deficiencies created compelling explanations for the legitimate exploitation of these groups. This is the reason why club members unabashedly claimed that it is futile to help caddies, because, as a golfer noted, "sooner or later they start drinking alcohol and that's the end. I've tried to help them, but it's impossible." In this scenario, the subordinated position of caddies is not the product of inequitable social relations but the result of the natural order of the world.

Class and racialized dynamics, however, are not the only elements that shape the privileged space of golf. As emphasized in previous chapters, golf clubs are sites regulated by a form of hegemonic masculinity. However, unlike the sexism commonly found in most other sports, the gender inequality present in these affluent sites operates alongside class and racialized practices. The confluence of class and racialized privilege, on the one hand, and gender marginalization, on the other, situates women in the paradoxical position of being dominated dominants, a point that I explore in the following chapter.

6

Gender on the Golf Course

I am a golfer, and people often ask, "since when?" or "for how long?" I can't answer that accurately, and my response is generally, "since my aunt took me out on early summer mornings when I was a youngster." Seven years old? Maybe nine or ten—I'm not sure. But I do recall my Red Ball Jets being thoroughly saturated by the morning dew. My aunt loved to play, and I loved it too. The etiquette, she reminded me often, was what really mattered. Little did I realize back then just how much that etiquette, especially as it relates to being a "lady," would speak to my place in the larger world.

—JANE STANGL (2017)

Introduction

I met Miguel in a peculiar way. Five different golfers from three different clubs suggested that I contact him. One of these golfers exclaimed, "You should talk to him, he knows a lot about golf [in Mexico]." Two of these golfers gave me his contact information. I called Miguel, and after describing my project, I asked him for an interview. He then posed the question that players inevitably asked upon meeting me: "Do you play golf?" When I responded affirmatively, he invited me to his club to talk. We met in the early afternoon in the middle of the week. After we shook hands in the club's reception area, he invited me to join him at the snack bar, an elegant kiosk at the intersection of two holes in the middle of the course (unlike the main bar, which was located at the end of the course). The snack bar had a pleasing atmosphere: the minimalist architecture, including panoramic glass walls, allowed for a superb view of the course from any of approximately 10 tables.

Miguel was a charming and friendly player in his early seventies who grew up in a family of golfers. He had an extensive knowledge of the sport, which alongside his gracious personality and strong playing skills contributed to make him a popular figure in the community. Before

I started asking the questions I had prepared for the interview, I asked Miguel if he could put me in touch with female golfers in high-ranked business/corporate positions so that my sample would include sets of female and male participants in similar socioeconomic and work positions. At the time, I was concerned about how skewed the sample was in favor of male participants, a situation that would only offer a masculine perspective of society. Miguel responded: "A woman in business or a corporation who plays golf is an oddity. I don't know any, but I'll think about it and let you know later."

As we talked, we saw about 12 male golfers pass in front of us on the course. Miguel commented on the playing skills of most of these golfers, highlighting good and bad shots. Near the end of our interview, a golf ball flew high and landed on the green near the hole (a shot that requires impressive technical skills). The dense trees did not allow us to see who had hit the ball because the player was far from the green. Miguel exclaimed, "Let's wait to see who's coming. That was a great shot." A moment later, a man and woman walked across the middle of the course, followed by two caddies carrying their golf bags. The woman walked in the direction of the ball that had caught our attention, while the man proceeded to hit a ball that had landed farther from the green. Miguel pointed at the woman on the course and said, "Claudia is an executive." Once the couple had finished playing the hole, Miguel invited Claudia and her playing partner (and husband) Raul, to come over and talk with us. They sat at our table for about 23 minutes while the caddies waited by the green, about 30 yards away.

Near the end of our conversation with Claudia—and with a notable degree of skepticism—Miguel began to ask her whether gender creates an unfair treatment for women in golf. After offering some examples of discrimination, Claudia concluded: "Women are discriminated against [in golf] by the fact of being women; there isn't any other reason." Miguel restated the question, obviously expecting to prompt a more complicated explanation: "But, are . . . are women discriminated against on the sole basis of being women?" Claudia quickly retorted, "Yes, that is true." Persistent in his skepticism, Miguel immediately asked again, "In golf?" to which Claudia instantly answered, "In golf, in work, everywhere." She provided three more examples of discriminatory experiences and then apologized for not being able to continue talking with us, saying, "I don't want to make Raul [who had remained silent for most of the conversation] wait any longer." Claudia and her husband returned to the course and disappeared behind a line of trees separating holes nine and ten, followed by the two caddies.

The combination of Miguel's extensive knowledge of golf and his complete ignorance of the discrimination faced by women golfers might seem paradoxical, but it is not an unusual pattern. The literature on gender in sports has extensively documented the rampant sexism that permeates the world of athletic games (Eastman and Billings 2000; Hargreaves 2002; Kane 1995; Messner 1988, 1992; Messner and Sabo 1990, 1994; Paradis 2012; Wacquant 2006). The present chapter uses the concept of hegemonic masculinity (Connell 1983; Connell and Messerschmidt 2005) to explain why women golfers have taken a subordinate position to their male peers. The analysis first examines how women club members occupy a higher-class position and white(r) racial identity, granting them a dominant position relative to lower-class women and men. Despite their advantaged position, the class-based hegemonic masculinity prevailing in these clubs produces a wide range of mechanisms that keep women in a secondary place. The gender distribution of playing time and the exclusion of women from the bar are two examples that illustrate how hegemonic masculinity dominates women golfers inside these clubs. The chapter ends by showing how some women possess enough privilege to subvert this form of gender subordination. Ironically, however, the possibility to create a more gender-inclusive space was hindered by the class and racial benefits that initially provided these women a privileged position in society at large.[1]

---

1. The interaction between gender, class, and race is complex and not fully understood. Arceo-Gomez and Campos-Vázquez (2014) conducted a study in which simulated resumes including pictures of the candidates were sent to employers. The researchers found that lighter-skinned, more European-looking women were more likely to get job interviews than darker-skinned, more indigenous-looking women with the same qualifications. Differences in epidermal schema did not affect men to the same degree. These findings suggest that racial dynamics influence judgments of middle-class women. This study dovetails with the argument presented in Chapters 4 and 5 about the racialization of class in Mexico. For middle-class women, the alignment of a higher class position and a white(r) epidermal schema generates an immediate form of racial and class distinction, which allows them to be perceived as more desirable workers. In contrast, this form of distinction is not immediately available for women whose epidermal schema does not seamlessly align with their class position (i.e., women with darker skin). Women in the latter group must demonstrate their white(r) identity by exhibiting objects and behaviors commonly associated with higher classes. They must interact with others in person to demonstrate their "true" class and racial identity. More research is needed to explain why the racialization of class does not affect men and women equally.

A Class-Based Hegemonic Masculinity

One of the very first times I formally presented my research on the connections between class and golf, before I met Miguel and Claudia, a female scholar asked about the role of women in these affluent settings. Thoroughly embarrassed, I stammered a response along the lines of "I don't know." When I began the project, I did not fully understand how the constitution of this privileged space was connected to gender dynamics. From the outside, women golfers appeared just as affluent as the men at the clubs, and thus class seemed to be the most productive lens through which to examine the organization of these sites. The topic of gender continued to crop up (usually in questions posed by women in the audience) as I presented further iterations of the project. While I did not want to disregard the argument that gender influenced the distribution of power in golf clubs, at the early stage of the research project I had not gathered enough data to understand exactly how experiences in the world of golf differed by gender.

While the strong influence of class on the organization of golf clubs initially obscured the way gender norms pushed women to the side, these early questions about the role of gender motivated me to begin exploring this topic. The more ethnographic and interview data I collected about the lack of women in both golf and high-ranking corporate positions, the more intrigued I became by the relationship between gender and privilege. When I began asking male golfers to put me in contact with their female colleagues, I repeatedly heard, "I don't know any women who are high-ranking executives and who play golf," after which some interivewees offered to put me in contact with their wifes or female relatives, yet adding, "but she doesn't work" or "she is not an upper-manager." These common responses revealed the strongly gendered aspect of privilege. The more I inquired about the topic and the more I learned about the organization of space inside golf clubs, the more it became apparent that the "problem" of women was not related to women themselves but rather was the result of the gender dynamics that shaped this privileged space.

In his classical study on sports, Michael Messner noted that athletic games "serve as a primary institutional means for bolstering a challenged and faltering ideology of male superiority" (1988:198). Sports contribute to promulgate the idea that men are naturally stronger, faster, and more skillful than women. This sense of supremacy is well captured in the concept of hegemonic masculinity (Connell 1983), which refers to "the pattern of practice (i.e., things done, not just a set of role expectations or an identity) that allowed men's dominance over women to continue" (Connell and Messerschmidt 2005:832). The prevailing hegemonic masculinity in golf, however, differs from that in most other athletic games due to the upscale character of this sport. Whereas the most common form of hegemonic masculinity present in athletic games focuses on violence, aggressive performances, and bodily contact (Bridges 2009; Magazine 2007; Messner and Sabo 1994; Thangaraj 2015), in golf this notion is articulated through well-mannered interactions. As Pyke (1996) noted, the civilized demeanors of polite gentility embraced by wealthy men should not be equated with support for gender equality. Instead, these non-aggressive attitudes are a class-based marker that separates better-off men from their poorer counterparts, who are commonly associated with displays of aggressive masculinity (Pyke 1996).

Indeed, the refined manners, politeness, and chivalry that characterize golf obscured the gender imbalance in the sport and thus reinforced the assumption that hegemonic masculinity (e.g., unfair gender practices) only affect popular sports. Moreover, the fact that Lorena Ochoa is the most important Mexican golfer of all time bolstered the perception that unequal gender dynamics are limited to sports practiced by the lower and middle classes. Hegemonic masculinity, however, produces a multitude of practical mechanisms that emphasize women's "inadequacy" and "deficiency," which, if accepted as legitimate, makes them unqualified to occupy a prominent role. These mechanisms were manifested, for example, in the gender separation of tees—where each player hits the ball for the first time—and the distribution of gender-exclusive time slots—points that I will return to later. These differences were not viewed as the expression of an unfair gender order but rather as the product of natural differences between male and female bodies. Hegemonic masculinity allowed men to hide concrete practices of gender differentiation and exclusion behind the masked of supposedly women's "weak" anatomical constitution.

The Number of Women on the Course

The subordinate position of women is manifested in their relative participation in the sport of golf—they constitute a small percentage of golfers in Mexico. The Mexican Golf Federation (FMG) has 27,631 registered members (IGF 2017). Because the website of the Mexican Women's Golf Association (AMFG) does not provide information about the number of members, I contacted the organization to inquire about what percentage of all golfers in Mexico were women. The organization's spokesperson told me that just under 1,000 women competed in their tournaments at the national level but did not know how many more women were affiliated with the FMG. The person claimed that it was the FMG's role to keep track of this type of data. I then contacted the FMG to find out exactly how many women play golf in Mexico, but the Federation's spokesperson explained that this information was not public.[2] In the absence of precise numbers, I continued to ask participants to estimate the proportion of golfers who were women.

A golf journalist responded to this question by noting, "I'm not sure. I don't know the exact number, but it is between 10 and 20 percent. There aren't many women on the course." The golf instructor at one of the clubs I visited offered a similarly low estimate:

The percentage of women who play golf is very low, I don't know what the number is at a national level; here in the club it's about 15 percent. Look, I commonly start with [a] similar number of girls and boys at about 9 years old, but by the time they're 13 there are only two girls for every eight or nine boys. Once they're 16, no more than one girl is in the group. Some women return [to the sport] later, but anyway, not many women [are] playing golf.

Robin, the owner of a consulting firm that organizes corporate golf tournaments, noted that while the number of women golfers has increased in recent years, women remain a small minority on the course:

One of my friends is the owner of a company that organizes a female-only tournament sponsored by a magazine. Before Lorena Ochoa became famous, no more than 50 participants attended this

2. The FMG's website provides extensive information about tournaments but little general information about golf in Mexico. There is no information about the total number of golfers affiliated with the organization, no statistics on the overall number of golf courses in the country, and no data about the number of clubs not affiliated with FMG. Two different golf journalists noted that the Federation has little interest in accurately tracking the development of the sport in Mexico. One remarked, "The Federation has no interest in keeping this information. They even recently threw away their historical archive, can you believe that, everything in the trash." Thus, I was not surprised when the FMG spokesperson said he could not tell me how many women were affiliated with the Federation, arguing privacy concerns.

tournament. But in recent years they have had up to 150 players, all of them women. The number of women playing has expanded amazingly. Now, in the tournaments I organize, you only see a handful of them. In the last two tournaments, for example—one was a charity, the other a corporate—out of 120 players there were 5 and 6 women, respectively. Women do not play golf at the same rate as men.

Alejandro and Hector, the owners of two other golf consulting firm, elaborated on the female-only tournament that Robin mentioned in his comment. First, Hector said,

There is an important tournament only for women sponsored by a magazine. In its first years, the total number of women competing did not even reach 30 players. I heard that in the last tournament they had a good turnout, about 100 or more participants, I'm not sure. This shows you the rapid increase of women in golf and part of this is due to the popularity of Lorena [Ochoa].

Alejandro clarified this assessment, saying,

Now, you asked about female golf players who were also executives or work in business. From that tournament [the one Hector referred to] no more than 10 percent [of those women] worked in high-ranked jobs; the other 90 percent are housewives or women who work in lower-ranked jobs.

Alvaro, a marketing director at a large corporation in his mid-forties, did not play golf but was very familiar with the sport because he had attended every round of the amateur tournament sponsored by his employer. His view of women's participation in the sport corroborated what the other golfers described. He explained,

Of the 17 rounds that have taken place this year [as part of a large annual tournament], only in six have I seen women competing, between four and six players [women] in each of them. In the last tournament, [out of 120 players] four women were competing.

Patricia, a golfer in her early thirties who learned to play golf in her childhood and worked at a consulting firm, was one of the few women who competed in corporate tournaments. When I asked her about the participation of women in golf, she responded, "I may be wrong, but I guess that we [are] about 10 percent of the overall number of players. I usually play one [mixed-gender] tournament a year, sometimes two. We [women] are always a minority, 6, 8, 10 [players], never more than that." Emilio, the general editor of a golf magazine, estimated that women composed about 20 percent of all golfers in Mexico, but added that only a small fraction play in amateur competitions. He said,

> Tournaments are especially important for networking, everybody knows that, but women do not participate because most of them do not work. You will find them [female golfers] at the internal and interclub tournaments, they compete there, but they are not interested in networking outside of clubs because they don't need to, they don't work.

In 2005, one of the most prestigious golf clubs in the city published a book celebrating its 100th anniversary. Based on the information in the book, of the club's 967 members, 203 (20.9 percent) were women (Krauze, Moreno, and Speckman Guerra 2005). Taken together, the data on women golfers and the interviewees' estimates all pointed toward marginal participation of women in the sport. Notably, this trend is replicated at a global scale (Crosset 1995; McGinnis, Gentry, and McQuillan 2008; McGinnis, McQuillan, and Chapple 2005; Reis and Correia 2013).[3]

The Paradoxical Relationship between Gender and Privilege

As described in Chapter 4, Laura, a golfer in her late fifties who had played at the same prominent club for about 30 years, invited me to interview her at her house. After Laura "corrected" the embarrassing situation that occurred when a domestic worker asked me to enter through the service door, we sat in her living room. The space featured Chippendale furniture,

---

3. Golf has long been perceived as a masculine space. In early twentieth-century Britain, for example, suffragettes specifically targeted golf courses to protest male domination (Evans 2016:540).

an antique grandfather clock, and what looked like a Persian rug covering most of the floor. The room reminded me of the style typical of aristo-cratic houses I had toured in Britain. As I described my project and talked about my time in England, a uniformed domestic worker entered the living room. She asked if we wanted a drink, adding, "Do you want water, lemon water, sparkling water, tea, or coffee?" We both asked for lemon water. She returned with a crystal pitcher, glasses, and napkins and then quickly disappeared from view after arranging everything on a coffee table in front of the main sofa. During my 90-minute conversation with Laura, the worker returned periodically to see if we needed anything else.

As part of the interview I asked Laura what she thought of the increased popularity golf had enjoyed in recent years. She responded by talking about professional tournaments. In Mexico, she argued, these events had to offer large economic prizes and be well attended to attract important international players. Laura believed that by holding such tournaments Mexico would acquire a respected place on the interna-tional golf scene. While the FMG had begun to offer relatively large monetary prizes, the organization struggled to increase attendance at its tournaments, although in the last two years large crowds had begun to show up to watch these contests. Laura's statement about tournaments being "well attended," however, referred to a specific type of attendee. She explained,

> The Federation gives tickets to the main sponsors and clubs. [The] clubs distribute them among [their] members, but the problem is with the sponsors. They don't give them to anyone passing by on the street, no, no, but still. . . . For example, at the last event, when Lorena Ochoa was about to hit the ball, someone's phone started ringing. That is awful, someone needs to take the phones away from these guys. They don't have a clue about what's happening on the course. But, you tell me, of all Mexicans, how many of us know how to play golf? Very few. We are a tiny minority, but there are many who want to try it, but they don't know anything about golf. It's impossible to educate these people about golf, they behave like a herd [of animals].

All of the women I interviewed generally agreed with the self-centered class-based arguments that male players frequently articulated. For example, Mercedes, a female golfer in her mid-fifties who was deeply involved in promoting the sport among female club members, expressed great surprise that golf clubs generated intensely negative reactions among poor communities. She specifically discussed impoverished communities with indigenous origins whose members still owned communal land, because these groups had strongly resisted the construction of golf facilities in their territories.[4] Mercedes explained her incredulity, saying,

> Did you hear about the possibility of constructing a public course [in one of the wealthiest municipalities around Mexico City that is surrounded by communities who own land communally]? A friend of mine was working on the project. This group of golfers already had an agreement with the municipality, but when the project was made public, some locals [who owned the land on which the public course was to be built] fought back against the idea. They stopped it . . . and the same thing happened in Tepoztlan. Locals opposed the construction of a course there; I don't know why these people are so afraid of golf, it would be a source of employment for them.

Mercedes's taken-for-granted privilege may have led her to overlook the lack of reciprocity between affluent groups and poorer communities (some of them of indigenous origins) in issues such as access to water and recreational spaces as well as fair use of other local resources. In most cases, women adhered to arguments that emphasized class distinction when talking about golfers and those outside of this affluent sport.

The Language of Class Differences

As discussed in previous chapters, most club members drew a clear distinction between themselves and outsiders who, because of their lower class position, were uninformed about the world of golf. Women were

---

4. After the Mexican revolution (1910–1921), the state recognized the legal right of communities to own land collectively, naming this property *ejido*. This type of ownership was strongly linked with indigenous groups. In most cases, the land was individually farmed, but was not considered individual property. It could not be legally sold because it was a communal asset. The neoliberal policies implemented in Mexico since the late 1980s changed the legal status of *ejidos*, allowing this land to be turned into private property (Perramond 2008; Weaver et al. 2012).

no exception to this rule. They commonly used their class position to mark boundaries between themselves and other women and men who did not have similar tastes, attitudes, and opinions. This type of class boundary-making was manifested in the way female golfers talked to workers inside the clubs. As noted in Chapter 5, almost all caddies had nicknames, and the men at the clubs almost always referred to caddies by these monikers. However, I heard some women referring to caddies by their actual names.

When talking to caddies and other workers at the club, some women used the informal second-person pronoun *tu* (you), which implies a degree of familiarity and equality, whereas others used the formal second-person pronoun *usted* (you), which conveys a higher degree of formality and respect. For example, I interviewed Nora, a golfer in her early forties who was involved in the promotion of golf among female club members, at her club's restaurant. After we had talked for about 25 minutes, she ended the conversation curtly by asking a waitress to call for her chauffeur. When the chauffeur entered the restaurant, Nora gave him instructions about the errands he needed to finish that afternoon, and then she excused herself from the interview and left the restaurant. Nora referred to both the waitress and chauffeur by their first names, although she used the second-person pronoun *usted*, which conveyed an attitude of respect. In contrast, the workers used the honorific title *Señora* (Mrs.) to address Nora and acknowledge her requests ("Yes, Señora"). Nora's use of first names and the workers' use of formal titles shows how the vast class differences between them were manifested in language (Bourdieu 1991).

An exchange that occurred during my conversation with Ruth inside the clubhouse further illustrates how language reflects class differences. Ruth, a golfer in her late fifties who, like Mercedes and Nora, was actively involved in promoting the sport among female club members, had begun playing golf after she married a golf enthusiast about 30 years before. As Ruth and I talked while sitting in a small open hall furnished with a sofa, armchairs, and plants as well as paintings on the wall and thus feeling like the living room of a large house, a female worker passed in front of us. Ruth interrupted our conversation to give the worker an instruction, using a diminutive form of her name (Juanita rather than Juana, similar to calling someone Janie rather than Jane). She said, "Juanita, how are you? Please, tell Luis [the caddy] that I'm going to play later than I had expected. I need my bag ready by 2:50." She then returned to our conversation.

Similarly, Laura, the female golfer I interviewed at her house, also referred to her domestic worker using a diminutive of the worker's name each time the worker checked to see if we needed anything else. While using a diminutive of someone's name is often regarded as a sign of affection, this linguistic form is also frequently used when adults talk to children. In the context of a significant class disparity, using a diminutive of an adult's name seemed like a subtle way to express recognition, domination, and condescension all at the same time. In contrast, when workers talked to club members, they used language that signified the highest degree of respect and referenced their subordinate position, such as formal pronouns or a combination of the golfer's professional title and first or last name (e.g., Doctor Luís or Doctor Gutiérrez).

Women's Perceptions of Class and Race

The privileged position of the women I interviewed was the result of not only their affluent class position but also their phenotypes, which closely resembled the epidermal schema of other members of the upper-middle and upper classes rather than the features associated with the working and middle classes (Nutini 1997, 2008). In the Mexican context, these women were white(r). The explanations the women gave for the impoverished condition of caddies, which closely resembled the class and racial tropes used by male club members, highlighted the women's racial positions. For example, Ruth maintained that caddies do not succeed as professional players because they do not have the natural abilities required to play golf. She said,

> I've heard that some caddies are good, that they are competing against one another, but if you take all of them together you don't even end up with one competitive player. They don't have the mental strength; they don't have the technique; they are not prepared to compete professionally. It's sad, but that is the reality.

Although Ruth's comment can be understood as a classist remark, it is important to remember that in Mexico, racialized ideas do not operate straightforwardly along color lines. Rather, class and racial dynamics are always intertwined. Her assertion that all the caddies combined would still not make a competitive (i.e., real) golfer expresses both classist and racialized notions. Ruth's comment implied that there was something intrinsically different about these workers that prevented them from embodying the best traits of golfers. Hence, caddies could never be professional players, not even all of them together. Mercedes also alluded to the inherent otherness of caddies to explain their lack of success, concluding,

> The fact that there are no caddies playing in the professional leagues is influenced by what people [caddies] eat and their mental strength. Look at what they [caddies] eat; they cannot cope with the pressure of playing with big names in the United States.

As noted in Chapters 4 and 5, comments about food express deep-seated notions about the racial otherness of lower-class individuals, who eat a diet supposedly closer to indigenous people rather than to the mestizo-European taste. An even more straightforward example of highlighting the inherent otherness of caddies occurred when Laura described Esteban Toledo, the Mexican professional golf player, as a *naco*. After describing the obstacles caddies must overcome to become professionals, she added,

> And then what happens with some of them, they have some success and become unbearable. That is what happened with the *naco* Esteban Toledo. The last time I tried to greet him he completely ignored us. He has no manners. He is a caddy.

As Chapter 4 elaborates, the word *naco* implies both a class and racialized statement about the lack of commonality between the accuser and the accused. Esteban's decision to ignore Laura, and the group of women golfers that was with her, demonstrated that despite his relative success as a professional player, he was not different from the other workers who populated the clubs; after all, Esteban was a caddy and will always be one, and by extension a *naco*.

The way women addressed workers, their perceptions of caddies, and their view of themselves as part of a small, sophisticated minority all exemplify the privileged position enjoyed by women club members. Within the larger society, these women belong to the upper-middle and upper classes, which represent the pinnacle of the Mexican class structure. Nevertheless, the class and racial privilege these women possessed evaporated when they were with men who enjoyed a similar affluent class position and epidermal schema. In these situations the privileged position of women succumbed, giving way to a class-based hegemonic masculinity (for an analogous scenario in the United States, see Ostrander 1980, 2010).

Gender, Class, and Space

All of the women I interviewed talked extensively about their passion for golf. They mentioned a wide range of factors when discussing what drew them to the sport. Mercedes, the golfer who was surprised at poor communities' reactions to the possibility of building a new course, emphasized competing with herself to improve her game. She explained, "This sport is the only one where you compete against yourself. It is not about others; it is about improving your own score. This is why I love golf." Laura, the golfer who had rectified the embarrassing moment in her house, rhapsodized about the beautiful landscapes along the course, noting, "I enjoyed so much walking the course, the trees, the birds, the vegetation. The club helps me relax after work; the club is great." Ruth, the player in her late fifties whom I had interviewed in the lavishly appointed hall, talked about how much she valued the constant opportunities to meet new people, explaining, "Golf helps extend your [social] contacts. I've met very nice people at interclub tournaments. I have friends all over the city because of golf." Nora, the golfer who had suddenly ended our interview by calling her chauffeur, touted the camaraderie among golfers. She said she enjoyed going to tournaments organized by the Mexican Female Golf Association with her female friends, explaining,

> I've got a group of [female] friends I made through golf and we've developed strong ties. We've traveled together, played in tournaments together, and supported each other outside of golf. This sport is amazing; it allows you to connect with people in a deeper way.

These fond descriptions of golf and its social surroundings, however, were interspersed with (sometimes subtle and sometimes explicit) references to feelings of marginalization.

The Gendered Nature of Tee Boxes and Handicaps

When I asked Mercedes about the limited participation of women in golf, she responded sarcastically, "Haven't you heard the joke that golf stands for [speaking in English] **G**entlemen **O**nly, **L**adies **F**orbidden?" and then laughed. Humor touches on deeply shared understandings to provoke laughs and smiles (Lowe 1986). Thus, unsurprisingly, the spatial organization of the golf course corroborated the joke. Each hole of golf starts at the tee box, where each player hits the ball for the first time. At the clubs I visited, there were three tee boxes at each hole. Golfers referred to the one closest to the green (scoring area) as the ladies' or red tees. These were between 5,600 and 5,900 yards from the site where the ball needs to enter (also called the hole). The middle ones were referred as the men's or white tees, which were between 6,300 and 6,800 yards from the hole. The ones farther from the scoring area as referred as the professional's or blue, sometimes black, tees. These are between 7,000 and 7,300 yards away from the hole.

Amateur women golfers were assigned to the ladies' tee regardless of their playing skills. As a beginner, I struggled to hit the ball both straight and far enough. Most times, I managed to hit it either straight but not very far, or far but not very straight; I could rarely accomplish both. However, no one ever recommended that I use the closer tee to speed up the game. Similarly, even though some of the older golfers (men) I played with lacked the strength to hit the ball a long distance, I never heard anyone suggest they should use the closer tee. In fact, in all the time I spent on golf courses, I never saw a man playing from the forward tees. These tees are perceived as a space for women, who, because of their "natural" weakness, must start the game closer to the green. Men commonly described women golfers as slower and weaker players. Hundley (2004) described a similar situation in the United States, where the forward tees are never used by men, and many clubs even use pink tees to signal that these are "ladies' tees." Hundley argued that the strong identification of the forward tees with women has turned these spaces into emasculated areas that men avoid, even those who could benefit from the shorter distance to the green, such as beginners and older players.

The gendering of the tee boxes is all the more striking because, unlike popular "contact" sports such as football, boxing, and basketball, golf is not based on notions of physical strength, bodily contact, and force. In fact, the use of handicaps in golf eliminates any possible need for separating tees by gender. Golf is the only global sport that includes clear rules of handicap, which means that two players with different skill levels and physical strength compete against each other on level playing field, offering the weaker and less dexterous player a chance to win.[5] The handicap (the number of strokes removed from a player's score) is

---

5. This code was originally introduced for betting purposes in nineteenth-century England (see Cerón-Anaya, 2010).

a numerical representation of a golfer's playing potential; the lower the number, the better the golfer, so a 5 handicap is better than a 13 handicap, which is better than a 26 handicap, and so on (in a game where the lowest score wins). The handicap is roughly based on a golfer's best score in recent games.

The use of handicaps implies that a game of golf is only fair if less-skilled players receive an advantage. A 60-year-old player (with a handicap of 30) can compete against a 40-year-old player (with a handicap of 10) and even have the opportunity to defeat his younger, stronger, and more skillful opponent. Notably, the rules of handicap are only used by amateur players, not professionals. Other popular sports have no parallel system, and thus the stronger, more skillful, and often younger competitor usually wins, even among amateur players. This notable distinction between golf and most other sports is based on class principles. Instead of embracing lower-class masculine ideals such as physical strength, bodily contact, and violence, golf embraces the upper-class idea of fair play (Bourdieu 1988; Crosset 1995). This unusual characteristic is linked to the gentrification of golf that occurred in late nineteenth- and early twentieth-century England (Cerón-Anaya 2010). Under the rules of the handicap system, it is not hard work, training, and physical strength that improves a player's chances of winning but rather a combination of experience, concentration, and a bit of luck.

The use of handicaps does not mean there is no competition in the game. After all, participants reported that being an outstanding player generated strong feelings of respect among other golfers. However, as explained in Chapter 3, golfers do not place competition at the center of the game, unlike athletes in popular sports where "winning at all costs" is a core principle. In golf, camaraderie, honor, and etiquette are just as important as competition. At least theoretically, the rules of handicap eliminate the "natural" differences between aged and gendered bodies, because when younger and older individuals and men and women play together, handicaps make the competition fair (McGinnis, Gentry, and McQuillan 2008). Yet even this system designed specifically to mitigate bodily differences does not eradicate players' perceptions of gender either on the course or beyond its walls.

Many women, for example, complained that in mixed-gender amateur tournaments, men frequently tinkered with their handicap to limit the possibility of a women defeating them. Mercedes, a very talented golfer in her mid-fifties, complained,

There is something we call here [in Mexico] *caimanismo* [being a caiman],[6] where people cheat on their handicap [to increase their possibility of winning]. That is common in amateur tournaments, when people fight for monetary prizes. It is awful. [. . .] But I've noticed another type of *caimanism*, one that is common whenever men play with women. Look, whenever I play with men, I straight away tell them, "What's your handicap? But don't forget that you have three, OK, one to show off, one to bet, and another for when you play tournaments." And I remind them, "To play tournaments, your handicap is higher than 20 [meaning that the person is a bad player]; to show off, it's about 10 [which means the person is a very good player]; and to bet, it's 15 [which is about average]." I cannot deal with this anymore. You know what, I stopped playing mixed-gender tournaments because it is impossible to win. All the winners are men who happened to have their best game ever on the day of the tournament. No way, that is impossible. Men do not like having women defeat them.

I asked Ruth about the idea of *caimanismo* and how men can get away with not having a well-defined handicap. She explained that women are generally very scrupulous, counting all their strokes and submitting their scorecards to the starter (the person who controls the pace of the course) at the end of every game. She said, "We all [women] follow the rules and if you see another woman forgetting to hand in her scorecard, you ask her to submit it. We never let another woman not hand in her scorecard. We police each other." Because the scores for every game are recorded, women have highly accurate handicaps. In contrast, Ruth explained, men do not always submit their scorecards, and neither caddies nor starters enforce the rule stating that players must submit their scorecards at the end of the game. The inconsistent recording of men's scores allowed them to modify their handicap at will (by not turning in scorecards with particularly low or high scores), and thus increased their chances of winning against women, who did not have the chance to modify their handicap.

I heard men golfers complaining about the *caimanismo* that occurred at amateur tournaments where people compete for large monetary prizes, but the type of gender-based cheating Mercedes and Ruth described went

---

6. The caiman, an animal that inhabits Central and South America, is similar to an alligator or crocodile. The word caiman implies that someone is a cheater.

unmentioned by the men I interviewed. This type of *caimanismo* acts as a concrete mechanism that reinforces hegemonic masculinity. Within the class-based hegemonic masculinity of the golf world in Mexico, men's inflation of their handicaps and the clubs' use of tee boxes to situate women as weaker players (regardless of their individual skill levels) both reinforce the myth of male superiority among golfers (for a parallel discussion of these practices in the United States, see Hundley 2004; McGinnis and Gentry 2006; McGinnis, Gentry, and McQuillan 2008; McGinnis, McQuillan, and Chapple 2005; Messner 1988). In this context, it was not surprising to hear Rafael, a 60-year-old golfer who owns a well-established advertising company, addressing the question of how women and men golfers differ, saying, "by nature women are slower and unfocused players, there are exceptions, but generally speaking, it is not fun to play with them."

Spatial Separation and the Invisibility of Women's Golf Skills

The customs and rules surrounding the 19th hole constitute another mechanism that helps maintain a class-based hegemonic masculinity in golf. Golf club interiors are characterized by their spatial openness (see Chapter 2 for a detailed discussion of the spatial characteristics of golf clubs). Visibility defines these spaces, and their design elements—from the vast and immaculate greens to the modern architecture in the restaurants and main halls—convey a sense of exposure. This spatial openness allows club members to see one another at all times, except while they are playing, when dense trees and the layout of the course restrict visibility to the members of one's own playing group and the groups playing directly in front of and behind one's group. The course becomes visible to everyone at the main bar, which is located at the end of the course and is known as the 19th hole. However, socialization at the bar is, for the most part, restricted to men. Because unspoken and unwritten rules discourage women from entering the bar, they usually socialize at the club restaurant after finishing a round of golf.

Men use the bar as a place to talk, joke, and recall key moments of past games. Men at adjoining tables sometimes intervene in the conversation, asking questions or recounting their own experiences. The bar functions as a space that renders visible what is otherwise invisible: the actions and behaviors of golfers on the course. At the bar, male club members learn information about other male golfers in the club, such as who is a good/bad player, who seems to have a lot of luck, who is a funny person, and who tends to get angry on the course. The fact that women are not welcomed at the bar renders their skills, sense of humor, character, and other personal traits invisible to the men at the club. I commonly asked the men I interviewed to talk about the difference in playing styles between men and women. About 20 percent of male golfers responded by talking about alleged differences, such as women being slower, more distracted, and weaker players. Raul, Claudia's husband who was mentioned in the opening vignette, was one of the few male golfers who portrayed female players in a positive light. Nearly 80 percent of the men I interviewed said that they could not answer the question because they had never played with a woman and had rarely seen them playing.

For example, Ernesto, a golfer in his mid-fifties who served as the director of a media company, noted, "I cannot tell you what the difference is [between women and men] because I don't know. I play early in the mornings [with men] and I am on my way out of the club by the time women start playing." Ruben, one of the golfers who invited me to his club, said, "That's a good question," and after a long paused added, "I need to think about it, I cannot give you an answer right now." However, he never answered the question later. Most of these men indicated that they commonly played with male colleagues and friends and women were never present in these groups. Agustin, one of the participants who had learned how to play at a driving range, remarked,

> I don't know [what the difference between men and women is] because I've never played with women, but I guess that it might be difficult to keep up a conversation between women and men [while playing together] because women start the game from different tee box.

In her seminal book *Space, Place, and Gender* (1994:186), Doreen Massey famously argued that "space and place, spaces and places, and our senses of them (and such related things as our degrees of mobility) are gendered through and through." In multiple ways, the experiences of women golfers suggest that she was correct to emphasize the gender-based organization of space. Massey also argued that all discussions concerning space must consider the inexorable relationship between space and time, a topic to which I now turn.

Gender, Class, and Time

According to Massey (1994), time plays an important role in the organization of space. For example, people and actions can be allocated to the same space but at different times, changing the way the space is perceived. A group's high status can be signaled by its access to a space during the period of greatest demand, while the less desirable time periods are allocated to groups and individuals perceived as less important. The organization of space through time conveys perceptions of prominence or irrelevance without openly articulating them.

The Gendered Nature of Time on the Course

All golf clubs in Mexico City have policies that use time to organize the course (and the golf world) by gender. Certain days and time slots are reserved almost exclusively for either men or women (I discuss certain exceptions later in the chapter). Women are almost never allowed to play during early-morning hours on the weekends, which is considered prime time. Further, women are generally not permitted to play during early-morning hours on most weekdays, except one day a week, which is known as "ladies day." In all the clubs I visited (and those I heard about from golfers), the best playing times were reserved for men. One of the women I interviewed said she had heard that the most expensive club in the city did not have this restriction, but none of the other interviewees could confirm the veracity of this assertion.

Claudia, the golfer described in the opening vignette, started our conversation about women's experiences on the golf course by noting, "There is a horrible gender discrimination in golf, just look who plays during prime time [i.e., men]." This was a common complaint among the women I interviewed. They explained that the best tee times (in the early mornings) were allocated based on gender rather than playing skills. Laura objected to this temporal distribution of playing times, saying, "In most clubs, women cannot play during early hours on most weekdays and not at all during early hours on weekends, which isn't fair." Early hours are considered the best time to play because a round of 18 holes of golf (the standard game) takes about four and a half hours to finish. A player starting around 6:30 a.m. will finish around 11:00 a.m. and thus can arrive at the office by late-morning. This schedule is also beneficial in a city with heavy traffic jams. Golfers who start early can drive to the course before the morning traffic jam and leave just as traffic begins to dissipate. Further, during the rainy season (June through September), playing early in the morning allows golfers to avoid the rain showers that are common in the afternoons.

In addition to reflecting the status difference between men and women, the decision to reserve early time slots for men and late-morning/afternoon slots for women is based on two premises. First, there is an assumption that women are not paid workers and, therefore, have plenty of time during regular working hours to play golf. Second, male players believe that women are slower and weaker players by "nature" and therefore benefit from playing when the course is less crowded. All the women I interviewed expressed frustration about gendered tee time policies. Mercedes asserted, "These policies are discriminatory, as simple as that. The argument that we are slow players is nonsense. I have a better handicap that the average man in my club." Laura voiced a similarly blunt assessment: "The distribution of time is horrible. It is sexist. Unfortunately, these policies are present in all clubs."

Because of these playing time policies, each club was a neatly organized universe, where space was masculine during the early mornings and slowly became feminine/mixed-gender during the course of the day; the exception was on "ladies' day," when the clubs were a feminine space even during the early morning. This space-time transformation reinforced the subordination of women inside clubs by justifying the temporal allocation of space based on the assumptions that men, but not women, have careers (Pyke 1996) and that female athletes are inherently weaker than male athletes (Hundley 2004). These set of ideas transmit a binary perception of gender, in which female and male are viewed as naturally opposing and hierarchically arranged categories. These notions also reinforces an heteronormative view, assuming that couples are naturally formed by a man (breadwinner) and a woman (homemaker). Women were aware of some of the most obvious elements of these narratives. Concerning the notion that women do not work, Mercedes observed,

> [Generally speaking] men restrict our right to play with the argument that as we don't work [and] that we have plenty of time to fit in a match during the afternoon, which is nonsense. Nowadays, half of the female population in Mexico works, so . . . if we work when are we going to play?

While it is true that a large percentage of women in today's Mexico work, the percentage is smaller among golfers than among the general population. Claudia remarked that "most women here [at her club] are housewives. . . . We [working women] are about a third of all women in the club." There are no statistics on the ratio of employed and non-employed female golfers, but all the sources I consulted agreed that the majority of women players are not paid workers. This fact, however, does not justify gendering tee times based on the assumption that non-employed women can easily fit in a match later in the day. On the contrary, gender-based temporal regulations directly penalize women who do not pursue tradi- tional gender roles because, as Mercedes noted, professional women have fewer opportunities to play (for a parallel discussion about golf in the northeastern United States see Sherwood 2012). Gendered tee times on the weekend also have negative consequences for women. In Mexico, the main meal of the day is served between 2:00 p.m. and 4:00 p.m., and this meal often serves as a significant family/social gathering on weekends. A man who starts a round during the early-morning hours can easily at- tend family/social gatherings in the early afternoon, while a woman who has to start later in the morning will need to rush to be present at these events.

The gender-based organization of the golf course extended to amateur tournaments. Claudia, Patricia, and Mercedes, all of whom were working women and very good golfers, explained that there were at least two am- ateur tournaments exclusively for women, one organized by a magazine and the other by an upscale retail store. However, while mixed-gender am- ateur tournaments, which were dominated by men, were always held on weekends, the women-only tournaments were played during the week, which made it hard for working women to participate. Mercedes described the problem this schedule created for her and other working women:

> Amateur tournaments for women only are held during the week. It is hard to take two or three days off from work to play in them. [. . .] Besides housewives, only a top female executive or the owner of a company can take enough time off to participate in these events.

Claudia expressed a similar conundrum: "I only play one of these two tournaments. I cannot play both of them; they are played during the week. It is hard to take so many days out of your work schedule." Finally, Patricia experienced the same problem. She explained, "I cannot take three days off from work on a regular week to play these [women-only] golf tournaments, I still don't have the seniority to do that. Weekdays tournaments are a no-no for me."

The Effects of Temporal Separation: The Perpetuation of Traditional Gender Narratives

Gendered time policies not only limit women's opportunities to play, they also reduce their visibility. The time restrictions limit interactions between male and female players. Most men have left the club by the time most women start to play. Thus, women's playing abilities—a major asset in the context of a golf club—are rendered invisible to the community of male players. This invisibility is one of the reasons the women I interviewed felt they were constantly belittled or ignored by their male colleagues. Beyond Lorena Ochoa, who was regularly cited as an outstanding player, most of the men I talked with were unable to list specific good women golfers and less talented ones, and many simply assumed that all women belonged in the second category. This assumption shows that men both believed and reinforced the hegemonic masculine narrative assumes that women are "naturally" weaker and incompetent athletes.

Women were very aware of these accounts. For example, Ruth, a golfer in her early sixties who had played the sport for about 30 years, reported that men often complained about women's skills, noting, "They say that we are slow and we take a lot of time to reach the hole," and then adding, in a sarcastic tone, "[however,] unlike many men I know, I calculate the distance [between the ball and the green] by myself and I don't expect caddies to tell me how to play." In a similar vein, Mercedes lamented, "I have heard so many jokes about women in golf—we are slow, clumsy, and so on and so forth—but despite playing better than many men, many [men] do not respect us." Claudia, the golfer whose shot Miguel admired in the opening story, also emphasized this point, observing,

> When there is a group of male players looking for an extra golfer [to make a standard group of four, called a foursome], they never want women to play with them. I have, many times, heard comments like, "No, dude! Why a gal? No way." Men don't like to play with women [. . .] because men feel inhibited by good women players.

The marginalization of women in golf was articulated through spatial dynamics that, in sometimes subtle and sometimes explicit ways, communicated ideas about belonging, affinity, inclusion as well as separation, disdain, and exclusion (Massey 1994). The gendered nature of the golf course shifts throughout the day. At prime playing times, the golf course is a masculine site in which almost all the female figures present are brown-skinned workers. Donaldson and Poynting (2007) argued that in Australia, upper-class men socialize in activities where women are never present, unless they are assistants, which allows affluent men to internalize a strong sense of hegemonic masculinity. The restricted presence of women in Mexican golf clubs follows a similar pattern, including the fact that those women who were present at male-only time slots were brown-skinned female workers.

The (Im)Possibility of Resisting Gender Inequalities

The findings and analysis I have presented so far might create the impression that there is no escape from hegemonic masculinity. The devaluation of women is articulated through a wide range of mechanisms such as the way men talk about women golfers as inherently weak and incompetent athletes and the way the placement of tee boxes reinforces this narrative. The power of hegemonic masculinity is also present in men's unethical practice of modifying their handicap to recreate the myth of masculine physical prominence as well as the gendering of tee times, which conceals women's playing skills, character, and personalities. While readers might be tempted to conclude that hegemonic masculinity renders affluent women completely powerless inside golf clubs, this is not the case. The privileged position these women occupy offers them multiple ways to resist and mitigate gender inequalities.

Resistance

Two of the women I interviewed had successfully fought against gender-based playing policies. At their respective clubs, each of these players was part of a group of two all-woman foursomes that could play during prime time (eight women in total per club). The first woman who described this type of resistance to gender inequality was Laura, who was in her early fifties and had started playing golf in her late teens after years of playing competitive tennis. Her previous athletic experience helped her become a very good golfer quite rapidly. Although she was in a comfortable economic position, early on in her marriage Laura had decided to start a business, which she continued to oversee at the time of the interviews. About 10 years ago, she became frustrated that her work schedule and her club's gendered tee times greatly limited her opportunities to play golf. Laura was not alone in this; another member of her foursome was also a business owner. Neither of them could play very often because the club's gender-based time rules conflicted with their work responsibilities.

The foursome asked to be permitted to play during prime time, showing evidence that half of them worked and could not come in the middle of the day or early afternoon. However, the most important argument they made, according to Laura, was that all four were excellent players who would not slow the pace on the course. She concluded by saying:

> The president of the club at the time let us play early in the morning. We even managed to gain another spot for a second all-woman foursome. These other women are also great players. Since then [10 years ago], every new president who takes office immediately wants to ban us [from playing at prime time], arguing that the number of men playing in the early mornings has increased and that they need our spots. We've kept both spots, but it's a constant fight. Men don't want us to play during the early-morning hours.

Mercedes was the second golfer who had fought for the right to play at prime time. She explained that she had invested a significant amount of time and money to take lessons when she began playing golf, adding, "I didn't like the idea that I was the wife of a golfer and that's why I play golf. I really wanted to become a very good player on my own." About six years ago, Mercedes's all-woman foursome and one other group won the right to play in the early mornings at her club. When the group first asked to be allowed to play during prime time, the president at the time rejected their request. But Mercedes remained firm in her desire to play during prime time. She asked me, "If we couldn't play early in the morning, at what time were we [working women] going to play?" When a new club president was elected, she and her playing partners once again requested an exemption to the gendered tee time restrictions. To strengthen their case, Mercedes noted that half of the money to pay for her family's club expenses came from her own earnings. The new president allowed two all-woman foursomes to play in the early-morning hours, but some club members were not happy about the situation. Mercedes explained,

> [Six years later] some men still ask us why we don't play with the rest of the women. Once a male member hit a ball that landed very close to my foursome. Angry, I asked him to wait until we had moved farther away. He replied that he didn't understand why we were playing at that time [early in the morning] and that we should go and play with the rest of the chicks,[7] adding that men were the ones who paid for the memberships. I got even angrier, telling him that he could not speak for every man and woman in the club. The fact that he paid for his family's membership was not my business and who was paying for my family's [membership] was not his [business]. I told him that I would report his rude behavior. He later came up to me to apologize, saying that he didn't intend to offend me.

Despite the multiple forms of spatial and discursive exclusion women faced (e.g., gendered time allocation and the notion that women are deficient players), the actions of Laura and Mercedes and their playing partners illustrated the ways in which some of these privileged women could subvert their clubs' gender-based temporal and spatial constraints. The possibility of successfully engaging in the struggle for gender equality, however, was connected to a golfer's financial, social, and cultural resources. Laura, for example, became a good player in her adolescence (her family had a membership in a well-established club), which reflected her upper-class origins. In addition, she was a highly skilled player and a well-known figure both within and beyond her club because she had played an active role in promoting amateur tournaments for women. In the case of Mercedes, although she did not learn to play until her early thirties, she had ample resources (time and money) to invest in developing her skills. Like Laura, Mercedes was known both within and beyond her club because she helped promote golf events for women. In addition, her husband was

---

7. The phrase Mercedes used to describe what the man had said was, "*Por qué no se van con el resto de las viejas.*" The word *vieja* is a slang term used to refer to a woman in Mexico. It is literally translated as "old woman" but is also used to talk about younger women. The word *vieja* encompasses the condescending meaning conveyed by the informal English term "chick."

an important figure in her club. When she described the apology offered by the rude golfer on the course, Mercedes added, "The man knew that my husband was part of the board [in the club]," implying that he knew he could get in trouble if he did not apologize.

These women had enough capital in its multiple forms (economic, social, and cultural, understanding the latter not in the academic sense but as the acquisition of playing skills) to have a certain degree of success when they fought to modify the gender-based dynamics that affected them. In spite of their resources, however, the success these women achieved was always fragile because it threatened to thoroughly disrupt a neatly organized space divided along clear gender lines (Massey 1994). The visibility of women who can keep up with male players, who do not rely on the knowledge of caddies, who can hit the ball with precision and strength, and who have a decent chance of defeating men represents a threat to the organization of "natural" gender hierarchies and the hegemonic masculinity that underpins these ideas.

The Limits of Resistance

While I was in the process of transcribing the interviews and analyzing the ethnographic data for this book, I constantly wondered why women did not come together to fight against the hegemonic masculinity that kept them in a dominated position. The answer to my question emerged unexpectedly in snippets spread throughout the interviews. My conversation with Patricia is a good example. Like most of the women I interviewed, she complained about the unfair restrictions on playing time that women experienced. She talked extensively about men not respecting women in the golf world and lamented that gender-based playing time policies were extremely frustrating because they did not take an individual's playing skills into consideration. Patricia repeated a comment I had heard from other women: "I am better than many of the men who play in the early mornings."

To validate her argument about gender discrimination, Patricia shifted our conversation to the topic of women in professional golf. She referred to Lorena Ochoa to demonstrate that women were capable of becoming outstanding golfers. At the same time, however, she belittled most other professional female players saying, "Have you followed the female professional league? Most of the players are lesbians. They look like men— have you seen their arms [she opened one of her hands around her arm, suggesting that professional players' arms were too muscular]?" She then reassured me that Lorena Ochoa was not a lesbian. Patricia did not see the connection between the unfair treatment she and other women experienced in golf clubs, based on a set of traditional gender norms and expectations, and her ridicule of professional players who did not conform to the traditional upper-class feminine physical ideals of slimness and delicacy (Mears 2011) and an overall heterosexual expectation (Wolter 2010).

Multiple scholars have coined terms to capture social dynamics in which the oppressed internalized the arguments used by the oppressor to justify unfair social relations. Marx's idea of false consciousness (1970 [1846]), DuBois's the veil (1999 [1903]), Fanon's inferiority complex (2008), and Bourdieu's symbolic violence (2001) are concepts that describe how the excluded sometimes explain their own exclusion in the terms set up by the dominant. These concepts do not seek to blame the oppressed for their oppression. Instead, they aim to explain that the efficacy of power resides in its capacity to convince the powerless of their own inadequacy, deficiency, uncivility, and scarcity. Persuaded of the legitimacy of the unfair treatment, the oppressed do not challenge the condition but contribute to its reproduction. The example presented in the above paragraph dovetails with the essence of these concepts. The derogatory comment Patricia made about professional female players, who do not follow traditional gender norms, closely follows the arguments many men expressed to justify the exclusion of women—including Patricia—from prime time. In both cases, a narrow definition of the role and appearance women must have in society were used to disparage and subordinate them. This example illustrates how some upper-middle- and upper-class women have internalized a view of themselves that is strongly shaped by hegemonic masculinity.

A second hint that shows the power of hegemonic masculinity in preventing women from unite and protest the discrimination all of them experience appeared in the existing division between working and notworking women. As mentioned above, the percentage of working women is smaller among club members than among the general population in Mexico. Describing her own club, Claudia remarked, "Most women here [in the club] do not work; they are housewives. We [salaried women] are about a third of all women in the club." She later added,

It's sad, but many of the [non-working] women here in the club look down on us [working women]; they are rude. [. . .] Years ago, when I joined the club, some of the older female players invited me to come to the cafeteria with them after I finished playing, but I couldn't because I work. I cannot stay to play cards, plan the next social event, and help with charitable stuff. I work. After I had been invited two or three times, but didn't go, they stopped inviting me. After that, I heard them making rude comments about me.

Claudia explained that non-working women organized events at times they knew working women like her would not be able to attend and then complained that the latter group did not contribute to the social life of the club. I asked the other women about this issue, but only Patricia acknowledged any tension. She divulged, "I don't have friends among the women who spend a lot of their time at the club," referring to the non-working women who invested a large part of their time socializing with other non-working women in the club. The rest of the women I interviewed said that they were unaware of any conflict. It is unclear whether they were genuinely unaware or simply did not want to address what seemed to be a thorny subject. This type of avoidance would be particularly understandable because these women were extensively involved in the organization of women-only amateur tournaments, and the participation of all female club members was very important to these contests. In contrast, Patricia and Claudia were not involved in the organization of tournaments for women; their primary interest was in their own careers.

These examples further illustrate the paradoxical relationship between privilege and gender. The class mechanisms and principles that benefit women club members vis-à-vis racialized lower-class women and men also limit their opportunities to adopt unconventional gender identities and practices, such as having their own careers or adopting unorthodox feminine looks. Ostrander (2010:152) reached the same conclusion in her analysis of upper-class women in the United States, noting that it is not in upper-class women's best interest "to challenge their gender-subordinated position, for to do so would seem to challenge the superiority of their class and the advantages that come from it." The paradoxical situation becomes clearer when looking at the work of Zweigenhaft and Domhoff (2006), who argued that the limited number of female corporate executives may be linked to women's limitations to access elite golf clubs in the United States. In other words, the same mechanisms that benefit women golfers, vis-à-vis racialized lower classes, also disadvantage them in relation to their male peers.

However, in Mexico, the conflict of interest did not preclude some women from challenging some gender norms—Laura and Mercedes fought for their right to play during prime time and work even though they had a comfortable economic situation. In addition, all of the golfers I interviewed noted that the enormous success of Lorena Ochoa had led to a growing number of women taking up the sport. Although these transformations are important, they do not suggest a linear progression toward the abolition of hegemonic masculinity. As Nora concluded, "I feel that things [related to gender inequality] are changing in golf, well, not at the pace we [women] would like to see. Change has been very slow." The slow change that Nora perceives is based on the uneven ways in which gender norms and identities are internalized, creating multiple degrees of challenging and passive personalities. In other words, whereas some women decide to fight back against gender inequalities, some others prefer to maintain the status quo.

Conclusion

This chapter describes the paradoxical position women occupy in the affluent world of golf in Mexico. These women were like most men at the clubs in that their class and racial identities granted them a higher status than most women and men in the middle and particularly lower classes. The chapter includes multiple examples of female golfers having access to the labor of workers both inside and outside the club, including caddies, chauffeurs, and domestic servants. The large class differences between women golfers and workers was manifested in the way they talked to each other. While women could use first names to refer to workers, the latter always used courtesy and professional titles when addressing these women. However, the class and racial elements that granted women an advantaged position in society disappeared when they interacted with fellow men inside the club. In these cases, a class-based form of hegemonic masculinity relegated women to a second-class position.

As Connell and Messerschmidt (2005:832) noted, hegemonic masculinity is not just a set of expectations, but also a set of practices that permits "men's dominance over women to continue." At the clubs I visited, these practices were both spatial and temporal. Women were relegated to the less crowded, and less desirable, time slots. Further, women were regarded as inherently weak players, a notion that was spatially reinforced by the tee boxes from where they started playing. The conventional rules prevented women from accessing the main bar, which made their playing skills—one of the most important assets a golfer possesses—nearly invisible to most of their fellow men golfers. Despite women's class and racial privilege, hegemonic masculinity subordinated them to men inside golf clubs.

Some women, however, successfully challenged one of these practices, gaining the right to play during prime time. Nevertheless, this victory seemed fragile as men often challenged women to return to their "natural" place. The men's hostility was a reaction to the (potential for) spatial chaos that these women introduced into the masculine space—the presence of highly skilled and defiant women threatens the organization of gender hierarchies by showing the inconsistency of men's athletic superiority. Paradoxically, women's ability to reduce gender inequality was hindered by the same principles that privileged them in the first place: changing the norms and principles that produced inequality could potentially transform the class, racial, and gender hierarchies that situated women club members in a highly privileged position.

Epilogue—Privilege

They are not going to play golf anymore. The upper-ranked civil servants at the SAT [the Mexican equivalent of the Internal Revenue Service] play golf all the time with the executives of the corporations that they should be demanding to pay taxes—yes, it happens. Do you think members of the SAT are going to tax them [after playing golf together]? [. . .] This is the end, there are no more privileges.

—ANDRÉS MANUEL LÓPEZ OBRADOR (Hernández, López, and Guerrero 2018)

THE INTRODUCTION OF this book discussed how the studying up field has generated limited interest among academics who study Mexico (see Appendix for extended analysis). The topic of social privilege, however, has sparked great interest among the broader Mexican public in recent years. The 2018 presidential elections in Mexico, for example, demonstrated that the average citizen was eager to discuss and debate many of the broader issues analyzed in this book. During the campaign, candidates and their supporters constantly referenced the intertwined connections between class, race, gender, and privilege in the form of denunciations, criticisms, accusations, and insults. Journalists and political commentators also contributed to the discussion of privilege as they condemned, disputed, and rebuked politicians for their comments and points of view. In this Epilogue, I show that social privilege has played a central role in recent public debates in this country.

On July 1, 2018, Mexicans held a crucial election—the results determined nine gubernatorial races (out of 32 states), the composition of both the federal chamber of representatives and the senate, and, most importantly, the next president of the country. National attention focused heavily on the presidential race, in part because the left-leaning candidate Andres Manuel Lopez Obrador, popularly known as AMLO, was making his third consecutive attempt to gain the presidency and the polls showed him with a commanding lead (his two previous unsuccessful efforts ended in highly contested results). In December 2017, AMLO became the center of a controversy concerning the connection between privilege, class, and racial dynamics. He publicly belittled his two main political rivals, declaring to the press that these politicians "don't know anything about the country, they are always indoors [away from the working classes], they have a pale complexion, they are *puxhos* [. . .] and *pirrurris.*" The latter term is associated with inherited wealth, elitism, arrogance, and spite for the lower classes; reproaching someone as a *pirrurris* represents a denunciation of class privilege (see Chapters 2 and 3 for an expanded analysis of relation between class and privilege).

Significantly, however, AMLO's accusation also incorporated a reference to race. In his comment, he associated the snobbish attitude of his opponents with not only their undeserved wealth but also their whiteness, which he emphasized with his use of the terms pale and *puxhos* (in his native southern state of Tabasco, the latter term refers to people with a white skin tone). The local audience clearly understood the racialized nature of AMLO's accusation. The following day, *El Universal*, a leading Mexican newspaper, covered the event in an article entitled, "Ricardo Anaya and José Meade, 'White Pirrurris,' Declares AMLO." Despite Mexico's national ideology of mestizaje, the newspaper did not explain why a racialized term—white—would be used to attack someone in an ostensibly raceless nation (Chapters 4 and 5 further examine the topic of race and racialization).

Immediately after the comment was made, Ricardo Anaya, one of the criticized candidates, accused AMLO of inciting racial hatred:

> AMLO's recent attacks on me are very dangerous; It is not only the issue of accusing me of being a *pirrurris*, but the insulting comment that I have white skin because I am never out in the sun. I believe talking about skin color brings up a divisive issue—this type of thing leads to discrimination. He should refrain from using this racist language. (Redaccion 2017)

Political pundits also chimed in. Leo Zuckermann, a well-known political commentator and a university professor, wrote an editorial entitled "The Rhetoric of 'We the Browns against You the Whites'" in the newspaper *Excelsior*, in which he criticized the remarks of the leftist politician. Zuckermann asked,

If AMLO wins the presidency, what type of country are we going to have? Would he promote unity and harmony or class and racial confrontation? [. . .] Up to the present, AMLO has typically exploited class polarization, the *poor* against the *rich*. Now, he just entered a dangerous road: racial rhetoric.

In the piece, Zuckermann acknowledged a recent study published by the National Institute of Statistics and Geography (INEGI 2016), which found a significant correlation between skin color and socioeconomic position in Mexico such that lighter skin tone correlates with higher status and greater wealth while darker skin tone correlates with lower status and less wealth. After sarcastically identifying himself as a white person, Zuckermann argued that the way to solve the problem (the correlation between skin color and socioeconomic position) was not to promote "divisive" racial rhetoric but rather to create more opportunities among the lower classes, those with darker skin tones. He ended the piece by asking, "Is it worth inciting racial hatred to win the presidency?"

This was not the first instance in which the complex relationship between class and racial dynamics surfaced in the political sphere. In 2014, AMLO founded a political party that he named Movimiento de Regeneración Nacional (Movement of National Regeneration). The party's acronym is MORENA, which, according to the *Dictionary of Spanish of Mexico*, means "someone of a darkened white skin or a brown skin tone." The name of AMLO's political party seemed to play with two ideas. First, morena (or moreno in its masculine form) insinuates a reference to the skin tones commonly found in Mexico, particularly among the middle and lower classes (Nutini 1997, 2008; Nutini and Isaac 2010). Second, the term implies a reference to the name of the Virgin of Guadalupe, the national saint of Mexico. Guadalupe is popularly called "the Morena Virgin" or "The Morena." Under both meanings, the name of the political party embraces the racialization of class logic, although in a reversal of the usual form by inspiring a feeling of pride in being moreno.

AMLO and other candidates associated with MORENA adopted a political discourse that situated corruption, inequality, and poverty as Mexico's critical problems. However, unlike the ubiquitous political narrative that blames poverty for the country's miserable situation and addresses corruption in abstract terms, AMLO directly identified the economic and political elites—who are, in general, white(r)—as the root of the problem. In his narrative, in recent decades the neoliberal state had almost exclusively benefited the dominant classes—the white *pirrurris*. The mainstream mass media regarded AMLO's rhetoric as naïve, delusional, and radical, but the narrative resonated strongly with the electorate. Almost every poll indicated that MORENA's candidates were leading their respective races.

A few months after AMLO's comment, on February 9, 2018, during a political rally in the southern state of Tabasco, Enrique Ochoa Reza, the leader of the Institutional Revolutionary Party (PRI), lashed out against former members of his party who had recently joined MORENA. Ochoa Reza mockingly said: "*A esos prietos desde aquí les decimos, les vamos a demostrar, son prietos pero ya no aprietan* [To those *prietos*, let us be very clear, we are going to show you, you are *prietos*, but you are worthless]." The last part of his comment, "*ya no aprietan*," has a strongly gendered connotation. The expression is a vulgar insult aimed at women that suggests their bodies—particularly their genitals—have become flaccid and sexually unattractive. In an abstract sense, the phrase degrades women by equating the alleged condition of being sexually undesirable ("*no apretar*") with being worthless. This offensive expression emerges from the perspective of hegemonic masculinity, suggesting that older women are less sexually attractive and that when women lose their sexual attractiveness, they become irrelevant (see Chapter 6 for an extended analysis of hegemonic masculinity). The fact that Ochoa Reza referred to former male members of his party in the same comment implied that these men were emasculated and useless. Unsurprisingly, this gender-based insult was deeply entwined with a racialized innuendo.

As Chapter 4 explains, the term *prieto* refers to dark brown or black skin tone. In popular language, however, the term is used not only to suggest skin color but also to indicate that someone is out of his or her racial place. Ochoa Reza's insult seems to touch on both meanings of the term. He clearly used the word *prieto* as a synonym of *moreno*, indicating skin color, but he also connected darker skin to being out of place. The comment suggested that the "*prietos*" had joined a political party that was above their subordinate position, implying that dark-skinned people cannot determine their political allegiances themselves but rather should follow orders. The reaction on social media was immediate and strong. People accused Ochoa Reza of being classist, racist, and sexist. Hours later, the PRI leader apologized for the remark via his Twitter account, insisting that he never meant to attack people based on their skin color. He emphasized the point by noting that he also had a brown skin tone "of which I feel very proud." Despite his apology, the comment was widely discussed in the mass media, most of the times in highly critical ways.

The well-known political journalist Sanjuana Martínez, for instance, addressed the incident in an editorial entitled "Prietos, Racism, and Classism in Mexico" in the online newspaper *Sin Embargo*. Her article referred to the INEGI study (2016) referenced in Zuckermann's piece that found a significant correlation between skin color and socioeconomic position. Martínez also discussed a recent study, "Discrimination in Mexico," that concluded that darker skin tone is a primary basis of prejudice in the country. She argued:

> Ochoa Reza's racist expression matches the image of his party's presidential candidate Jose Antonio Meade, who is white, has Irish origins, has a foreign last name, studied at a private [and expensive] university in Mexico and has a Ph.D. from Yale University. Obviously, Ochoa Reza insulted the "prietos" because his candidate is white and rich.

The article concludes,

> If the PRI excludes those regarded as prietos, it is excluding 90 percent of the Mexican population. This way of thinking brings us back to the caste regime that for three centuries [the colonial period, 1521–1821] left deep social wounds that are still reflected in today's racism, in everyday exclusion and discrimination, in the words "naco," "indio," "mestizo," and "prieto."

Notably, Martínez referenced both class-based and racialized reproaches in her criticisms of Ochoa Reza's comment.

Political rivals were even quicker to use a combination of class-based and racialized arguments to attack one another in the unregulated universe of social media. These insults, however, changed according to the perceived privilege of the person issuing the insult. For example, Juan Pedro Vera Martínez, a mid-ranking politician in the coastal state of Colima, used his personal social media account to remark that supporters of his MORENA-backed opponent would not need a pen to mark their ballots on the day of the election, saying, "You can use the dirt in your elbows to mark your preference" (Redacción 2018). His comment implied that only uneducated and destitute people who worked in the fields or on construction sites—and who lacked access to running water for a shower—would be voting for the MORENA candidate. Meanwhile, AMLO's supporters also incorporated a racialized class logic into the insults they launched against their political opponents, although in the converse way. Terms such as *blanquito* ("little white"), *sangre azul* ("blue blood"), *pirrurris* ("inherited wealth"), and *riquín* ("rich") were used interchangeably to criticize their political adversaries. In short, MORENA supporters accused their political opponents of being too privileged to understand the Mexican reality.

On July 1, 2018, AMLO won the presidency by a landslide, receiving 53 percent of the popular vote, a 30 percent margin over the second-place finisher. In addition, MORENA became the leading force in both the federal chamber of representatives and the senate and won five of the nine gubernatorial races. A whole host of factors, including the high level of criminality, the persistence of corruption, meager economic growth, economic insecurity, and the incompetence of the political elite, likely played a role in AMLO's victory. However, the overwhelming triumph of a political candidate who openly criticized the intertwined relationship between the socioeconomic hierarchy and racialized principles and repeatedly blasted the economic elite for their excessive privilege suggests that a significant portion of the Mexican population seek to disrupt (or at least acknowledge as problematic) the strong connection between class, race, and privilege. Further, the strong reaction generated by Ochoa Reza's sexist comment showed that some Mexicans are aware of the relationship between privilege and gender. Yet the continued underrepresentation of women in positions of power and even more tragic the alarming high rates of feminicides reflects the persistent ability of hegemonic masculinity to tilt power in favor of men in this contry. While the outcome of this political struggle remains to be seen, the analysis presented in this book offers insights into the future of the conflict.

The extreme inequality in the distribution of resources in Mexico has created strong resentment against the dominant groups. This anger is based on both the excessive material benefits the upper classes have accumulated and the paradoxical way in which racial perceptions are deployed to erect social barriers in a purportedly raceless nation. This reaction does not mean that there is a coherent political movement to dismantle the system that privileges dominant groups, just as there is not a campaign to ban golf in Mexico. Instead, the strong political reaction against the excessive benefits of the upper classes—including the privileged space of golf, as indicated in the quote at the beginning of the

Epilogue—shows that power, domination, and privilege are social relations that are part of a constant struggle in every society. Although those at the top of the socioeconomic pyramid have a disproportionate influence on the distribution of resources and the crafting of class, racial, and gender narratives, the elite is not a unified block, and diversity within this group paves the way for social change.

Throughout the process of crafting this book, more than one person has asked, "So what?" followed by, "As long as people have amassed their fortunes legally, why should we care about wealthy people?" The answer to the questions is linked to a persistent trend of wealth concentration benefiting the upper classes all over the world in the last forty years (Ratcliff 2019; Piketty 2014). There is a growing consensus on two issues among scholars examaining this process. First, high levels of wealth concentration produces dysfunctional societies (Elizondo Mayer-Serra 2017; Collier 2018; Esquivel 2015c; Lindsey and Teles 2017). Second, poverty cannot be understood as an isolated element but rather must be conceptualized as the integral flip side of wealth concentration (Cattani 2009; Donaldson and Poynting 2007; Reeves 2017; Friedman and Laurison 2019). Hence, this book represents a renewed "call to arms" for social scientists interested in studying privilege. It is necessary, even urgent, to show that privilege and the lack of privilege—together with the interwoven influences of class, race, and gender—are two sides of the same coin. We cannot understand impoverished groups without paying attention to the other face of the same coin, the privileged.

An Un/Ethical Approach

It is my own view that a lack of knowledge about elites contributes to obscuring and therefore maintaining their position in society, a better understanding of methodologies for elite study may also play a part in challenging that position.

—SUSAN OSTRANDER (1993:7)

I began researching golf and golf clubs in Mexico after learning that during the economic crisis of 1982, the Mexican state had targeted a golf club to stop the rebellion of the local upper class. I discovered that the incident had occurred at one of the four most exclusive clubs in the country, which charges a one-time membership fee of over $120,000. After I decided to study golf clubs, I realized that it was not feasible to use the methods social scientists have traditionally employed to gain access to groups they want to study—joining a club to meet people and build social relationships (Wacquant 2006), using the status that higher education generates among communities with limited education to gain initial acceptance (Goffman 2015), and working alongside the focal group to capture their life experiences (Gomberg-Muñoz 2011). I lacked the economic resources to pay for a club membership, and my status as a graduate student was not valued enough to obtain a type of honorary membership in the golf community. I considered caddying, but in most Mexican clubs, especially the more prestigious ones, prospective caddies must undergo a vetting process.

As I considered these methodological constraints, I realized that my goal of studying golf by becoming an embodied researcher, a social scientist who physically engages in the subject he wants to explain intellectually, would be more difficult than I had originally imagined. My own class background, situated near the boundary between the middle and the lower-middle class, meant that before starting this research I knew almost nothing about golf. My previous understanding of the sport was based on nothing more than stereotypical film scenes in which wealthy individuals discuss top-secret information on the course, TV series featuring shots of a verdant golf course and affluent characters socializing in a country club–style setting, and several rounds of mini-golf played at a beach resort.

I decided to start the project by learning as much as possible about the sport (Durkheim 1982[1895]). I traveled to Scotland to visit the most iconic golf sites in Britain (I discuss the privilege implied in this statement later in this chapter); learned more about the Professional Golfers' Association of America (PGA), the professional golf league in the United States; read about the history of the game; and perused contemporary golf magazines. The office of research at the university I attended at the time reluctantly gave me a grant of £100 ($140) to take a short introductory course and pay for four visits to a golf range (a *tiradero*, as some golfers in Mexico called these training sites). One year later, after an internal audit, the new dean of research asked me to provide further explanation of the suspicious grant of £100 that the university had invested in my golfing skills. In spite of all my preparation— taking the introductory course, visiting the golf range a few times, and playing at in-expensive courses six times—my golf skills remained mediocre. Hitting a small ball with a big-headed club is much more difficult than it sounds or than it looks on TV.

Britain is home to inexpensive municipal public golf courses, which might seem to suggest that the game is accessible to all. However, my own experience indicates otherwise. As a graduate student, my income was similar to that of the working class. Only a few courses were affordable for members of the working class in the city where I lived, and all of them were on the outskirts of town. Each trip to the closest inexpensive course required an initial 20-minute bike ride carrying my old, heavy golf bag on my back, followed by a 10-minute train ride and another 15-minute bike ride. The public course I visited lacked any leisure facilities beyond the actual course (e.g., no clubhouse, cafeteria, or bar). A vending machine stocked with candy, cookies, and soda was the only hint this might be a place to meet up with friends and relax. Because I played with a heavy set of old iron clubs and a leather bag (the cheapest available options), I often left three or four clubs at home to reduce the weight of the bag. During every trip I made to the course, I thought of a state-ment I had read in the August 22, 1902, issue of *Golf Illustrated*: "Golf is not a poor man's game."

In this Appendix I describe how I navigated class barriers to gain access to golfers and golf clubs in Mexico, paying particular attention to those instances in which I did not fully disclose the motives underlying the research. For example, I some-times presented the project as an analysis of the relationship between business and golf and other times answered affirmatively when players asked the inevitable ques-tion of whether I was a golfer. These instances might suggest that I deliberately attempted to deceive participants during the fieldwork, which would be unethical by traditional standards. However, here I present a more nuanced explanation of my methods by situating the research in the broader context of the "studying up" literature, and from this position I join the call to shift the common understanding of ethical/unethical practices.

THE BEGINNING

I decided not to conduct research at the Mexican golf club that originally inspired my interest in golf (the club targeted by the government during the economic crisis of 1982) because I had no contacts in the area, even among the working class. Instead, I used my social capital—trust embedded in social networks—to contact golfers in Mexico City, where I grew up. Originally, I established contact with three golfers. Only one of these early connections was part of my social circle before I had entered a graduate program at a British university. The other two contacts were established when I socialized with fellow Mexican students enrolled in British and other European institutions. With the assistance of these three individuals, I eventually extended the research to include 58 participants.

The first person I contacted was Sergio, a man in his late forties who was married to a woman in my social circle. I called him to request an interview, explaining that I was doing a research project on class and social networks. The words "networks" and "class" made Sergio quite anxious, and he proceeded to ask several clarifying questions, including "What do you mean by networks?" and "How exactly is class related to your research?" After I had offered a long explanation, he finally agreed to be interviewed, but only after claiming that "there are no social networks in golf clubs." As Ostrander (1993) and Hirsch (1995) suggested, Sergio's concerns and anxiety might have arisen from the fact that I used the language of social sciences rather than his own language—the language of the upper-middle class—to explain the project. However, it would have been quite a challenge to use the expressions of affluent individuals to explain that I was interested in understanding how class and privilege were manifested in daily interactions.

I interviewed Sergio in a pleasant café with mid-range prices that was located on his route home from work. We both ordered coffee and chatted for about 35 minutes. I started by asking two questions: "How do you define a golfer?" and "What do you think are the most important transformations golf has experienced in your lifetime?" I then shifted to the issue of class by asking, "Why is golf popular among business people?" Whereas he provided relatively brief answers to the first two questions, Sergio discussed the third question extensively, using a multitude of concrete examples. At the end of the interview, I asked him if he could put me in contact with other golfers; he said he would try but that his friends were very busy. In the end, he did not pass along contact information for any other players.

The second participant was Fernando. As described in the vignette at the beginning of Chapter 3, Fernando was a friend of an acquaintance I had made in England. In this case, I purposely decided to omit the word "class" when I introduced my project. Instead, I explained that my research was about social networks, business, and golf. Fernando immediately accepted my request for an interview, asking if we could meet at a restaurant near his workplace. The place he suggested was ideal for me because it was located near a metro station. Our interaction was quite amiable until he realized that I commonly moved about by public transportation (which is a strong indicator of class in Mexico City). He was not rude, but his once-lengthy answers became stilted. Despite having tacitly agreed to help me find other golfers, Fernando never answered my calls or replied to my messages. My own socioeconomic position in the lower-middle/middle class might have alienated him. As Gaztambide-Fernández and Howard argue, the status of the researcher is "always implied in their ability to access other elites" (2012:292).

My third informant was a close friend of an acquaintance I made in England. Daniel, a golfer in his early thirties, did not belong to a golf club himself but had friends at multiple clubs because he often participated in amateur tournaments. When I contacted him by phone, I purposely presented my project as a study about business and golf. He immediately agreed to be interviewed based on the trust established through having a mutual acquaintance. We met at the conference room in his office, a modern corporate building in an upscale neighborhood in the northern part of Mexico City. At the beginning of the interview, I spent about 10 minutes talking about London and describing my trips to iconic golf courses in Scotland (which I visited for research purposes but did not play). My interview with Daniel lasted an hour and a half, and at the end I asked him if he could put me in contact with other golfers. A few days later, he sent me an email with contact information for three of his friends who had agreed to talk to me. The contrast between the first two interviews and the third one made it clear that the "management of my identification [was] an important aspect of my research strategy" (Hoffman 1980:47).

Rafael, a golfer in his early sixties who had played for over 30 years in two different clubs, was one of the three contacts Daniel put me in touch with and became a key figure in the research project. As I had in Daniel's interview, I began by offering vivid descriptions of my time in London and the "majestic" golf courses I had visited in Scotland. Rafael found my project on business and golf amusing and intriguing and decided to help me as much as he could. When I asked him for contact information for other golfers at the end of the interview, he immediately picked up his phone, pressed the speaker option, and began to call his friends as I sat across from him. During each call, after greeting his friend, he exclaimed, "You won't believe what a researcher in England is working on . . . business and golf!" and then introduced me. One of the people Rafael called was Emilio, the editor of an important golf magazine.

Interestingly, I was already aware of the magazine and knew Emilio was the editor. Using the telephone number on the magazine's website, I had attempted to contact Emilio four times in the previous weeks. Each time, his secretary asked me to leave my contact information and a message and indicated that Emilio would get back to me as soon as possible. He never did. After greeting Emilio, Rafael told him about the "researcher in England" who was working on "business and golf" and said, "You two should meet." Emilio responded, "Hugo, you're the person who's been calling me, aren't you?" I replied in a non-confrontational tone, "Yes I am, but your secretary told me that you were out of the office." Emilio immediately exclaimed, "I'm sorry Hugo, I didn't know you were a friend of Rafael. Why didn't you start there [saying that I was Rafael's friend]? When do you want to come to the office?"

This was not the first time a golfer's secretary had impeded my attempts to communicate with a potential interviewee. Indeed, this type of interaction was the norm. My experience with Emilio highlighted the importance of making my social capital visible as soon as possible in the process of negotiating an interview. When I contacted Arturo, a golfer in his early fifties who was an active promoter of amateur tournaments, his secretary asked me to leave a message because he was not in the office at that moment (mid-morning on a weekday). I found it difficult to explain to the secretary why I wanted to talk to Arturo, so I told her I would call him later that same day. She insisted on taking a message, claiming that her boss would probably be out of the office in the afternoon. I responded that, in that case, I would just call him tomorrow. The secretary swiftly replied that he would probably be out of the office tomorrow and more than likely the rest of the week as well, saying that she was not sure when he would be at the office again. The best way to contact him was to leave a message, she reiterated. I left a message in which I clearly mentioned who had given me Arturo's contact information and then told the receptionist "Please tell him that I am a friend of X." I called Arturo a few days later, and this time the secretary put my call through immediately. He apologized, saying, "I'm sorry that I didn't take your call the other day. My secretary didn't recognize your name. You should have started by telling her that you were a friend of X."

Based on this type of interaction, I realized that the moment my social capital—with all its class implications—became evident to a golfer, a basic form of trust materialized, allowing me to connect with a potential interview subject. These early interviews also made it clear that it was important for me to emphasize my cultural capital by talking about my academic degrees, particularly the part obtained in Europe. The fact that I had graduated from a British institution played an even greater role in the "management of my identification" (Hoffman 1980:47). I spent the first moments of most interviews with golfers conveying my cultural capital by mentioning the British and European institutions that I had visited for workshops, conferences, and other types of academic meetings. These conversations often evolved into an exchange of anecdotes and vivid memories about places that the interviewee and I had both toured in Europe or about trips other golfers had taken in the region. These interactions shifted some participants' racialized perceptions of me—I became whiter in their eyes as they realized we had common life experiences (see Chapter 4 for a detailed discussion of the racialization of class).

Not every interaction generated further contacts, however. My capital—in its multiple forms—was simply not sufficient to allow me to connect with certain golfers. This was the case in my extremely short "interview" with Omar. I had contacted him at the beginning of a golf tournament after one of the event's organizers informed me that he was the most important corporate executive playing in the tournament that day. I approached Omar and told him that I was a researcher who had been invited to the tournament by the organizing company and that I hoped to interview him to talk about the relationship between business and golf. Omar agreed be interviewed but asked me to look for him after the end of the event (six hours later). When the tournament was over, I approached him and again asked for an interview. He graciously agreed and sat down with me at the 19th hole. He answered my first three questions rapidly, in about three and a half minutes, and as I was trying to rephrase the questions so he would elaborate, he promptly excused himself, saying, "I am sorry but I need to catch up with someone else." He then moved to the adjacent table and began chatting enthusiastically with other golfers about the tournament they had just played. In this case, I did not possess social capital that would allow me to reach out to Omar via a common acquaintance or friend, and my cultural capital—including its racialized component—was only enough to create a momentary bond of trust.

ETHICS

From the beginning, I struggled with the question of how to ethically conduct research among wealthy individuals. Like any other researcher in the social sciences, I had been trained in the best practices concerning ethnographic and interview projects (Irwin 2006; Lassiter 2005; Murphy and Dingwall 2001, 2007). I was aware of the need for respect, consideration for privacy, use of a consent form, and allowing participants access to the results, as well as other ethical practices researchers must implement when studying human subjects (ASA 1999). I also knew that in certain circumstances a research project could become a highly exploitative endeavor (Paris and Winn 2013; Simpson 2007). Therefore, my desire to gain access to affluent golfers to study privilege was intermixed with a set of ethical considerations about the project.

Before starting my fieldwork, I contacted a handful of scholars who had previously conducted research on wealthy groups in Mexico to ask about their experiences. They described the difficulties they had faced and offered advice about how to salvage challenging situations (for an international discussion, see Aguiar and Schneider 2016; Donaldson and Poynting 2007, 2013; Hay and Muller 2012; Pierce 1995; Yeager and Kram 1990). Although they were encouraging and offered some valuable advice, one of the scholars candidly stated that he had chosen to adopt a historical approach to his research because he found it impossible to gain access to upper-class sites and people. Another explained that he had developed indirect methods to study corporate executives because "wealthy people don't want outsiders to peek inside their world." A third researcher noted that the best studies in the field usually included members of the upper class among the research team (for similar cases in Portugal and the United States, see, respectively, Baltzell 1985; Marcus and Mascarenhas 2005). My conversations with these researchers revealed why, despite the value of interview-based and ethnographic research, most studies of the dominant classes in Mexico are based on discourse analysis on public data and focus on institutional relations (Alba Vega 2001; Anzaldua and Maxfield 1987; Arriola 1991; Basañez 1990; Luna and Pozas 1993; Tirado 1994; Zabludovsky 2007).

While Khan maintained that "honesty is essential to ethnographic projects" (2010:202), my early encounters with golfers suggested that divulging my interest in class inequalities, gender segregation, and racial animosity would have required me to provide extensive clarification before starting each interview and, more importantly, would have provoked a certain level of anxiety among interviewees. This early assessment was reinforced during the interviews. Golfers often seemed self-conscious about making negative statements about others, especially fellow golfers (less so for statements about caddies). For example, club members commonly paused, as if carefully selecting their words, before making a belittling comment about a peer. I interpreted this recurrent act as a desire to offer a criticism but not paint a negative portrayal of their peers. Hence, a candid explanation of the connection between privilege, racial ideas, and social inequalities would have made most club members extremely self-conscious. Lastly, I worried that disclosing my goals would scare away underprivileged workers, who would likely fear being fired for speaking critically about golf and golfers. Given these constraints, the fieldwork represented a series of ethical dilemmas.

These considerations are recurring themes in the "study up" literature (Cattani 2009; Donaldson and Poynting 2007; Galliher 1980; Gaztambide-Fernández 2015; Ostrander 1993; Sherwood 2012; Sieber 1989). Scholars have repeatedly posed the question of how researchers should interpret the ethical considerations commonly employed in the social sciences, which were created to protect marginalized communities (Tuck 2009), when studying groups who hold a considerable amount of power. Based on this literature, I wondered whether my desire to explore social inequalities was sufficient justification for ignoring the disciplinary codes of ethics. Was my work deceptive and therefore unethical? Was it even possible for an outsider to conduct a critical study of privilege in Mexico by explicitly discussing inequalities with participants?

At first glance, it had seemed clear that my research project should adhere to the code of conduct expected in the discipline (ASA 1999), meaning I would inform all interviewees of the goals of the project. I began to wonder, however, whether the answers to the ethical dilemmas related to my research required a different set of considerations given that the broader aim of my work was to understand the extreme social and economic inequality in Mexico City—to discern how the city could have the second largest number of private helicopters per capita in the world (Quesada 2016) and 15 Mexicans could be on the *Forbes* list of billionaires, including one of the 10 wealthiest individuals in the world (Peterson-Withorn 2015), while at the same time the salaries of the city's workers were the lowest of all members of the OECD (2017) and almost half of the country's population lived in poverty (CONEVAL 2014).

UN/ETHICS

Social scientists have discussed ethical/unethical methods of studying powerful groups for a long time (Galliher 1980). Those who have advocated for conducting more research on these groups have argued that it is necessary to consider that the privileged are considerably different from average individuals (Domhoff 1967; Gaztambide-Fernández 2015; Gaztambide-Fernández and Howard 2012; Mills 1956; Sherwood 2012; Sieber 1989). As Sieber noted, " 'The powerful,' as a research population, are notably different from the typical research subject in many ways which are pertinent both to the justification for studying them and to the difficulties of studying them" (1989:1). This does not imply, however, that the desire to understand social inequalities justifies ignoring the rights, dignity, and worth of affluent individuals. No "study up" scholar has suggested that researchers should completely dismiss the code of ethics. Indeed, studies in this field commonly use pseudonyms, modify situations (e.g., jobs, locations), and obscure recognizable characteristics to maintain the anonymity and privacy of informants to the fullest extent possible.

These scholars have sought to refocus the debate by noting that the discussion of research ethics originated because many human subjects were powerless and marginalized, but affluent individuals fit neither of these descriptions. Gaztambide-Fernández offered one of the most recent arguments in the long debate about the ethics of "studying up," concluding that "in the context of studies about elites and the production of elite status as it is directly related to the production (and justification) of inequality, we need a different understanding of the ethics of representation" (2015:1141). Again, this is not to say that researchers should employ unethical methods, but rather that it is necessary for scholars in the field to develop what Gaztambide-Fernández (2015) called an "un/ethical" approach.

This un/ethical approach differs from an unethical attitude: the former "demands an examination of how a procedural concern with research ethics itself becomes a way to avoid the difficult question of when it is imperative to reveal what elite institutions [and wealthy individuals] are invested in keeping hidden" (Gaztambide-Fernández 2015:1141). An un/ethical approach seeks to lift the veil that an ethical code of research imposes on scholars and thus allow them to critically examine the way the upper strata contribute to the perpetuation of their own privileged positon (Sieber 1989). This approach shifts the focus of ethical concerns from the powerful subjects of the research to society's need to understand the mechanisms, patterns, and social elements that allow affluent groups to maintain their privilege. Adopting an un/ethical approach allows researchers to make visible the otherwise invisible mechanisms of privilege reproduction (Gaztambide-Fernández 2015). The possibility of illuminating these mechanisms in Mexico City resonated strongly with a handful of marginalized individuals in my research, who urged me to move beyond the common celebratory accounts of golf in Mexico.

On four different occasions, people at the bottom of the status hierarchy in the world of golf asked me to write a "true book" about this sport. The first request occurred near the end of an interview with a golf journalist who had covered the sport for several years. I asked him if he knew of any books about golf in Mexico, in hopes of finding sources that I had not yet identified. The journalist listed several books I was already aware of and then said, "There is still the need to write a less flattering history of golf [in Mexico]. Most of the authors are golfers themselves; they write for their buddies. I hope your work will contribute in a new direction." A similar appeal occurred during an interview with another journalist. When I asked him the same question about books, he named the books I was already familiar with and then added, "These books were written by club members or people who want to flatter golfers, because the style sells well and the writers know it will help them get other jobs. You have the opportunity to do something different."

The other two requests for a "true" account of golf came from caddies. When I interviewed caddies, I did not describe my work as research on business and golf but rather as a study of the recent history of the sport. I switched to this framing of the research to encourage caddies to talk in detail about their own perspectives and experiences working at these affluent sites. While I was unsure whether caddies would be put off by an accurate description of the project, I feared that their jobs might be jeopardized if golfers or someone at the administrative level became aware that caddies were talking about class, social inequalities, and privilege with an outsider. I used a purposely vague description to protect them from any possible retaliation. Like the journalists, two caddies urged me to take a more critical approach to the history of golf.

In the first case, a caddy in his mid-forties expressed excitement that I was investigating caddies' perspectives on golf. After I asked him why caddies do not become professional players, he said, "I like that you are doing this [research]. Nobody asks us our opinion about these issues and when a reporter does talk to us about this stuff, our words are never included in the newspaper article." After this statement, the caddy offered an extensive description of the structural problems caddies faced in their efforts to advance their careers. In the final instance, as I was expressing my gratitude to an older caddy for giving me an interview, he said emphatically,

I hope that you write a book about golf from the perspective of us [caddies]. We are the ones who really make this sport happen, but we are never included in the books [about golf]. In most books there is one mention [of caddies] here, another one there, but that's it.

This caddy's critique of books about golf in Mexico was a legitimate one. In the institutional books published on golf in Mexico, caddies were mentioned only in reference to their humorous nicknames, laughable anecdotes, and the charitable work members has done for them and were rarely described in terms of their work ethic, knowledge of the sport, or playing skills (Castellanos 1999; Horta 1989; Krauze, Moreno, and Speckman Guerra 2005; Morales y Favela 1996; Wray 2002; Wright 1938).

The un/ethical approach I used in this project is based on a central theme running throughout the "study up" literature. As Sieber explained, "The point of studying up is not to serve as a tool with which the powerful may manipulate to their advantage the public's perception of them. The point of studying up is precisely to penetrate that facade" (1989:3). Gaztambide-Fernández (2015) highlighted the role of the researcher within this approach, concluding that the researcher can only access privileged spaces as far as he brings with him a degree of privilege (my use of binary gendered language here is intentional). In other words, there is a degree of entanglement between the researcher and the privileged setting being researched.

PRIVILEGE

In the same way that social forces prevented people from moving freely inside golf clubs or kept them from seeing these sites at all, my own class, gender, and racialized identity played a fundamental role in allowing me to gain access to the clubs I researched. While my class origins hindered social contact on multiple occasions, especially among members of the upper class, my relatively extensive cultural capital (a class indicator), particularly my experience with British institutions, was a fundamental asset in the research process. One of the researchers who met with me to discuss his own research experiences and thoughts about "studying up" candidly explained, "The fact that you are studying outside [of Mexico] helps. If you were doing your doctoral studies at any public institution here [in Mexico], golfers would immediately be suspicious of you and your project." In Mexico (and other countries), there is a very strong association between class and the public or private status of institutions, organizations, and spaces, such that golfers would assume that someone attending a public university had a middle-class or lower-class background (for a detailed discussion of this issue, see Chapter 4).

Early in the research process, I realized that having an animated conversation about Britain, and Europe more generally, helped me generate a sense of rapport and trust with members of the upper-middle class and some members of the upper class. Specifically, my visits to iconic golf courses in Scotland (even though I only went for research purposes) and other European destinations allowed me to talk with club members about our "common" life experiences, and this commonality led people to make assumptions about my own class identity and views about society. Many club members articulated a feeling of common identity based on these shared experiences. As E. P. Thompson asserted, "Class happens when some men, as a result of common experiences (inherited or shared), feel and articulate the identity of their interests as between themselves, and as against other men whose interests are different from (and usually opposed to) theirs" (1963:9). Despite these shared experiences, however, as a dark-skinned individual I found myself in an ambiguous situation inside golf clubs and among golfers. On many occasions, I was the only dark-skinned person in a club who was not serving members, cleaning, or taking care of the space in some way, and my epidermal schema led people to doubt my status and position in this privileged world.

To adapt West and Zimmerman's (1987) famous phrase, whenever someone doubted my position, I found myself "doing class"—enacting or referring to markers that revealed my middle-class status, such as my role of "researcher" at a Western university or my ability to express ideas in language that denoted a high level of formal education (in a country where people, on average, complete only nine years of school, stopping after the equivalent of the first year of high school in the United States). I also purposely mentioned other golfers I had already interviewed, particularly those who were well known, to demonstrate my social capital. These actions not only reassured people that I inhabited an "acceptable" class position but also changed the way they perceived me racially. Notably, as someone who was socialized into the Mexican national myth of racial equality, it took me a relatively long time to coherently articulate the racial dynamics that were constantly at play among these privileged club members.

Despite my conscious commitment to "doing class," my lower-middle-/middle-class origins, including my cultural capital, dwindled in value and utility at the invisible but perceptible boundary between the upper-middle class and the upper class. The few contacts I made with members of the upper class produced amicable interactions but rarely led to introductions to other members of the same group. Despite constant requests, for example, I was never able to find a golfer who could or was willing to introduce me to golfers at one of the two clubs in Mexico City that charged more than $100,000 in membership fees. This situation emphasizes that the status of the researcher is "always implied in their ability to access other elites" (Gaztambide-Fernández and Howard 2012:292).

My class advantages and limitations were not the only elements that shaped the fieldwork process. I entered these clubs with a degree of gender privilege that was not initially visible to me. The influence of gender on every aspect of golf was something I did not immediately notice. After I had crossed the class barrier via an invitation from a club member, I easily walked into the 19th hole and sat down without being asked to leave. Indeed, some male golfers even invited me to play with them. The gender-based organization of the space was initially imperceptible to me. Over time, however, the gender order become visible as I heard innumerable arguments justifying the lack of women on the golf course. The extensive influence of gender finally became fully obvious when Claudia, a woman golfer, boldly argued that "women are discriminated against [in golf] by the fact of being women, there isn't any other reason."

Claudia's comment clarified the relationship between the masculine order that characterizes privileged sites and the lack of women at the golf clubs, helping me to finally make sense of some common patterns I had witnessed at these clubs; including a lack of women golfing during prime playing times, the absence of women at the 19th hole, and men's perception of female golfers in positions of power as "oddities." My male gender identity was fundamental to my ability to gain access to these sites but also obscured the practical ways in which hegemonic masculinity organized these privileged spaces. A female researcher studying golf in Mexico would likely have been forced to take a different approach (for example, see Kendall 2008; Sherwood 2012).

There is one final aspect of privilege that is necessary to address. In the current neoliberal era when academic posts, especially those in the social sciences, have been eliminated and defunded across the globe, holding a permanent academic position that allows me to write and publish an academic book examining privilege, is, paradoxically, its own form of privilege. In other words, my own status as an academic researcher, including all the advantages that come with this status, is connected to the broader patterns of privilege analyzed in this book (for a discussion of how class, gender, and racial privilege play a role in organizing academic institutions, see Ahmed 2012; Delgado 1984; Gutiérrez y Muhs et al. 2012; Tokarczyk and Fay 1993). The acknowledgment that my position as an academic who analyzes privilege is deeply intertwined with privilege itself does not extend to the cynical argument that privilege can never be fruitfully examined. Rather, this admission simply recognizes the complex way in which academic scholars can participate, in some cases unwittingly, in the reproduction of privilege.

CONCLUSION

To sum up, understanding the relationship between poverty and the concentration of wealth requires the development of a robust "studying up" literature. Yet this literature cannot be developed without corresponding methodological discussions. As Susan Ostrander asserted in the quote presented at the beginning of this Appendix, developing better methodologies for studying the elite will illuminate and challenge the way privileged groups have maintained their position in society.

References

Adler-Lomnitz, Larissa. 2014. *Networks and Marginality: Life in a Mexican Shantytown.* New York, NY: Elsevier Science.

Aguiar, Luis L. M., and Christopher J. Schneider. 2016. *Researching Amongst Elites: Challenges and Opportunities in Studying Up.* London, UK: Routledge.

Aguirre Beltrán, Gonzalo. 1946. *La Población Negra De México.* Mexico City, Mexico: Fondo de Cultura Económica.

Ahmed, Sara. 2012. *On Being Included: Racism and Diversity in Institutional Life.* Durham, NC: Duke University Press.

Alba Vega, Carlos. 2001. "Los Empresarios En La Transición Política Mexicana." Pp. 209–39 in *Caminos a La Democracia*, edited by R. Ortega Ortiz. Mexico City, Mexico: Colmex.

Alchian, Armen. July 13, 1977. "Of Golf, Capitalism and Socialism." *Wall Street Journal.* Vol. 190 (8), P. 28.

Alder Lomnitz, Larissa, and Marisol Pérez Lizaur. 1987. *A Mexican Elite Family, 1820–1980.* Princeton, NJ: Princeton University Press.

Alexander, Michelle. 2012. *The New Jim Crow: Mass Incarceration in the Age of Colorblindness.* New York, NY: The New Press.

AMAI (Asociación Mexicana de Agencias de Investigación de Mercado y Opinión Pública). 2018. "Nivel Socioeconómica AMAI 2018." AMAI.org. Retrieved June 1, 2018 (http://www.amai.org/nse/wp-content/uploads/2018/04/Nota-Metodolo%CC%81gico-NSE-2018-v3.pdf).

An, Minseok, and George H. Sage. 1992. "The Golf Boom in South Korea: Serving Hegemonic Interests." *Sociology of Sport Journal* 9(4):372–84.

Anderson, Elijah. 2011. *The Cosmopolitan Canopy: Race and Civility in Everyday Life.* New York, NY: W.W. Norton.

Andrisani, J. 2002. *Everything I Learned About People, I Learned from a Round of Golf.* Indianapolis, IN: Alpha.

Anzaldua, Ricardo, and Sylvia Maxfield, eds. 1987. *Governmnent and Pritvate Sector in Contemporary Mexico*. San Diego, CA: Center for U.S.-Mexican Studies, University of California Press.

Appelbaum, Nancy P., Anne S. Macpherson, and Karin A. Rosemblatt. 2003. *Race and Nation in Modern Latin America*. Chapel Hill, NC: University of North Carolina Press.

Arbena, Joseph L. 1991. "Sport, Development, and Mexican Nationalism, 1920–1970." *Journal of Sport History* 18(3):350–64.

Arceo-Gomez, Eva, and Raymundo Campos-Vázquez. 2014. "Race and Marriage in the Labor Market: A Discrimination Correspondence Study in a Developing Country." *American Economic Review* 104(5):376–80.

Arriola, Carlos. 1991. *Los Empresarios Y El Estado, 1970–1982*. Mexico City, Mexico: Miguel Angel Porrua.

Arzate Salgado, Jorge. 2005. *Pobreza Extrema En México: Evaluación Microsociológica*. Toluca, Mexico: UAEM, Facultad de Ciencias Políticas y Administración Pública.

ASA, American Sociological Association. 1999. *Code of Ethics*. Washington, DC: American Sociological Association.

Atkinson, Anthony, and Andrea Brandolini. 2014. "On the Identification of the Middle Class." Pp. 77–100 in *Income Inequality: Economic Disparities and the Middle Class in Affluent Countries*, edited by J. C. Gornick and M. Jäntti. Stanford, CA: Stanford University Press.

Auyero, Javier. 2012. *Patients of the State: The Politics of Waiting in Argentina*. Durham, NC: Duke University Press.

Babb, Sarah L. 2002. *Managing Mexico: Economist from Nationalism to Neoliberalism*. Princeton, NJ: Princeton University Press.

Badenhausen, Kurt 2012. "The World's Highest-Paid Athletes 2012." Forbes.com. Retrieved June 18, 2012 (https://www.forbes.com/sites/kurtbadenhausen/2012/06/18/mayweather-tops-list-of-the-worlds-100-highest-paid-athletes/#1f4d5ea35f66).

Badenhausen, Kurt 2013. "The World's Highest-Paid Athletes 2013." Forbes.com. Retrieved June 5, 2013 (https://www.forbes.com/sites/kurtbadenhausen/2013/06/05/the-worlds-highest-paid-athletes-2013-behind-the-numbers/#7359ed451eee).

Badenhausen, Kurt 2014. "The World's Highest-Paid Athletes 2014." Forbes.com. Retrieved June 11, 2014 (https://www.forbes.com/sites/kurtbadenhausen/2014/06/11/the-worlds-highest-paid-athletes-2014-behind-the-numbers/#16475f4478ed).

Badenhausen, Kurt. 2017. "The World's Highest-Paid Athletes 2017." Forbes.com. Retrieved June 15, 2017 (https://www.forbes.com/sites/kurtbadenhausen/2017/06/15/full-list-the-worlds-highest-paid-athletes-2017/#566d3679d583)

Baltzell, E. Digby. 1985. *Philadelphia Gentlemen: The Making of a National Upper Class*. Glencoe, IL: Free Press.

Barot, Rohit, and John Bird. 2001. "Racialization: the genealogy and critique of a Concept." *Ethnic and Racial Studies* 24(4):601–18.

Basañez, Miguel. 1990. *La Lucha Por La Hegemonía En México*. Mexico City, Mexico: Siglo XXI.

Boltvinik, Julio, and Susan Archer Mann. 2016. *Peasant Poverty and Persistence in the Twenty-First Century: Theories, Debates, Realities and Policies*. New York, NY: Zed Books.

Bourdieu, Pierre. 1983. "The Field of Cultural Production, Or: The Economic World Reversed." *Poetics* 12(3):11–56.

Bourdieu, Pierre. 1986a. "The Forms of Capital." Pp. 241–58 in *Handbook of Theory and Research for the Sociology of Education*, edited by J. G. Richardson. New York, NY: Greenwood Press.

Bourdieu, Pierre. 1986b. *Distinction: A Social Critique of the Judgment of Taste*. Cambridge, MA: Harvard University Press.

Bourdieu, Pierre. 1988. "Program for a Sociology of Sport." *Sociology of Sport Journal* 5(2):153–61.

Bourdieu, Pierre. 1991. *Language and Symbolic Power*. Cambridge, UK: Polity Press.

Bourdieu, Pierre. 2000. *Pascalian Meditations*. Stanford, CA: Stanford University Press.

Bourdieu, Pierre. 2001. *Masculine Domination*. Stanford, CA: Stanford University Press.

Bourdieu, Pierre, and Loïc Wacquant. 1992. *An Invitation to Reflexive Sociology*. Chicago, IL: University Of Chicago Press.

Bourdieu, Pierre, and Loïc Wacquant. 1999. "On the Cunning of Imperialist Reason." *Theory, Culture & Society* 16(1):41–58.

Bridges, Tristan S. 2009. "Gender Capital and Male Bodybuilders." *Body & Society* 15(1):83–107.

Brownell, Susan, ed. 2008. *The 1904 Anthropology Days and Olympic Games: Sport, Race, and American Imperialism*. Lincoln, NE: University of Nebraska Press.

Caldeira, Teresa Pires do Rio. 2000. *City of Walls: Crime, Segregation, and Citizenship in São Paulo*. Berkeley, CA: University of California Press.

Camp, Roderic A. 1982. "Family Relationships in Mexican Politics: A Preliminary View." *The Journal of Politics* 44(3):848–62.

Camp, Roderic Ai. 2002. *Mexico's Mandarins: Crafting a Power Elite for the Twenty-First Century*. Barkeley, CA: University of California Press.

Carrión, Juan Manuel. 1993. "The National Question in Puerto Rico." Pp. 67–75 in *Colonial Dilemma: Critical Perspectives on Contemporary Puerto Rico*, edited by E. Meléndez and E. Meléndez. Boston, MA: South End Press.

Castellanos, Ana María de la O. 1999. *Guadalajara Country Club: Los Primeros Noventa Años De Una Tradición Tapatía*. Guadalajara, Mexico: Guadalajara Country Club.

Castillo Negrete, Miguel Rovira del. 2017. "Income Inequality in Mexico, 2004–2014." *Latin American Policy* 8(1):93–113.

Cattani, David, ed. 2009. *Riqueza E Desigualdad Na América Latina*. Porto Alegre, Brazil: Zouk.

Cave, Damien. 2008. "This Ho Chi Minh Trail Ends at the 18th Hole." *New York, NY Times*, March 9. Section: Travel, P. 1.

Centeno, Miguel Aangel. 1994. *Democracy Within Reason: Technocratic Revolution in Mexico*. University Park, PA: Pennsylvania State University Press.

Cerón-Anaya, Hugo. 2010. "An Approach to the History of Golf: Business, Symbolic Capital, and Technologies of the Self." *Journal of Sport & Social Issues* 34(3):339–58.

Cerón-Anaya, Hugo. 2017. "Not Everybody Is a Golfer: Bourdieu and Affluent Bodies in Mexico." *Journal of Contemporary Ethnography* 46(3):285–309.

Chambers, Marcia. 1990. "A Revolution in Private Clubs." *Golf Digest* 41 (May):123–36.

Chambers, Marcia. 1995. *The Unplayable Lie: The Untold Story of Women and Discrimination in American Golf*. New York, NY: Pocket Books.

Cock, Jacklyn. 2008. "Caddies and 'Cronies': Golf and Changing Patterns of Exclusion and Inclusion in Post-Apartheid South Africa." *South African Review of Sociology* 39(2):183–200.

Colby, Benjamin N., and Pierre L. Van Den Berghe. 1961. "Ethnic Relations in Southeastern Mexico." *American Anthropologist* 63(4):772–92.

Cole, C. L. 2002. "The Place of Golf in U.S. Imperialism." *Journal of Sport & Social Issues* 26(4):331–36.

Collier, Paul. 2018. *The Future of Capitalism: Facing the New Anxieties*. Milton Keynes, UK: Penguin

Collins, Patricia Hill. 2015. "Intersectionality's Definitional Dilemmas." *Annual Review of Sociology* 41:1–20.

Collinson, D., and K. Hoskin. 1994. "Discipline and Flourish: Golf as a Civilising Process?" Pp. 739–47 in *Science and Golf Ii: Proceedings of the World Scientific Congress of Golf*, edited by A. Cochran. London, UK: Taylor & Francis.

Collinson, Jacquelyn Allen. 2008. "Running the Routes Together: Corunning and Knowledge in Action." *Journal of Contemporary Ethnography* 37(1):38–61.

CONEVAL (Consejo Nacional de Evaluación de la Política de Desarrollo Social). 2014. "Pobreza En México." Retrieved August 10, 2017 (https://www.coneval.org.mx/Medicion/MP/Paginas/Pobreza_2014.aspx).

Connell, Robert W., and James W. Messerschmidt. 2005. "Hegemonic Masculinity: Rethinking the Concept." *Gender & Society* 19(6):829–59.

Connell, Robert William. 1983. *Which Way Is Up?: Essays on Sex, Class, and Culture*. Sydney, Australia: Allen & Unwin Academic.

Coy, Martin. 2006. "Gated Communities and Urban Fragmentation in Latin America: The Brazilian Experience." *GeoJournal* 66(1–2):121–32.

Crichlow, Warren. 2013. *Race, Identity, and Representation in Education*. London, UK: Routledge.

Crosset, Todd W. 1995. *Outsiders in the Clubhouse: The World of Women's Professional Golf*. Albany, NY: State University of New York Press.

Davis, Bob. 1935. "Senor Harry Wright, Successor to Zapata." Pp. 30–31 in *The American Golfer*, edited by Grantland Rice. New York, NY: Conde Nast & Company.

Delgado, Richard. 1984. "The Imperial Scholar: Reflections on a Review of Civil Rights Literature." *University of Pennsylvania Law Review* 132(3):561–78.

DEM (Diccionario del Español de México). 2017. "Naco." Mexico City, Mexico: El Colegio de México, A.C. Retrieved January 15, 2018 (http://dem.colmex.mx).

Demas, Lane. 2017. *Game of Privilege: An African American History of Golf*. Chapel Hill, NC: University of North Carolina Press.

Desmond, Matthew, and Mustafa Emirbayer. 2010. *Racial Domination, Racial Progress: The Sociology of Race in America*. New York, NY: McGraw-Hill Higher Education.

Diaz-Cayeros, Alberto, Federico Estévez, and Beatriz Magaloni. 2016. *The Political Logic of Poverty Relief: Electoral Strategies and Social Policy in Mexico*. New York, NY: Cambridge University Press.

Dinzey-Flores, Zaire Z. 2017. "Spatially Polarized Landscapes and a New Approach to Urban Inequality." *Latin American Research Review* 52(2):241–52.

Dinzey-Flores, Zaire Zenit. 2013. *Locked in, Locked out Gated Communities in a Puerto Rican City*. Philadelphia, PA: University of Pennsylvania Press.

Dirks, Nicholas B. 2000. *Colonialism and Culture*. Ann Arbor, MI: University of Michigan Press.

Domhoff, G. William. 1967. *Who Rules America?* Englewood Cliffs, NJ: Prentice-Hall.

Donaldson, Mike. 2003. "Studying Up: The Masculinity of the Hegemonic." Pp. 156–79 in *Male Trouble. Looking at Australian Masculinities*, edited by S. Tomsen and M. Donaldson. Melbourne, Australia: Pluto Press.

Donaldson, Mike, and Scott Poynting. 2007. *Ruling Class Men: Money, Sex, Power*. London, UK: Peter Lang.

Donaldson, Mike, and Scott Poynting. 2013. "Peering Upwards: Researching Ruling-Class Men." Pp. 157–69 in *Men, Masculinities and Methodologies*, edited by B. Pini and B. Pease. London, UK: Springer.

Doremus, Anne. 2001. "Indigenism, Mestizaje, and National Identity in Mexico During the 1940s and the 1950s." *Mexican Studies/Estudios Mexicanos* 17(2):375–402.

Duany, Jorge. 2002. "Neither White nor Black: The Representation of Racial Identity Among Puerto Ricans on the Island and in the U.S. Mainland." Pp. 236–60 in *The Puerto Rican Nation on the Move: Identities on the Island and in the United States*. Chapel Hill, NC: University of North Carolina Press.

Du Bois, W. E. B. 1999 [1903]. The Souls of Black Folk. New York, NY: Norton.

Durkheim, Emile. 1982. *Rules of Sociological Method*. New York, NY: The Free Press.

Eastman, Susan Tyler, and Andrew C. Billings. 2000. "Sportscasting and Sports Reporting: The Power of Gender Bias." *Journal of Sport & Social Issues* 24(2):192–213.

Eckstein, Susan Eva. 1977. *The Poverty of Revolution: The State and the Urban Poor in Mexico.* Princeton, NJ: Princeton University Press.

Eichberg, Henning. 1986. "The Enclosure of the Body—on the Historical Relativity of 'Health,' 'Nature' and the Environment of Sport." *Journal of Contemporary History* 21(1):99–121.

Eichberg, Henning. 1990. "Forward Race and the Laughter of Pygmies: On Olympic Sport." Pp. 115–31 in *Fin De Siècle and Its Legacy*, edited by M. Teich and R. Porter. London, UK: Cambridge University Press.

Elias, Norbert. 1983. *The Court Society.* New York, NY: Pantheon Books.

Elias, Norbert. 1987. "The Retreat of Sociologists into the Present." *Theory, Culture & Society* 4(2):223–47.

Elias, Norbert. 1991. *Society of Individuals.* New York, NY: Continuum.

Elizondo Mayer-Serra, Carlos 2017. *Los de adelante corren mucho: Desigualdad, privilegios y democracia.* Mexico City, Mexico: Random House

Elsey, Brenda. 2011. *Citizens and Sportsmen: Fútbol and Politics in Twentieth-Century Chile.* Austin, TX: University of Texas Press.

Emirbayer, Mustafa. 1997. "Manifesto for a Relational Sociology." *American Journal of Sociology* 103(2):281–317.

Esquivel, Gerardo 2015a. "La Verdad Sobre La Clase Media En México: Respuesta a Roger Bartra." *Horizontal.* Retrieved September 1, 2016 (http://horizontal.mx/la-verdad-sobre-la-clase-media-en-mexico-respuesta-a-roger-bartra/).

Esquivel, Gerardo 2015b. "Más Sobre La Clase Media: Contrarréplica a Roger Bartra." *Horizontal.* Retrieved September 1, 2016 (http://horizontal.mx/mas-sobre-la-clase-media-contrarreplica-a-roger-bartra/).

Esquivel, Gerardo. 2015c. *Desigualdad Extrema en México: Concentración del Poder Económico y Político.* Mexico City, Mexico: Oxfam México.

Evans, Richard J. 2016. *The Pursuit of Power: Europe 1815–1914.* New York, NY: Penguin.

Fanon, Frantz. 2008. *Black Skin, White Masks.* New York, NY: Grove Press.

Fernández-Kelly, Patricia. 2016. *The Hero's Fight: African Americans in West Baltimore and the Shadow of the State.* Princeton, NJ: Princeton University Press.

FMG, Federacion Mexicana de Golf. 2017. "Acerca Del Golf." Retrieved October 10, 2017 (http://www.fmg.org.mx/InformacionView/Informacion?idSeccion=6).

Forbes, Staff. 2015. "The World's Highest-Paid Athletes 2015." Forbes.com. Retrieved June 10, 2015 (https://www.forbes.com/sites/forbespr/2015/06/10/forbes-announces-2015-list-of-the-worlds-100-highest-paid-athletes/#5d445582283c).

Forbes, Staff. 2016. "The World's Highest-Paid Athletes 2016." Forbes.com. Retrieved June 8, 2016 (https://www.forbes.com/sites/forbespr/2016/06/08/forbes-releases-the-worlds-highest-paid-athletes-list-2016/#30235885b965).

Foucault, Michel. 1995. *Discipline & Punish: The Birth of the Prison.* New York, NY: Vintage.

French, John D. 2000. "The Missteps of Anti-Imperialist Reason: Bourdieu, Wacquant and Hanchard's Orpheus and Power." *Theory, Culture & Society* 17(1):107–28.

Freyre, Gilberto. 1938. *Casa-Grande & Senzala: Formação Da Familia Brasileira Sob O Regimen De Economia Patriarchal.* Rio de Janeiro, Brazil: Schmidt.

Friedman, Sam, and Daniel Laurison. 2019. *The Class Ceiling: Why It Pays to be Privileged.* Bristol, UK: Bristol University Press.

Gall, Olivia. 2004. "Identidad, Exclusión Y Racismo: Reflexiones Teóricas Y Sobre México." *Revista Mexicana de Sociologia* 66(2):221–59.

Gall, Olivia. 2007. *Racismo, Mestizaje y Modernidad: Visiones desde Latitudes Diversas.* Mexico City, Mexico: UNAM.

Galliher, John F. 1980. "Social Scientists' Ethical Responsibilities to Superordinates: Looking Upward Meekly." *Social Problems* 27:298–308.

Garrido, Celso. 1994. "Grupos privados nacionales en México, 1988–1993." *Revista de la Cepal* 5(3):159–76.

Gaztambide-Fernández, Rubén A. 2009. *The Best of the Best: Becoming Elite at an American Boarding School.* Cambridge, MA: Harvard University Press.

Gaztambide-Fernández, Rubén A. 2015. "Elite Entanglements and the Demand for a Radically Un/Ethical Position: The Case of Wienie Night." *International Journal of Qualitative Studies in Education* 28(9):1129–47.

Gaztambide-Fernández, Rubén A., and Adam Howard. 2012. "Access, Status, and Representation: Some Reflections from Two Ethnographic Studies of Elite Schools." *Anthropology & Education Quarterly* 43(3):289–305.

Gems, Gerald R. 2006. *The Athletic Crusade: Sport and American Cultural Imperialism.* Lincoln, NE: University of Nebraska Press.

Gerth, Karl. 2011. "Lifestyles of the Rich and Infamous: The Creation and Implications of China's New Aristocracy." *Comparative Sociology* 10(4):488–507.

Gewertz, Deborah B., and Frederick K. Errington. 1999. *Emerging Class in Papua New Guinea: The Telling of Difference.* London, UK: Cambridge University Press.

Gibson, Heather J. 1998. "Active sport tourism: who participates?" *Leisure Studies* 17(2):155–70.

Gieryn, Thomas F. 2000. "A Space for Place in Sociology." *Annual Review of Sociology* 26(1):463–96.

Gilbert, Dennis L. 2007. *Mexico's Middle Class in the Neoliberal Era.* Tucson, AZ: University of Arizona Press.

Godreau, Isar P. 2008. "Slippery Semantics: Race Talk and Everyday Uses of Racial Terminology in Puerto Rico." *Centro Journal* 20(2):5–33.

Goffman, Alice. 2015. *On the Run: Fugitive Life in an American City.* New York, NY: Picador.

Goffman, Erving. 1959. *The Presentation of Self in Everyday Life.* New York, NY: Anchor Books.

Goffman, Erving. 1961. *Encounters: Two Studies in the Sociology of Interaction.* Indianapolis, IN: Bobbs-Merrill.

Goldberg, David Theo. 2002. *The Racial State.* New York, NY: Wiley.

Goldberg, David Theo. 2009. *The Threat of Race: Reflections on Racial Neoliberalism.* New York, NY: John Wiley.

Gomberg-Muñoz, Ruth. 2011. *Labor and Legality: An Ethnography of a Mexican Immigrant Network.* New York, NY: Oxford University Press.

González Casanova, Pablo. 1965. *La Democracia en México.* Mexico City, Mexico: ERA.

Gordon, John Steele. 1990. "The Country Club." American Heritage, September/October, pp. 75–84.

Grecko, Témoris. 2017. "Afromexicanos: La Discriminación Visible." *Proceso.* Retrieved March 27, 2017. (https://hemeroteca.proceso.com.mx/?page_id=2789 58&a51dc26366d99bb5fa29cea4747565fec=416024).

Guimarães, Antonio Sergio Alfredo. 2012. "The Brazilian System of Racial Classification." *Ethnic and Racial Studies* 35(7):1157–62.

Gutiérrez y Muhs, Gabriella, Yolanda Flores Niemann, Carmen G. González, and Angela P. Harris, eds. 2012. *Presumed Incompetent: The Intersections of Race and Class for Women in Academia.* Logan, UT: Utah State University Press.

Guttmann, Allen. 1994. *Games and Empires: Modern Sports and Cultural Imperialism.* New York, NY: Columbia University Press.

Hansen, Thomas B. 2018. "Civics, Civility and Race in Post-Apartheid South Africa." *Anthropological Theory* 18(2–3):296–325.

Hargreaves, Jennifer. 2002. *Sporting Females: Critical Issues in the History and Sociology of Women's Sport.* London, UK: Routledge.

Harris, Marvin. 1970. "Referential Ambiguity in the Calculus of Brazilian Racial Identity." *Southwestern Journal of Anthropology* 26(1):1–14.

Hart, John Mason. 2002. *Empire and Revolution: The Americans in Mexico Since the Civil War.* Berkeley, CA: University of California Press.

Hartigan, John. 2013. "Looking for Race in the Mexican 'Book of Life': Inmegen and the Mexican Genome Project." Pp. 125-151 in *Anthropology of Race: Genes, Biology, and Culture,* edited by J. Hartigan. Santa Fe, NM: SAR Press.

Harvey, David. 1989. *The Urban Experience.* Baltimore, MD: Johns Hopkins University Press.

Harvey, David. 2003. *Paris, Capital of Modernity.* New York, NY: Psychology Press.

Harvey, David. 2007. *A Brief History of Neoliberalism.* New York, NY: Oxford University Press.

Hay, Iain, and Samantha Muller. 2012. "'That Tiny, Stratospheric Apex That Owns Most of the World'—Exploring Geographies of the Super-Rich." *Geographical Research* 50(1):75–88.

Hay, Iain, and Jonathan V. Beaverstock. 2016. *Handbook on Wealth and the Super-Rich.* London, UK: Edward Elgar.

Hernández, Érika, Mayolo López, and Claudia Guerrero. 2018. "Prometen Bajar Publicidad Y Puestos De Confianza." *Reforma.* Retrieved July 12, 2018. (https://

www.reforma.com/aplicacioneslibre/articulo/default.aspx?id=1441432&md5=d
a1978900f5814381b819f02360305f2&ta=odfdbac11765226904c16cb9ad1b2efe).

Hirsch, Paul M. 1995. "Tales from the Field: Learning from Researchers' Accounts."
Pp. 72–80 in *Studying Elites Using Qualitative Methods*, edited by Rosanna Hertz
and Jonathan B. Imber. Thousand Oaks, CA: SAGE.

Hirst, David. 2001. "The Emirs in the Internet Era: Dubai, a Sheikhdom Happy
to Embrace Globalization." *Le Monde Diplomatique (English Version).* February.
Retrieved May 10, 2008, (https://mondediplo.com/2001/02/06dubai).

Hochschild, Arlie Russell. 1983. *The Managed Heart: Commercialization of Human
Feeling.* Berkley, CA: University of California Press.

Hoffman, Joan Eakin. 1980. "Problems of Access in the Study of Social Elites and
Boards of Directors." Pp. 45–56 in *Field Work Experience: Qualitative Approaches
to Social Research*, edited by W. Shaffir and R. A. Stebbins. New York, NY: St.
Martins.

Horta, Raul. 1989. *Golf En México II: Club Campestre De La Ciudad De México.* Mexico
City, Mexico: Litógrafos Unidos.

Huerta Nava, Raquel. 2005. *Agustín Legorreta García, Líder Empresarial.* Mexico City,
Mexico: Vila.

Hundley, Heather L. 2004. "Keeping the Score: The Hegemonic Everyday Practices
in Golf." *Communication Reports* 17(1):39–48.

IGF (International Golf Federation). 2017. "Mexican Golf Federation, Statistics."
Retrieved October 10, 2017 (https://www.igfgolf.org/nationalmembers/mexican-
golf-federation/).

INEGI (Instituto Nacional de Estadística y Geografía). 2015. "Grado Promedio de
Escolaridad de la Población de 15 Años y Más. Mexico" Retrieved March 10, 2017
(http://www.beta.inegi.org.mx/temas/educacion/).

INEGI (Instituto Nacional de Estadística y Geografía). 2016. "Módulo De Movilidad
Social Intergeneracional. Mexico." Retrieved October 20, 2017 (http://internet.
contenidos.inegi.org.mx/contenidos/Productos/prod_serv/contenidos/espanol/
bvinegi/productos/nueva_estruc/702825094867.pdf).

Inglis, Patrick. 2019. Narrow Fairways. New York, NY: Oxford University Press.

Irwin, Katherine. 2006. "Into the Dark Heart of Ethnography: The Lived Ethics
and Inequality of Intimate Field Relationships." *Qualitative Sociology*
29(2):155–75.

Iturriaga Acevedo, Eugenia. 2016. *Las Élites De La Ciudad Blanca. Discursos
Racistas Sobre La Otredad.* Mexico City, Mexico: UNAM- Centro Peninsular en
Humanidades y en Ciencias Sociales.

Janoschka, Michael, and Axel Borsdorf. 2004. "The Rise of Private Residential
Neighbourhoods in Latin America." Pp. 89–104 in *Private Cities: Global and
Local Perspectives*, edited by G. Glasze, C. Webster, and K. Frantz. New York,
NY: Routledge.

Kane, Mary Jo. 1995. "Resistance/Transformation of the Oppositional Binary: Exposing
Sport as a Continuum." *Journal of Sport & Social Issues* 19(2):191–218.

Kelly, William W. 2007. "Is Baseball a Global Sport? America's 'National Pastime' as Global Field and International Sport." *Global Networks* 7(2):187–201.

Kendall, Diana. 2008. *Members Only: Elite Clubs and the Process of Exclusion*. New York, NY: Rowman & Littlefield.

Khan, Shamus Rahman. 2010. *Privilege: The Making of an Adolescent Elite at St. Paul's School*. Princeton, NJ: Princeton University Press.

Khan, Shamus Rahman. 2012. "The Sociology of Elites." *Annual Review of Sociology* 38:361–77.

Klein, Bradley. 1999. "Cultural Links: An International Political Economy of Golf Course Landscapes." Pp. 211–26 in *Sportcult*, edited by T. Miller and R. Martin. Minneapolis, MN: University of Minnesota Press.

Knight, Alan. 1990. "Racism, Revolution, and Indigenismo: Mexico, 1910–1940." Pp. 71–113 in *The Idea of Race in Latin America, 1870–1940*, edited by R. Graham. Austin, TX: University of Texas Press.

Krauze, Enrique. 2014. "Latin America's Talent for Tolerance." *New York, NY Times*. Op Ed., July 10. Retrieved March 10 2016 (http://nyti.ms/1xWTonq).

Krauze, Enrique, Francisco Martin Moreno, and Elisa Speckman Guerra. 2005. *Mexico Country Club: 100 Años Club Campestre De La Ciudad De Mexico 1905–2005*. Mexico City, Mexico: Editorial Club Campestre de la Ciudad de Mexico.

Lamont, Michele 1992. *Money, Morals, and Manners: The Culture of the French and the American Upper-Middle Class*. Chicago, IL: University of Chicago Press.

Lancaster, Roger N. 1991. "Skin Color, Race, and Racism in Nicaragua." *Ethnology* 30(4):339–53.

Lassiter, Luke E. 2005. *The Chicago Guide to Collaborative Ethnography*. Chicago, IL: University of Chicago Press.

Lindsey, Brink, and Steven M Teles. 2017. *The Captured Economy: How the Powerful Enrich Themselves, Slow Down Growth, and Increase Inequality*. New York, NY: Oxford University Press.

Loveman, Mara. 2009. "Whiteness in Latin America: Measurement and Meaning in National Censuses (1850–1950)." *Journal de la société des américanistes* 95(2):207–34.

Le, Long S. 2010. "Anger on the Farm: The Displacement of Rural Vietnam." *Global Asia* 5(1):84–89.

Lefebvre, Henri. 1991. *The Production of Space*. Oxford, UK: Blackwell.

Leonard, David J., and King Richard, eds. 2010. *Commodified and Criminalized: New Racism and African Americans in Contemporary Sports*. New York, NY: Rowman & Littlefield.

Lewis, Oscar. 1961. *The Children of Sánchez: Autobiography of a Mexican Family*. New York, NY: Vintage Books.

Lezcano, Norma. 2005. "Ella Gana Campeonatos; Su Hermano Gestiona La Marca. El Swing Ochoa." *Expansión* 36(920):112–23.

Lipsitz, George. 2006. *The Possessive Investment in Whiteness.* Philadelphia, PA: Temple University Press.

López Beltran, Carlos, Peter Wade, Eduardo Restrepo, and Ricardo Ventura Santos (eds.), 2017. *Genómica Mestiza: Raza, Nación y Ciencia en Latinoamérica.* Mexico City, Mexico: Fondo de Cultura Económica.

López-Durán, Fabiola. 2018. *Eugenics in the Garden: Transatlantic Architecture and the Crafting of Modernity.* Austin, TX: University of Texas Press.

Loveman, Mara. 2014. *National Colors: Racial Classification and the State in Latin America.* New York, NY: Oxford University Press.

Low, Setha. 2001. "The Edge and the Center: Gated Communities and the Discourse of Urban Fear." *American Anthropologist* 103(1):45–58.

Low, Setha. 2004. *Behind the Gates: Life, Security, and the Pursuit of Happiness in Fortress America.* New York, NY: Routledge.

Lowe, John. 1986. "Theories of Ethnic Humor: How to Enter, Laughing." *American Quarterly* 38(3):439–60.

Luna, Matilde, and Ricardo Pozas. 1993. "Los Empresarios En El Escenario Del Cambio. Trayectoria Y Tendencias De Una Acción Colectiva." *Revista Mexicana de Sociologia* 55(2[Apr–Jun]):243–271.

Lund, Joshua. 2012. *The Mestizo State: Reading Race in Modern Mexico.* Minneapolis, MN: University of Minnesota Press.

Lowerson, John. 1994. "Golf and the Making of Myths." Pp. 75–90 in John Lowerson, *Scottish Sport in the Making of the Nation: Ninety Minute Patriots?* Leicester, UK: Leicester University Press.

Lowerson, John. 1995. *Sport and the English Middle Classes, 1870–1914.* Manchester, UK: Manchester University Press.

Luna, M. 1992. "Inconsistencias De La Modernización: El Caso Del Consejo Coordinador Empresarial." *El Cotidiano* 50:136–41.

Magazine, Roger. 2007. *Golden and Blue Like My Heart: Masculinity, Youth, and Power Among Soccer Fans in Mexico.* Tucson, AZ: University of Arizona Press.

Maguire, Joe. 1991. "The Media-Sport Production Complex: The Case of American Football in Western European Societies." *European Journal of Communication* 6(3):315–35.

Mahar, Cheleen Ann-Catherine. 2011. *Reinventing Practice in a Disenchanted World: Bourdieu and Urban Poverty in Oaxaca, Mexico.* Austin, TX: University of Texas Press.

Maharaj, Gitanjali. 1997. "Talking Trash: Late Capitalism, Black (Re)Productivity, and Professional Basketball." *Social Text* (50):97–110.

Manzo, Diana. 2017. "Señalan Afromexicanos Racismo Y Discriminación De Autoridades." *La Jornada.* March 28, Section: Estados, p 31.

Marcus, George E., and Fernando Mascarenhas. 2005. *Ocasião: The Marquis and the Anthropologist, a Collaboration.* Walnut Creek, CA: Altamira.

Martínez, María Elena. 2008. *Genealogical Fictions: Limpieza De Sangre, Religion, and Gender in Colonial Mexico*. Stanford, CA: Stanford University Press.

Marx, Karl 1993. *Grundrisse, Foundations of the Critique of Political Economy*. Translated by M. Nicolaus. New York, NY: Penguin.

Marx, Karl, and Friedrich Engels. 1970 [1846]. *The German Ideology*. New York, NY: International Mason Publisher.

Massey-Gilbert, Co. 1901. *The Massey-Gilbert Blue Book of Mexico*. Mexico City, Mexico: Massey-Gilbert Company.

Massey, Doreen. 1992. "Politics and Space/Time." *New Left Review I* 196:65.

Massey, Doreen. 1994. *Space, Place, and Gender*. Cambridge, UK: Polity Press.

Maza, Enrique. 1984. "La Crisis De La Deuda, Principios De La Hegemonía Del Fmi." *Proceso*, August 4. Retrieved 2005 (https://www.proceso.com.mx/139191/la-crisis-de-la-deuda-principio-de-la-hegemonia-del-fmi).

McGinnis, Lee, Julia McQuillan, and Constance L Chapple. 2005. "I Just Want to Play: Women, Sexism, and Persistence in Golf." *Journal of Sport & Social Issues* 29(3):313–37.

McGinnis, Lee Phillip, and James W. Gentry. 2006. "Getting Past the Red Tees: Constraints Women Face in Golf and Strategies to Help Them Stay." *Journal of Sport Management* 20(2):218–47.

McGinnis, Lee Phillip, James W. Gentry, and Julia McQuillan. 2008. "Ritual-Based Behavior That Reinforces Hegemonic Masculinity in Golf: Variations in Women Golfers' Responses." *Leisure Sciences* 31(1):19–36.

Mears, Ashley. 2011. *Pricing Beauty: The Making of a Fashion Model*. Berkeley, CA: University of California Press.

Mears, Ashley. 2015. "Working for Free in the Vip: Relational Work and the Production of Consent." *American Sociological Review* 80(6):1099–122.

Messner, Michael A. 1988. "Sports and Male Domination: The Female Athlete as Contested Ideological Terrain." *Sociology of Sport Journal* 5(3):197–211.

Messner, Michael A., and Donald F. Sabo. 1990. *Sport, Men, and the Gender Order: Critical Feminist Perspectives*. Champaign, IL: Human Kinetics Books.

Messner, Michael A. 1992. *Power at Play: Sports and the Problem of Masculinity*. Boston, MA: Beacon Press.

Messner, Michael A., and Donald F. Sabo. 1994. *Sex, Violence & Power in Sports: Rethinking Masculinity*. Freedom, CA: Crossing Press.

Middlebrook, Kevin, and Eduardo Zepeda. 2003. *Confronting Development: Assessing Mexico's Economic and Social Policy Challenges*. Stanford, CA: Stanford University Press.

Mills, C. Wright. 1956. *The Power Elite*. New York, NY: Oxford University Press.

Minushkin, Susan. 2002. "Banqueros and Bolseros: Structural Change and Financial Market Liberalisation in Mexico." *Journal of Latin American Studies* 34(4):915–44.

Mitchelson, Ronald L., and Michael T. Lazaro. 2004. "The Face of the Game: African Americans' Spatial Accessibility to Golf." *Southeastern Geographer* 44(1):48–73.

Monsivais, Carlos. 1976. "No Es Que Esté Feo, Sino Que Estoy Mal Envuelto Je-Je (Notas Sobre La Estética De La Naquiza)." *Siempre! [La cultura en México]*, 20 de enero, P. 1.

Mora, Mariana. 2017. *Kuxlejal Politics: Indigenous Autonomy, Race, and Decolonizing Research in Zapatista Communities*. Austin, TX: University of Texas Press.

Morales Oyarvide, César. 2016. "Vulnerable Clase Media." *Horizontal*. Retrieved March 09, 2016. (http://horizontal.mx/vulnerable-clase-media/).

Morales, Vicente., and Manuel Caballero. 1908. *El Señor Root En Mexico*. Mexico City, Mexico: Arte y letras.

Morales y Favela, Alfonso Morales. 1996. *México a Través De Sus Campos De Golf*. Mexico City, Mexico: Asociación Mexicana Femenil de Golf.

Moreno Figueroa, Mónica. 2010. "Distributed Intensities: Whiteness, Mestizaje and the Logics of Mexican Racism." *Ethnicities* 10(3):387–401. Moreno Figueroa, Mónica, and Emiko Saldívar Tanaka. 2016. "'We Are Not Racists, We Are Mexicans': Privilege, Nationalism and Post-Race Ideology in Mexico." *Critical Sociology* 42(4–5):515–33.

Murji, Karim, and John Solomos. 2005. "Introduction: racialization in theory and practice." Pp. 1–27 in *Racialization: Studies in Theory and Practice*, edited by Karim Murji and John Solomos. New York, NY: Oxford University Press.

Nader, Laura. 1972. "Up the Anthropologist Perspectives Gained from Studying Up." Pp. 284–311 in *Reinventing Anthropology*, edited by D. H. Hymes. New York, NY: Pantheon Books.

Napton, Darrell E., and Christopher R. Laingen. 2008. "Expansion of Golf Courses in the United States." *Geographical Review* 98(1):24–41.

Navarrete, Federico. 2016. *México Racista: Una Denuncia*. Mexico City, Mexico: Grijalbo.

Navarrete, Federico. 2017. *Alfabeto Del Racismo Mexicano*. Mexico City, Mexico: Malpaso.

Nee, Victor, Jimy M. Sanders, and Scott Sernau. 1994. "Job Transitions in an Immigrant Metropolis: Ethnic Boundaries and the Mixed Economy." *American Sociological Review* 59(6 [Dec]):849–72.

Nelson, Lee, Paul Potrac, David Gilbourne, Ashley Allanson, Laura Gale, and Phil Marshall. 2013. "Thinking, Feeling, Acting: The Case of a Semi-Professional Soccer Coach." *Sociology of Sport Journal* 30(4):467–86.

Nemser, Daniel. 2017. *Infrastructures of Race: Concentration and Biopolitics in Colonial Mexico*. Austin, TX: University of Texas Press.

Ngai, Mae M. 2004. *Impossible Subjects: Illegal Aliens and the Making of Modern America*. Princeton, NJ: Princeton University Press.

Norman, Greg. 2006. *The Way of the Shark: Lessons on Golf, Business, and Life*. New York, NY: Atria Books.

Nutini, Hugo G. 1997. "Class and Ethnicity in Mexico: Somatic and Racial Considerations." *Ethnology* 36(3):227–38.

Nutini, Hugo G. 2008. *The Mexican Aristocracy: An Expressive Ethnography, 1910–2000:* Austin, TX: University of Texas Press.

Nutini, Hugo, and Barry Isaac. 2010. *Social Stratification in Central Mexico, 1500–2000.* Austin, TX: University of Texas Press.

Ochoa, Marcia. 2014. *Queen for a Day: Transformistas, Beauty Queens, and the Performance of Femininity in Venezuela.* Durham, NC: Duke University Press.

OECD. 2017. "Average annual wages." OECD Employment and Labour Market Statistics (database). Accessed July 10, 2018. (https://doi.org/10.1787/f5dc582e-en).

Omi, Michael, and Howard Winant. 2014. *Racial Formation in the United States.* New York, NY: Routledge.

Ostrander, Susan A. 1980. "Upper Class Women: The Feminine Side of Privilege." *Qualitative Sociology* 3(1):23–44. Ostrander, Susan A. 1993. " 'Surely You're Not in This Just to Be Helpful': Access, Rapport, and Interviews in Three Studies of Elites." *Journal of Contemporary Ethnography* 22(1):7–27.

Ostrander, Susan. 2010. *Women of the Upper Class.* Philadelphia, PA: Temple University Press.

Paradis, Elise. 2012. "Boxers, Briefs or Bras? Bodies, Gender and Change in the Boxing Gym." *Body & Society* 18(2):82–109.

Paris, Django, and Maisha T. Winn, eds. 2013. *Humanizing Research: Decolonizing Qualitative Inquiry with Youth and Communities.* Thousand Oaks, CA: SAGE.

Pérez Moreno, Argisofía. 2017. "La identificación de personas afrodescendientes por primera vez en un proyecto estadístico nacional en México." Paper presented at Quinta Conferencia sobre Etnicidad, Raza y Pueblos Indígenas, Morelia, Mexico, October 4–6, 2017. ERIP-LASA.

Perramond, Eric P. 2008. "The Rise, Fall, and Reconfiguration of the Mexican Ejido." *Geographical Review* 98(3):356–71.

Peterson-Withorn, Chase. 2015. "Forbes Billionaires: Full List of the 500 Richest People in the World 2015." *Forbes.* Retrieved March 2, 2017 (https://www.forbes.com/sites/chasewithorn/2015/03/02/forbes-billionaires-full-list-of-the-500-richest-people-in-the-world-2015/#1708024a45b9).

Pierce, Jennifer. 1995. "Reflections of Fieldwork in a Complex Organization: Lawyers, Ethnographic Authority, and Lethal Weapons." Pp. 94–110 in *Studying Elites Using Qualitative Methods,* edited by R. Hertz and J. B. Imber. Thousand Oaks, CA: SAGE.

Piketty, Thomas. 2014. *Capital in the Twenty-First Century.* Cambridge, MA: Harvard University Press.

Pitt-Rivers, Julian. 1968. "Race, Color, and Class in Central America and the Andes." Pp. 264–81 in *Color and Race,* edited by J. H. Franklin. Boston, MA: Houghton Mifflin.

Pitt-Rivers, Julian. 1977. "Race in Latin America." Pp. 317–32 in *Race, Ethnicity, and Social Change: Readings in the Sociology of Race and Ethnic Relations,* edited by J. Stone. Pacific Grove, CA: Duxbury Press.

Portes, A. 1995. *The Economic Sociology of Immigration: Essays on Networks, Ethnicity, and Entrepreneurship*. New York, NY: SAGE.

Portes, Alejandro. 1987. "The Social Origins of the Cuban Enclave Economy of Miami." *Sociological Perspectives* 30(4):340–72.

Pow, Choon-Piew. 2017. "Elite Informality, Spaces of Exception and the Super-Rich in Singapore." Pp. 209–28 in *Cities and the Super-Rich: Real Estate, Elite Practices and Urban Political Economies*, edited by R. Forrest, S. Y. Koh, and B. Wissink. New York, NY: Palgrave Macmillan.

Puga, C. 1994. *México: Empresarios Y Poder*. Mexico City, Mexico: Miguel Angel Porrua.

Pyke, Karen D. 1996. "Class-Based Masculinities: The Interdependence of Gender, Class, and Interpersonal Power." *Gender & Society* 10(5):527–49.

Quesada, Javier. 2016. "México Tiene La Segunda Ciudad En El Mundo Con Más Helicópteros Privados." *Forbes Mexico*. Retrieved September 20, 2016. (https://www.forbes.com.mx/mexico-la-segunda-ciudad-mundo-mas-helicopteros-privados/).

Ratcliff, Anna (2019). Billionaire fortunes grew by $2.5 billion a day last year as poorest saw their wealth fall. *Oxfam*. Retrived 1 Feb, 2019. (https://oxf.am/2Rypmsp).

Redaccion. 2017. "Anaya Acusa a Amlo De Usar Racismo Para Dividir." *El Financiero*. December 12. Retrieved July August 01, 2018 (http://www.elfinanciero.com.mx/nacional/anaya-acusa-a-amlo-de-usar-racismo-para-dividir).

Redacción. 2018. "Funcionario Plantea Votar Por Amlo 'Con La Mugre De Los Codos'." *Politico Mx*. June 07. Retrieved July August 5, 2018 (https://politico.mx/central-electoral/elecciones-2018/presidencial/funcionario-plantea-votar-por-amlo-con-la-mugre-de-los-codos/).

Reeves, Richard V. 2017. *Dream Hoarders: How the American Upper Middle Class Is Leaving Everyone Else in the Dust, Why That Is a Problem, and What to Do About It*. Washington, DC: Brookings Institution Press.

Reis, Helena, and Antónia Correia. 2013. "Gender Inequalities in Golf: A Consented Exclusion?" *International Journal of Culture, Tourism and Hospitality Research* 7(4):324–39.

Reygadas, Luis, and Paul Gootenberg, eds. 2010. *Indelible Inequalities in Latin America: Insights from History, Politics, and Culture*. Durham, NC: Duke University Press.

Rivera Lauren, A. 2015. *Pedigree: How Elite Students Get Elite Jobs*. Princeton, NJ: Princeton University Press.

Roberts, Elizabeth. 2012. *God's Laboratory: Assisted Reproduction in the Andes*. Berkeley, CA: University of California Press.

Roberts, Daniel. 2015. "Donald Trump: Let Golf Stay for the Rich Elites." *Fortune. com*. Retrieved July 10, 2015. (http://fortune.com/2015/07/01/donald-trump-golf-rich-elite/).

Robinson, Cedric J. 2005. *Black Marxism: The Making of the Black Radical Tradition*. Chapel Hill, NC: University of North Carolina Press.

Rodriguez, Darinka. 2014. "Golf, ¿Un Deporte Sólo Para Ricos?" *El Financiero*. Feb 26. ElFinanciero.com. Retrieved March 20, 2016. (http://www.elfinanciero.com.mx/mis-finanzas/golf-un-deporte-solo-para-ricos).

Rodriguez Diaz, E. 1975. "La Camara Americana De Comercio." *Estudios Politicos* 1(1):33–63.

Roitman, Karem. 2009. *Race, Ethnicity, and Power in Ecuador: The Manipulation of Mestizaje*. Boulder, CO: First Forum Press.

Rosas, Alejandro. 2014. "¿Classistas or Racistas?" *Milenio*. December 10. Milenio.com. Retrieved September 10, 2016. (https://www.milenio.com/tribuna/clasistas-o-racistas).

Rosas, María. 1997. *Tepoztlan, Cronica De Desacatos Y Resistencia*, Vol. 1. Mexico City, Mexico: Era.

Said, Edward W. 2006. *Orientalism*. London, UK: Penguin.

Saldívar, Emiko. 2014. "'It's Not Race, It's Culture': Untangling Racial Politics in Mexico." *Latin American and Caribbean ethnic studies* 9(1):89–108.

Saldívar, Emiko, and Casey Walsh. 2014. "Racial and Ethnic Identities in Mexican Statistics." *Journal of Iberian and Latin American Research* 20(3):455–75.

Saliba, Armando. July 1, 2003. "Hitting the Tropical Links: Growth of Golf Stunted by Heavy Price Tag, Limited Interest." *Business Mexico* 13(7):42–43.

Saldívar, Emiko, and Casey Walsh. 2014. "Racial and Ethnic Identities in Mexican Statistics." *Journal of Iberian and Latin American Research* 20(3):455–75.

Salverda, Tijo, and Iain Hay. 2014. "Change, Anxiety and Exclusion in the Post-Colonial Reconfiguration of Franco-Mauritian Elite Geographies." *Geographical Journal* 180(3):236–45.

Sanjek, Roger. 1971. "Brazilian Racial Terms: Some Aspects of Meaning and Learning." *American Anthropologist* 73(5):1126–43.

Saragoza, Alex M. 1988. *The Monterrey Elite and the Mexican State: 1880–1940*. Austin, TX: University of Texas Press.

Savage, Mike, and Karel Williams, eds. 2008. *Remembering Elites*. Oxford, UK: Wiley-Blackwell.

Schneider, Benn Ross. 2002. "Why Is Mexican Business So Organized?" *Latin American Research Review* 37(1).

Schrag, Peter. 2011. *Not Fit for Our Society*. Berkeley, CA: University of California Press.

Schwartzman, Luisa Farah. 2007. "Does Money Whiten? Intergenerational Changes in Racial Classification in Brazil." *American Sociological Review* 72(6):940–63.

Seda-Bonilla, Eduardo 1968. "Dos Modelos De Relaciones Raciales: Estados Unidos Y América Latina." *Revista de Ciencias Sociales* (4):569–97.

Sennett, Richard. 1996. *Flesh and Stone: The Body and the City in Western Civilization*. New York, NY: W. W. Norton.

Serna, Enrique. 1996. "El Naco En El País De Las Castas." Pp. 747–54 in *Las Caricaturas Me Hacen Llorar*, edited by E. Serna. Mexico City, Mexico: Joaquín Mortiz.

Sheriff, Robin E. 2000. "Exposing Silence as Cultural Censorship: A Brazilian Case." *American Anthropologist* 102(1):114–32.

Sherman, Rachel. 2017. *Uneasy Street: The Anxieties of Affluence.* Princeton, NJ: Princeton University Press.

Sherwood, Jessica H. 2012. *Wealth, Whiteness, and the Matrix of Privilege: The View from the Country Club.* New York, NY: Lexington Books.

Sieber, Joan E. 1989. "On Studying the Powerful (or Fearing to Do So): A Vital Role for Irbs." *IRB: Ethics & Human Research* 11(5):1–6.

Simpson, Audra. 2007. "On Ethnographic Refusal: Indigeneity, 'Voice' and Colonial Citizenship." *Junctures: The Journal for Thematic Dialogue* (9):67–80

Simmel, Georg. 1950. *The Sociology of Georg Simmel.* New York, NY: Simon & Schuster.

Skidmore, Thomas E. 1993. "Bi-Racial U.S.A. Vs. Multi-Racial Brazil: Is the Contrast Still Valid?" *Journal of Latin American Studies* 25(2):373–86.

Smith, Peter H. 1979. *Labyrinths of Power: Political Recruitment in Twentieth-Century Mexico* Princeton, NJ: Princeton University Press.

Stack, Carol B. 1975. *All Our Kin: Strategies for Survival in a Black Community.* New York, NY: Basic Books.

Stangl, Jane 2017, "Golfing with the Ladies" *Engaging Sports.* The Society Pages. Retrieved November 1, 2017 (https://thesocietypages.org/engagingsports/2017/09/19/golfingwith-the-ladies/).

Starn, Orin. 2006. "Caddying for the Dalai Lama: Golf, Heritage Tourism, and the Pinehurst Resort." *South Atlantic Quarterly* 105(2):447–63.

Starn, Orin. 2012. The Passion of Tiger Woods: An Anthropologist Reports on Golf, Race, and Celebrity Scandal. Durham, NC: Duke University Press.

Stepan, Nancy. 1991. *The Hour of Eugenics: Race, Gender, and Nation in Latin America.* Ithaca, NY: Cornell University Press.

Stoddart, Bryan. 1999. "Joe Kirkwood, Orientalism, and the Globalisation of Golf." Pp. 337–44 in *Science and Golf III: Proceedings of the World Scientific Congress of Golf,* edited by M. Farrally and A. Cochran. Leeds, UK: Human Kinetics Publishers.

Stutzman, Ronald 1981. "El Mestizaje: An All-Inclusive Ideology of Exclusion." Pp. 45–94 in *Cultural Transformations and Ethnicity in Modern Ecuador,* edited by N. Whitten. Chicago, IL: University of Illinois Press.

Sue, Christina A. 2013. *Land of the Cosmic Race: Race Mixture, Racism, and Blackness in Mexico.* New York, NY, Oxford University Press.

Sue, Christina A., and Tanya Golash-Boza. 2013. "'It Was Only a Joke': How Racial Humour Fuels Colour-Blind Ideologies in Mexico and Peru." *Ethnic and Racial Studies* 36(10):1582–98.

Székely, Miguel, ed. 2005. *Desmitificación Y Nuevos Mitos Sobre La Pobreza: Escuchando "Lo Que Dicen Los Pobres."* Mexico City, Mexico: Ciesas.

Telles, Edward. 2014. *Pigmentocracies: Ethnicity, Race, and Color in Latin America*. Chapel Hill, NC: University of North Carolina Press.

Telles, Edward, and René Flores. 2013. "Not Just Color: Whiteness, Nation, and Status in Latin America." *Hispanic American Historical Review* 93(3):411–49.

Terry, Thomas Philip. 1911. *Terry's Mexico, Handbook for Travellers*. New York, NY: Gay and Hancock.

Teruel, Graciela, and Miguel Reyes. 2017. "México: País De Pobres Y No De Clases Medias." Puebla, Mexico: Universidad Iberoamericana-Fundación Konrad Adenauer.

Thangaraj, Stanley. 2012. "Playing Through Differences: Black–White Racial Logic and Interrogating South Asian American Identity." *Ethnic and Racial Studies* 35(6):988–1006.

Thangaraj, Stanley I. 2015. *Desi Hoop Dreams: Pickup Basketball and the Making of Asian American Masculinity*. New York, NY: New York University Press.

Thiranagama, Sharika, Kelly, Tobias, & Forment, Carlos (2018). Introduction: Whose civility? Anthropological Theory, 18(2–3), 153–174.

Thompson, Edward Palmer. 1963. *The Making of the English Working Class*. London, UK: Pantheon Books.

Tirado, Ricardo. 1998. "Mexico: From the Political Call for Collective Action to a Proposal for Free Market Economic Reform." Pp. 183–209 in *Organized Business, Economic Change, and Democracy in Latin America*, edited by F. Duran and E. Silva. Oxford, OH: Miami University Press.

Tokarczyk, Michelle M., and Elizabeth A Fay, eds. 1993. *Working-Class Women in the Academy: Laborers in the Knowledge Factory*. Amherst, MA: University of Massachusetts Press.

Tuck, Eve. 2009. "Suspending Damage: A Letter to Communities." *Harvard Educational Review* 79(3):409–28.

Twine, France Winddance, and Bradley Gardener, eds. 2013. *Geographies of Privilege*. New York, NY: Routledge.

United States Investor. 1910. "New York Bankers Meet: Response of David R. Forgan." *United States Investor*. July 23, P. 46

Vamplew, Wray. 2012. "Concepts of Capital: An Approach Shot to the History of the British Golf Club Before 1914." *Journal of Sport History* 39(2):299–331.

Vaugh, Bobby. 2005. "Afro-Mexico: Blacks, Indígenas, Politics, and the Greater Diaspora." Pp. 117–36 in *Neither Enemies nor Friends: Latinos, Blacks, Afro-Latinos*, edited by A. Dzidzienyo and S. Oboler. New York, NY: Palgrave Macmillan.

Villarreal, Andrés. 2010. "Stratification by Skin Color in Contemporary Mexico." *American Sociological Review* 75(5):652–78.

Wacquant, Loïc. 1995. "Pugs at Work: Bodily Capital and Bodily Labour Among Professional Boxers." *Body & Society* 1(1):65–93.

Wacquant, Loïc. 2006. *Body & Soul: Notebooks of an Apprentice Boxer*. New York, NY: Oxford University Press.

Wade, Peter. 1995. *Blackness and Race Mixture: The Dynamics of Racial Identity in Colombia.* Baltimore, MD: Johns Hopkins University Press.

Wade, Peter. 2005. "Rethinking Mestizaje: Ideology and Lived Experience." *Journal of Latin American Studies* 37(2):239–57.

Wade, Peter. 2009. "Race in Latin America." Pp. 175–92 in Deborah Poole (ed.), *A Companion to Latin American Anthropology.* Oxford, UK: Blackwell.

Wade, Peter. 2010. "The Presence and Absence of Race." *Patterns of Prejudice* 44(1):43–60.

Weaver, Thomas, James B. Greenberg, William L. Alexander, and Anne Browning-Aiken. 2012. *Neoliberalism and Commodity Production in Mexico.* Boulder, CO: University Press of Colorado.

Weinstein, Barbara. 2015. *The Color of Modernity: São Paulo and the Making of Race and Nation in Brazil.* Durham, NC: Duke University Press.

West, Candace, and Don H. Zimmerman. 1987. "Doing Gender." *Gender and Society* 1(2):125–51.

Whyte, William Hollingsworth. 1980. *The Social Life of Small Urban Spaces.* New York, NY: Project for Public Spaces.

Wolter, Sarah. 2010. "The Ladies Professional Golf Association's Five Points of Celebrity: 'Driving' the Organization 'Fore-Ward' or a Snap-Hook Into the Next Fairway?." *International Journal of Sport Communication* 3(1):31–48.

Womack, John. 2011. *Zapata and the Mexican Revolution.* New York, NY: Vintage.

Wray, Maria. 2002. *Golf En Hidalgo: Un Legado Para México.* Pachuca, Mexico: Gobierno del Estado de Hidalgo.

Wright, Harry. 1938. *A Short History of Golf in Mexico and the Mexico City Country Club.* New York, NY: Country Life Press.

Yeager, Peter C., and Kathy E. Kram. 1990. "Fielding Hot Topics in Cool Settings: The Study of Corporate Ethics." *Qualitative Sociology* 13(2):127–48.

Zabludovsky, Gina. 2007. "Las Mujeres En México: Trabajo, Educación Superior Y Esferas De Poder." *Política y Cultura* (28):09–41.

Zentella, Ana Celia. 2007. "'Dime Con Quién Hablas, Y Te Diré Quién Eres': Linguistic (in)Security and Latina/o Unit." Pp. 25–38 in A Companion to Latina/O Studies, edited by J. Flores and R. Rosaldo. Oxford, UK: Blackwell.

Zweigenhaft, Richard L., and G. William Domhoff. 2006. *Diversity in the Power Elite: How It Happened, Why It Matters.* Lanham, MD: Rowman & Littlefield.

Index